PRAISE *for*

A Book *of* AGES

"A witty compilation of fun facts."
—*San Francisco Examiner*

"[Hanson] has scored with his first book."
—*Minneapolis Star Tribune*

"Hanson has compiled delicious tidbits . . . [and] he's woven them together with great care and wit."
—*San Jose Mercury News*

"There are lots of simple oddities and peculiar foreshadowings."
—*Booklist*

A Book *of* AGES

AN ECCENTRIC MISCELLANY *of*

GREAT & OFFBEAT MOMENTS

IN THE LIVES *of* THE FAMOUS

& INFAMOUS, AGES 1 TO 100

ERIC HANSON

Eric Hanson

THREE RIVERS PRESS
NEW YORK

Published in the United States by Three Rivers Press, an imprint of the
Crown Publishing Group, a division of Random House, Inc., New York.
www.crownpublishing.com

Three Rivers Press and the Tugboat design are registered
trademarks of Random House, Inc.

Originally published in hardcover in the United States by Harmony Books,
a division of Random House, Inc., New York, in 2008.

Permissions acknowledgments can be found on page 298.

Library of Congress Cataloging-in-Publication Data

Hanson, Eric.
A book of ages: an eccentric miscellany of great and offbeat moments
in the lives of the famous and infamous, ages 1 to 100 /
Eric Hanson.
1. Celebrities—Biography—Miscellanea.
2. Celebrities—Biography—Anecdotes.   I. Title.
CT105.H256 2008
920.02—dc22   2008012631
ISBN 978-0-307-40902-7

Printed in the United States of America

Design by Lauren Dong

1   3   5   7   9   10   8   6   4   2

First Paperback Edition

for FAITH *and* EVAN *and* MADELINE

PREFACE

WHEN A WRITER FRIEND OF MINE TURNED THIRTY A FEW YEARS AGO, I gave him three books, without any explanation attached: a volume of Keats, a book of Shelley, and a small collection of stories by Stephen Crane. The point being that each of these writers had done great things and had died before they were thirty years old. The gift struck just the right notes of nihilism and narcissism appropriate to the age.

In our twenties we all harbor a private belief that we will flame out before reaching thirty. Thirty and middle age represent an annulment of everything. Thirty is a risible age. Forty is unimaginable. People who are forty-five were born old to begin with. Sixty is a different species; ambition shifts to shooting one's age at golf.

Time makes decisions for us. If we are past seven years old and are not Mozart or Heifetz, what is the point of practicing an instrument at all? Writing careers that do not vault immediately into glowing reviews in the *New York Times* are humdrum. Everybody is writing a shallow intelligent novel at twenty-one. Everybody has a garage band in their thirties. As we age, we pass the time by keeping score.

Chronology has always fascinated me. The measure of our days. Career stats. Great moments. Crossed paths. Generational chasms and rivalries. Time is an accumulation of facts and moments. The way these moments resonate off each other comprises the plot, such as it is, of everyday life. Consider synchronicity: Did you know, for instance, that Shakespeare and Cervantes died on the very same day in 1616? Or that Charles Darwin and Abraham Lincoln were born on the same day in 1812? (Nobody in my eighth-grade English class knew, or cared, but I did.) Even ordinary lives are full of significant moments. Even the great stub their toes and fall down stairs.

Around the time my own first novel wasn't being published, this too-clever gift of Keats and Shelley and Crane gave me an idea. I began collecting data and writing it down. Who had done what in their tenth, their eleventh, their twentieth, their thirty-ninth year? I scribbled notes in the margins of articles I was writing, on the endpapers of books I was reading. The fragments of other writers' lives, but not only writers'. Lives of artists, composers, boxers, and quarterbacks, all the celebrated dead, accumulated like a kind of poetry. As I assembled the entries year by year, it seemed as if they were all swimming together in the same stream. That was the point.

I began by going through the standard literary references. I read diaries and collected letters. I read biographies. I bought a dictionary of biographies and books of obituaries. I clipped obits from the papers. I took notes. My favorite sources of all were the various anthologies of anecdotes—sports, political, military, literary, royal, theatrical. Often it isn't the accomplishments that define a life, but the stories people tell about their contemporaries, the gossip and the scandal.

Years passed and my collection grew, and as it grew a curious thing happened: the entries and the people in them developed a conversation among themselves. Juxtaposed lives began commenting on one another. What intrigues me is the simple fact of people doing things or not doing them, succeeding and failing, living forever and dying young—not along some infinite timeline but simultaneously, as if everybody who ever lived were a contemporary and lived cheek by jowl.

In a way, I am there with them, as are we all, in our own years of life, looking backward, looking forward, not as young as the phenomenal Mozart or as old as Noah. This book is the product of more than a decade of reading and sorting and writing things down. I suggest you do what everyone else will do—that is, turn to the age that you are now. After that you are on your own. Leaf through it at random. Look at the year that you remember most vividly. Or start at the beginning. Even as crowded and selective a canvas as this one does have a plot to it. Jot your own story in the margin.

Eric Hanson

A Book *of* AGES

INFANCY

Whether I shall turn out to be the hero of my own life, or whether that station will be held by anybody else, these pages must show.

—CHARLES DICKENS, *David Copperfield* (1849)

JOSEPH FRANCIS KEATON JR., the youngest member of a theatrical family, falls down the stairs. He isn't seriously injured and is christened Buster by family friend Harry Houdini, 1896.

ALFRED NOBEL's father declares bankruptcy, 1833.

ISAAC NEWTON is born premature and half dead on Christmas Day, 1642. He is small enough to fit into a quart pot.

ANDERSON COOPER is photographed by Diane Arbus. The photograph, titled "A very young baby, N.Y.C., 1968," is published in *Harper's Bazaar*. Cooper's mother is socialite Gloria Vanderbilt.

Essayist MICHEL DE MONTAIGNE is sent by his parents to live with a peasant family, 1533. The idea is to teach the child to love the lower classes. When Michel is returned home three years later, his father instructs everyone in the household to speak Latin at all times so it will be the boy's first language. This rule will be observed until Montaigne is six years old.

KEITH RICHARDS is evacuated from suburban London during the Blitz, 1944.

When King Herod orders the massacre of newborns, Joseph, Mary, and their infant son JESUS move to Egypt, where they will live for two years, 5 B.C.

HUMPHREY BOGART's father is a New York surgeon who is secretly addicted to opium, 1900. His artist mother paints infant Humphrey's portrait for the label of a popular baby food, but contrary to legend the baby on jars of Gerber is not Humphrey Bogart.

MARY STUART is crowned Queen of Scots before her first birthday in 1543, earning the enmity of all of the other heirs of Henry VIII. She will be raised in France under the supervision of her French uncles, the Duc de Guise and the Cardinal of Lorraine.

ONE

~

Parents who want a fresh point of view on their furniture are advised to drop down on all fours and accompany the nine or ten month old on his rounds. It is probably many years since you last studied the underside of a dining room chair. The ten month old will study this marvel with as much concentration and reverence as a tourist in the Cathedral of Chartres.

—SELMA H. FRAIBERG, *The Magic Years* (1959)

When his father is banished, PRINCE PHILIP OF GREECE arrives in England in a crib made out of an orange crate, 1922.

GIUSEPPE BONANNO, "Joe Bananas," moves with his parents from Sicily to Brooklyn, where his father opens a restaurant, 1906.

CHRISTOPHER ROBIN MILNE receives a stuffed bear for his birthday, August 21, 1921. He gets a stuffed donkey for Christmas. Christopher also has a small stuffed pig, a gift from a neighbor.

SEABISCUIT loses his seventeenth race in a row, June 1935. Although he's just passed his first birthday, he's listed as a two-year-old.

HELEN KELLER can see and hear as well as any child until the age of one year and seven months, but then suddenly loses both senses, probably as a result of meningitis or scarlet fever, 1882. She reacts with rages and tantrums.

TWO

There are many things children accept as "grown-up things"
over which they have no control and for which they have no
responsibility—for instance, weddings, having babies, buying
houses, and driving cars.

—FRED ROGERS, *Mister Rogers Talks with Parents* (1983)

When his parents return to Hong Kong, P. G. WODEHOUSE is left in the care of his maternal aunts. He won't see his mother and father for another four years. Strong-willed, often terrifying aunts will always populate his fiction.

EDGAR ALLAN POE is orphaned in 1811 when both of his parents die of tuberculosis. He is taken in by a wealthy merchant named John Allan, who will raise him and send him to university.

ALEKSANDR PUSHKIN's earliest memory is of the earthquake that strikes Moscow in 1801.

In 1949 STEPHEN KING's father, a merchant seaman, abandons his family, leaving behind a box of science fiction paperbacks.

In 1937 the fourteenth incarnation of the DALAI LAMA is found living in a small village in northeastern Tibet. After answering a series of questions, Lhamo Dhondrub is renamed Jetsun Jamphel Ngawang Lobsang Yeshe Tenzin Gyatso and is taken to be educated for his 1940 enthronement in Lhasa.

FRANCES "BABY" GUMM makes her stage debut in her parents' theater in Grand Rapids, Minnesota, on the day after Christmas, 1924. She sings "Jingle Bells."

PRINCESS ELIZABETH ALEXANDRA MARY OF YORK meets Winston Churchill, 1928. Churchill tells his wife: "She has an air of authority and reflectiveness astonishing in an infant."

SEABISCUIT is purchased by Charles Howard, a California car dealer, August 1936. Within a month Seabiscuit wins the Governor's Handicap at the Detroit Fairgrounds.

THREE

Three years she grew in sun and shower,
Then Nature said, "A lovelier flower
On earth was never sown;
This Child I to myself will take . . ."

—WILLIAM WORDSWORTH, "Lucy" (1787)

On his third birthday JOHN F. KENNEDY JR. is photographed saluting the caisson carrying his father's flag-draped coffin as it passes through the streets of Washington, D.C., November 25, 1963.

ERNEST HEMINGWAY is taken fishing for the first time by his father at Walloon Lake, Michigan, 1902.

RALPH ELLISON's father dies while delivering ice, 1916.

ALLEN STEWART KONIGSBERG sees *Snow White* at a Brooklyn movie theater, 1939.

ADOLF HITLER's family moves to Germany, 1892. His mother smothers him with affection, and his father beats him.

SAMUEL CLEMENS moves with his family from Florida, Missouri, to the town of Hannibal that he will later make famous, 1835.

JAMES STEWART lives in Indiana, Pennsylvania, where his father owns a hardware store, 1911.

JOHN HUSTON lives in Nevada, Missouri, a town his grandfather won in a card game, 1909.

JASCHA HEIFETZ takes violin lessons, 1904.

Albert Einstein learns to talk, 1882.

Sigmund Freud sees his mother naked, 1859.

Louis Braille is playing with an awl in the workshop where his father makes shoes when the tool slips and pierces his eye, 1810. By the time he is four, the sight in his remaining eye will be lost due to an infection.

Elizabeth Taylor enrolls in ballet classes, 1935.

Among Frida Kahlo's earliest memories is the sound of gunfire from the Mexican Revolution, 1910. Her mother sometimes makes tea for revolutionaries hiding in their garden.

Anne Frank flees with her family from Hitler's Germany to the safety of the Netherlands, 1933.

Shirley Temple makes her screen debut, 1931.

Rin Tin Tin is put under contract by Warner Brothers, 1922. At the peak of his career he will earn $1,000 a week and be provided with a chauffeur and a personal chef by the studio.

Mozart learns to play the harpsichord, 1759.

Isaac Newton is abandoned by his mother, 1646. He will be raised by an uncle.

Gore Vidal is the first child to fly across the United States, 1929. His father is the assistant to the general manager of TAT, the first major airline in America.

f O U R

Clear? Why a four-year-old child could understand this report! Run out and get me a four-year-old child. I can't make head or tail out of it.

—GROUCHO MARX in *Duck Soup* (1933)

RAY KROC is taken to a phrenologist who can tell from the bumps on his head that the boy is best suited for the food service industry, 1906.

CHRISTOPHER ROBIN MILNE suddenly becomes very famous when his father publishes a book of poems, 1924.

Poet WILLIAM BLAKE is terrified when he sees God looking in his bedroom window, on Broad Street in London, 1762.

MICK JAGGER meets Keith Richards, 1947.

JAMES THURBER's family purchases a dog that bites people, 1899.

MIKE NICHOLS has complications from a whooping cough vaccine and loses all his hair, including his eyebrows, 1936. They will never grow back.

JERRY GARCIA loses the end of his right middle finger while chopping wood, 1948. Later in the year his father drowns while on a camping trip.

MALCOLM X's Lansing, Michigan, home is firebombed, 1929. His father is an outspoken Baptist minister.

In November 1938 one-to-four underdog SEABISCUIT beats War Admiral at Pimlico. Forty million listen to the race on the radio. In December, Seabiscuit is named one of the top newsmakers of 1938, along with FDR and Hitler, by columnist Walter Winchell.

GERTRUDE STEIN's family moves from Paris to Oakland, California, 1878. Stein will later say of Oakland, "There is no there there."

*f*IVE

It is a great shock at the age of five or six to find that in a world of Gary Coopers you are the Indian.

—JAMES BALDWIN (1924–87)

MOZART begins composing, 1761.

WALT WHITMAN is embraced by the Marquis de Lafayette when the Revolutionary War hero visits Brooklyn on July 4, 1825.

HOWARD HUGHES's mother is teaching him to be very careful about the germs carried by other children, 1910.

E. B. WHITE is dragged kicking and screaming to his first day of kindergarten at P.S. 2 in Mount Vernon, New York, 1904.

THEODOR SEUSS GEISEL lives in Springfield, Massachusetts, where rifles are made, 1909. His father is a world champion marksman. Ted is good at wiggling his ears.

YO-YO MA is learning to play Bach's Suites for Unaccompanied Cello, 1960. His father has him memorize several bars at a time, working for a half hour each day.

JERRY LEWIS has spent most of his childhood with relatives, only joining his parents during the summer when they are entertaining in the Catskills, 1931.

Israel Baline arrives in New York City from Russia, 1893. The clerk at Ellis Island thinks IRVING BERLIN sounds more American.

JOHN LENNON's mother moves in with her new boyfriend, March 1946. The boyfriend doesn't like kids, so John stays on with his aunt Mimi at 251 Menlove Avenue. He is expelled from kindergarten.

FLANNERY O'CONNOR is photographed by newsreel cameramen with her chicken, which can walk backward, 1930. It is a moment that the writer will later characterize as the high point in her life.

Six

At the age of six I wanted to be a cook. At seven I wanted to be Napoleon. And my ambition has been growing steadily ever since.

—Salvador Dali, *Secret Life of Salvador Dali* (1948)

George Washington is given a hatchet by his father, which (if you believe Parson Weems's story) he uses to chop down his father's cherry tree, 1738.

Shirley Temple stops believing in Santa Claus when her mother takes her to see him in a department store and Santa asks for her autograph, 1934.

J. K. Rowling writes her first story, about a rabbit who has measles, 1971.

Roman Polanski's parents are sent to the Krakow ghetto, 1939. The future film director escapes and will spend the rest of his childhood avoiding his own extermination. His mother will die at Auschwitz.

Alfred Hitchcock's father sends him down to the police station with a note instructing the officer in charge to lock him in a cell for ten minutes, 1906.

Frida Kahlo is stricken with polio, 1913. She recovers but will wear long skirts to hide a deformed foot. It does not keep her from athletics. She enjoys boxing.

Eleanor Roosevelt's family vacation in Europe is spoiled when her father, an opium addict, becomes violent and has to be committed to an asylum, 1891.

TRUMAN CAPOTE, whose real name is Truman Streckfus Persons, is living in Monroeville, Alabama, next door to four-year-old Nelle Harper Lee, 1930.

WILLIAM F. BUCKLEY JR. attends first grade in Paris and learns to speak French, 1932. Until now he's only spoken Spanish. English will become his third language when the family moves to London later in the year.

BOBBY FISCHER takes up chess, 1949.

In November 1905 FRED ASTAIRE debuts at the summer resort of Keyport, New Jersey, dancing a bride-and-groom routine with his sister Adele. The pair are soon earning $150 a week on the Orpheum circuit.

WOLFGANG AMADEUS MOZART makes his debut at the Hapsburg palace at Schönbrunn, 1762. After his keyboard performance he sits in the empress's lap. Also in the audience is the empress's seven-year-old niece, Marie Antoinette.

JAMES BARRIE's adored brother David dies at age fourteen after a skating accident, 1867. When his mother falls into a depression, the future playwright dresses up in his older brother's clothes and does things around the house that his brother used to do.

THEODORE ROOSEVELT watches as the procession carrying the casket of Abraham Lincoln passes below his grandfather's window in New York City, 1865.

FREDERICK DOUGLASS is taken from his grandmother, who has raised him, and is put to work on the plantation of Colonel Edward Lloyd, 1824.

RAY CHARLES loses his sight, 1937.

Poet ALLEN GINSBERG sees his mother committed to a psychiatric hospital for the first time, 1932.

MARY MCCARTHY loses both her parents in the 1918 influenza epidemic.

POL POT is living in Phnom Penh, Cambodia, where his brother is an official at the royal palace, 1931.

The prophet MUHAMMAD's mother dies in the year 576, his father having died before he was born. Muhammad will be raised by his paternal grandfather.

GANDHI is betrothed to Kasturbai, the daughter of a merchant, 1876. She is his third fiancée.

HELEN KELLER is taken to meet Alexander Graham Bell, a well-known champion of the deaf, 1886. Bell suggests that the Perkins Institution might provide a tutor; Perkins sends Annie Sullivan. Sullivan finds a child who shrieks, throws silverware, and turns over furniture. Helen knocks out one of Sullivan's front teeth. Within a month the young girl is learning language from words that Sullivan writes in the palm of her hand.

Future film director PRESTON STURGES is traipsing around Europe with his mother and her best friend, the dancer Isadora Duncan, 1905.

SEVEN

"Seven years and six months!" Humpty Dumpty repeated thoughtfully. *"An uncomfortable sort of age. Now if you'd asked my advice, I'd have said 'Leave off at seven'—but it's too late now."*

—Lewis Carroll, *Through the Looking-Glass* (1872)

His father and his teacher believe Thomas Edison is too stupid to be educated in school, so his mother begins teaching him at home, 1854.

Orville Wright and his older brother Wilbur are given a bamboo flying toy by their father, 1878. It soon breaks.

John Wayne is playing cowboy and going to the movies four or five times a week in Glendale, California, 1914.

John Stuart Mill masters Greek, 1813.

Mike Nichols and his younger brother are sent out of Germany to escape the Nazis, 1939. His only English phrases are "I do not speak English" and "Please do not kiss me."

Agnes Gonxha Bojaxhiu's father is murdered, leaving the family in poverty, 1917. The child will be educated by Irish missionary nuns. She will later change her name to Mother Teresa.

Shirley Temple is given an Oscar, 1935, mostly for being brave and cheerful and helping Americans look on the bright side of the Great Depression. In 1936 she signs a new contract for $50,000 a picture.

While playing at bow-and-arrow with his brothers, James Thurber is shot in one eye, 1901. Over the years the sight in the other eye will deteriorate, leaving him blind.

George Herman Ruth is sent to St. Mary's Industrial School for Boys, a Catholic school for orphans and delinquents, 1902.

Tammy Wynette is picking cotton on her grandparents' farm in Itawamba County, Mississippi, 1949.

EIGHT

Not to expose your true feelings to an adult seems to be instinctive from the age of seven or eight onwards.

—GEORGE ORWELL, *Such, Such Were the Joys* (1947)

JANE GOODALL receives *The Story of Doctor Doolittle* for Christmas, 1942.

MOZART plays the piano for George III, 1764.

SYLVIA PLATH's father dies, 1940.

ADOLF HITLER dreams of entering the priesthood, 1896. Across the street from his home is a Benedictine monastery. A swastika is the most prominent feature of its coat of arms.

ALEKSANDR PUSHKIN writes his first verses, in French, 1807. Everybody in his family speaks French. He will learn Russian, eventually, from the household serfs.

TUTANKHAMEN becomes King of Egypt, 1333 B.C.

SAUL BELLOW spends six months in Ward H of the Royal Victoria Hospital in Montreal, recovering from a respiratory infection, 1923. He passes the time reading the comics and *Uncle Tom's Cabin*. He decides to become a writer. The following year his family will move to Chicago.

HANK WILLIAMS's family moves into a house by the railroad tracks in Georgiana, Alabama, 1931. Hank is given a guitar for his birthday.

EDWARD KENNEDY "DUKE" ELLINGTON begins piano lessons, 1907.

John Updike writes a short story, 1940.

William Somerset Maugham loses his mother, 1886. He will keep three pictures of her next to his bedside for the rest of his life. He develops a stammer.

Allen Stewart Konigsberg discovers the work of playwrights George S. Kaufman and Moss Hart in the library of his public school in Brooklyn, 1944. He makes the selection because it's the smallest book he can find.

Adolf Eichmann is living in Linz, Austria, 1914. His classmates make fun of his dark complexion, calling him "Jew Boy."

Norma Jeane Baker leaves her foster home and goes to live with her mother for the first time, in a house just off Highland Avenue, in Hollywood, California, 1933.

NINE

~

Even a nine-story pagoda must be built up level by level.

—Chinese proverb

SAMUEL CLEMENS takes his first steamboat ride, to St. Louis, 1845.

ARCHIBALD Leach arrives home from school and is told that his mother has gone to the seaside, 1914. Actually she has been committed to an insane asylum. He won't see her again for almost twenty years, by which time he will have changed his name to CARY GRANT.

HANK WILLIAMS learns to drink liquor while living for a year with his cousins' family in Fountain, Alabama, 1933.

ORSON WELLES's mother dies, 1924. To make themselves feel better, father and son embark on a trip around the world.

While visiting Peckham Rye, in suburban south London, WILLIAM BLAKE has a vision of "a tree filled with angels, bright angelic wings bespangling every bough with stars," 1767.

JONI MITCHELL is stricken with polio, 1953. While staying in a children's hospital, she learns that she enjoys singing and that the other patients enjoy listening to her sing. She will teach herself to play the guitar using a Pete Seeger instruction book.

SERGE PROKOFIEV composes his first opera, 1900.

EHRICH Weiss forms a five-cent circus with neighborhood friends, 1883. Wearing red woolen stockings, he is billed as "Ehrich, Prince of the Air." He will become famous as HARRY HOUDINI.

Jeanne-Antoinette Poisson is taken by her mother to a fortune-teller who predicts that she will become the mistress of Louis XV, 1730. She will become famous as MADAME DE POMPADOUR.

SONNY ROLLINS's family moves to Harlem's Sugar Hill neighborhood, 1939. His mother buys him his first saxophone.

PAUL SIMON hears Arthur Garfunkel sing in the fourth grade and decides he'd like to sing too, 1950.

MARCEL PROUST suffers his first asthma attack, 1881.

DANTE sees Beatrice for the first time, 1274.

RICHARD NIXON moves to Whittier, California, where his father, Frank Nixon, opens a grocery store and gas station, 1922. Two of Richard's four siblings will die of tuberculosis. Richard sometimes eats ketchup sandwiches for lunch.

KURT COBAIN's parents divorce, and he goes to live in a trailer park with his father, 1976.

Poet SAMUEL TAYLOR COLERIDGE is sent to school at Christ's Hospital, London, where he is dressed in the school uniform of blue coat and yellow stockings, 1782. The yellow hose are to discourage rats from biting the students' ankles.

TEN

I would there were no age between ten and three-and-twenty, or that youth would sleep out the rest; for there is nothing in the between but getting wenches with child, wronging the ancientry, stealing, fighting.

—WILLIAM SHAKESPEARE, *The Winter's Tale* (1610)

George Gordon becomes LORD BYRON, 1798.

PETER THE GREAT becomes tsar, 1682.

CHRISTOPHER ROBIN MILNE leaves the nursery and goes to school at Boxgrove, in 1930, then at Stowe. The other boys mock him, chanting: "Hush, hush, whisper who dares! Christopher Robin is saying his prayers!"

MARTIN LUTHER KING JR. sings in a boys' choir at the premiere of *Gone with the Wind* in Atlanta, December 1939.

ALBERT EINSTEIN enrolls at Luitpold Gymnasium, 1888. He barely speaks and is considered dull by everyone, probably because he prefers mathematics and philosophy to the school's Latin and Greek. In his free time he plays the violin and enjoys building enormous houses of cards.

INGMAR BERGMAN trades a hundred toy soldiers for a cinematograph, which was his brother Dag's Christmas present from Aunt Anna, 1929.

Xerox inventor CHESTER CARLSON's favorite possession is a toy typewriter, 1916.

CLARE BOOTHE is understudy to Mary Pickford on Broadway, 1913.

She will add Luce to her name when she meets and marries the famous publishing tycoon.

BEVERLY CLEARY is kissed by a boy, 1926.

BENJAMIN FRANKLIN has had only two years of formal schooling when he is put to work in his father's candle and soap shop in Milk Street, Boston, 1716.

ELVIS PRESLEY stands on a chair in front of a microphone and sings "Old Shep" in a youth talent contest at a fair in Tupelo, Mississippi, 1945. He wins second prize: five dollars and free admission to all the rides.

COLE PORTER's first composition is called "The Song of the Birds," 1901.

MICHAEL JACKSON has his first gold record in 1968, plus three more. The first four singles that the Jackson Five record with Motown Records—"I Want You Back," "ABC," "The Love You Save," and "I'll Be There"—all make it to number one.

JOHN LENNON receives a mouth organ from George, the conductor on the Liverpool-Edinburgh bus, 1950.

JAMES JOYCE's family's furniture is seized by the moneylenders, and the Joyces are all forced to leave their home in Blackrock for a dwelling in the city of Dublin, 1892. Joyce sees the Christmas panto of *Sinbad the Sailor.*

ELIZABETH TAYLOR makes her screen debut opposite Carl "Alfalfa" Switzer in *There's One Born Every Minute,* 1942.

NORMAN MAILER writes his first short story, titled "The Martian Invasion"; it is 35,000 words long, 1933.

Not yet a colonel, HARLAND SANDERS is doing farmwork for two dollars a month, 1900.

LEONARD BERNSTEIN's Aunt Clara sends her upright piano to the Bernsteins' to be stored, 1928. Leonard asks to have lessons.

Eleven

Seven to eleven is a huge chunk of life, full of dulling and for-
getting. It is fabled that we slowly lose the gift of speech with
animals, that birds no longer visit our windowsills to converse.
As our eyes grow accustomed to sight they armour themselves
against wonder.

—Leonard Cohen, *The Favourite Game* (1963)

Charles Schulz's family gets a new black and white dog, 1934. His name isn't Snoopy.

Princess Elizabeth Alexandra Mary of York joins the Girl Guides, 1937.

Anaïs Nin begins keeping a diary, 1914.

Giacomo Casanova experiences his first orgasm, 1736.

Henry James has his picture taken by Mathew Brady, 1854.

Lou Gehrig swims across the Hudson River to New Jersey, 1914.

Elizabeth Taylor signs a contract that ties her to MGM from 1943 until the early 1960s.

Jascha Heifetz plays the Mendelssohn violin concerto at a private party in Berlin, 1912. He is accompanied on the piano by the famed violinist Fritz Kreisler, who remarks, "Well, gentlemen, we can now all break our violins across our knees."

Gore Vidal flies a prototype airplane in a Pathé newsreel, 1935.

Stevie Wonder signs with Motown Records, 1961.

ELVIS PRESLEY wants a bicycle for his eleventh birthday, but it costs too much, so he gets a guitar instead. The guitar from Tupelo Hardware costs $12.95.

After his father dies, ROBERT FROST's mother moves the family back east, 1885. Robert sees his first New England farm.

ALEXANDER HAMILTON is an impoverished orphan, with few prospects, living on an island in the West Indies, 1768.

GROUCHO MARX leaves P.S. 86 after the sixth grade, 1901, never to darken its doors again.

BILL CODY leaves his family and goes west, 1857.

Philosopher BERTRAND RUSSELL is introduced to Euclid's geometry, a moment he would later call "one of the greatest events of my life," 1883.

TWELVE

~

The son will run away from the family not at eighteen but at twelve, emancipated by his gluttonous precocity; he will fly not to seek heroic adventures, not to deliver a beautiful prisoner from a tower, not to immortalize a garret with sublime thoughts, but to found a business, to enrich himself and to compete with his infamous papa.

—CHARLES BAUDELAIRE, "Squibs," sect. 22,
Intimate Journals (1887)

ERNEST HEMINGWAY's mother wants him to grow up to be a concert cellist, 1911.

ALICE LIDDELL receives an early Christmas present from a mathematics tutor at Christ Church College, Oxford, November 1864. The gift is a book containing a story that Mr. Dodgson told her two years before on an afternoon spent along the river, about Alice falling down a rabbit hole.

PAUL SIMON and ARTHUR GARFUNKEL sing together for the first time in a sixth-grade production of *Alice in Wonderland*, at P.S. 164 in Queens, New York, 1953. Paul plays the White Rabbit, Arthur is the Cheshire Cat.

ADOLF HITLER attends a performance of Wagner's *Lohengrin*, 1901.

NERO is adopted by the Emperor Claudius, A.D. 50.

Painter EDWARD HOPPER is already six feet tall, 1894.

POCAHONTAS saves Captain John Smith's neck, 1607. Her father, chief of the Powhatan, had ordered his execution.

Ralph Lifshitz is the best-dressed twelve-year-old in the Bronx, 1952. He will later change his name to RALPH LAUREN.

CHARLES DICKENS's father is imprisoned for debt, 1824.

JESUS amazes the priests in the Temple with his scripture knowledge, A.D. 7. Of course, back then it was only the Old Testament.

DANTE ALIGHIERI is betrothed to Gemma di Donati, 1277. But he is still in love with Beatrice Polinari, whom he has glimpsed only once.

RAY BRADBURY goes to see a traveling carnival, 1932. There he meets a magician named Mr. Electrico, who talks to him about reincarnation and immortality.

PAUL MCCARTNEY meets eleven-year-old George Harrison on a Liverpool bus, September 1954.

ELIZABETH TAYLOR stars in *National Velvet*, 1944.

Future director PETER BOGDANOVICH begins his film career, writing down the credits and a short review of every picture he sees, on three-by-five cards, 1952. When he stops after eighteen years, he will have compiled more than five thousand cards.

LOUIS BRAILLE is a scholarship student at the Royal Academy for the Blind, where students are taught to read raised print with their fingers. It is a slow, confusing way to read. But Braille is introduced to the military system called night writing, which employs a system of twelve raised dots that convey words phonetically, like shorthand. He begins work on a less complicated system of his own, employing six dots, 1821.

THOMAS EDISON is selling candy and newspapers on trains, 1859. He prints his own newspapers in the train's baggage car.

On an afternoon in 1910, a secondhand upright piano is hoisted up through the window of the GERSHWINS' Manhattan apartment on Second Avenue. George, who has never touched a piano before, sits down and begins to play.

BOB HOPE wins a contest imitating Charlie Chaplin at Luna Park in Cleveland, 1915. He uses his winnings to buy his mother a new stove.

LOUIS ARMSTRONG is arrested for firing a revolver on New Year's Eve 1913 and is remanded to the New Orleans Colored Waif's Home for Boys, where he will join the band.

IGOR SIKORSKY, inspired by the drawings of Leonardo da Vinci, makes a working toy helicopter powered by rubber bands, 1901.

FEDERICO FELLINI runs away to join the circus, 1932, but the police catch up with him and return him to the strict Catholic boarding school where he has lived for several years.

After his bicycle is stolen, CASSIUS CLAY takes boxing lessons at a neighborhood gym in Louisville, Kentucky, 1954.

STEVEN SPIELBERG receives his first movie camera, an 8mm Kodak, 1959. His first film is a 3½-minute western. Budget: $8.50.

PHILO T. FARNSWORTH moves with his family from Utah to a farm in Idaho, 1919. The new place has electricity as well as a stack of science magazines in the attic.

ANNIE OAKLEY can shoot the head off a running quail, 1872.

JOAN OF ARC begins to hear voices, 1424. The specific instructions of Saint Michael, Saint Catherine, and Saint Margaret are to cut her hair, wear men's clothes, and join the army in order to free France from the English invaders.

THOMAS CHATTERTON writes the first of his Rowley poems and tries to pass them off as undiscovered medieval masterpieces, 1765. His invention fools the experts, including Horace Walpole. The young forger spends his earnings on books.

BLAISE PASCAL masters Euclid's *Elements,* 1635.

CARL VON CLAUSEWITZ joins the army, 1792.

HORATIO NELSON enters the Royal Navy as a midshipman aboard the *Raissonable*, 1770.

ANNA Mary Robertson goes to work as a hired girl on a neighboring farm in Greenwich, New York, 1872. Many years later she will become better known as the painter GRANDMA MOSES.

THIRTEEN

I remember a very important lesson that my father gave me when I was twelve or thirteen. He said, "You know, today I welded a perfect seam and I signed my name to it." And I said, "But, Daddy, no one's going to see it!" And he said, "Yeah, but I know it's there." So when I was working in kitchens, I did good work.

—TONI MORRISON (1994)

ALBERT EINSTEIN isn't bar mitzvahed, 1892.

SPANKY MCFARLAND retires from *Our Gang*, 1942.

LAURENCE OLIVIER has his stage debut in the role of Katharina in *The Taming of the Shrew* at All Saints School, 1920.

WERNHER VON BRAUN receives a telescope as a confirmation gift from his mother, 1925.

ANNE FRANK receives a diary for her birthday, 1942. Before the year is out, she and eight members of her family will go into hiding.

L. RON HUBBARD is made an Eagle Scout on April Fool's Day, 1924.

MALCOLM X tells a teacher that his goal in life is to become a lawyer, 1939. She tells him being a lawyer is not a realistic goal for a "nigger" and maybe he'd better try to be a carpenter instead. Malcolm's mother is committed to the state mental hospital in Kalamazoo. He is placed in a juvenile home.

WILLIAM F. BUCKLEY JR. takes up sailing, 1939.

EVEL KNIEVEL steals his first motorcycle, 1952. A Harley.

GEORGE III feels sad when his father dies after being hit in the head by a cricket ball, 1751. He says, "I feel something, here, just as I did when I saw the two workmen fall from the scaffold at Kew."

KATHARINE HEPBURN discovers her idolized older brother's body hanging from a rafter, 1921. She will always maintain it was a prank, and for many years she will give out Tommy's November birthday as her own.

Since 1902 LANGSTON HUGHES has lived in Joplin, Missouri; Buffalo; Cleveland; Lawrence, Kansas; Topeka; Colorado Springs; and Lincoln, Illinois. At Lincoln Central he is elected eighth-grade class poet, 1915.

ALEXANDER THE GREAT is being tutored by Aristotle, the greatest philosopher of the age, 343 B.C.

FREDERICK DOUGLASS teaches himself the art of rhetoric from a book titled *The Columbian Orator*, 1831.

PRINCESS ELIZABETH develops a crush on her cousin, Prince Philip of Greece, 1939. He is eighteen and a naval cadet.

GANDHI is married, 1883.

Upon graduation from grammar school in 1889, JACK LONDON goes to work in a cannery, sometimes working eighteen hours a day.

BILL GATES begins fooling around with computers while a student at the private Lakeside School in Seattle, 1968.

JUDY GARLAND has a personal audition with Louis B. Mayer at MGM, 1935. She is signed to a contract for $100 a week.

SEABISCUIT, a lifelong bachelor, dies of an apparent heart attack, on May 7, 1947, six days short of his fourteenth birthday.

AUGUSTE RENOIR is apprenticed to a porcelain painter in Limoges, 1854.

ANDREW CARNEGIE emigrates from Scotland to the United States, settling with his family in Pittsburgh, 1848. He gets a job as a bobbin boy in a textile mill, earning $1.20 a week.

THOMAS PAINE goes to work making women's underwear, 1750.

*f*OURTEEN

When I was a boy of fourteen, my father was so ignorant I could hardly stand to have the old man around. But when I got to be twenty-one I was astonished at how much he had learned in seven years.

—MARK TWAIN, "Old Times on the Mississippi,"
Atlantic Monthly (1874)

LEONARDO DA VINCI is apprenticed to the Florentine artist Verrochio, 1466.

MARIE ANTOINETTE is packed off to be married to the heir to the throne of France, 1770. She is stripped naked and carefully inspected at the French border. Because of Louis's medical condition, the marriage will not be consummated for another seven years. Louis publicly blames the lack of issue on her. The French will call her "the Austrian Whore."

JOSEPH SMITH goes into the woods near Manchester, New York, to pray, 1820. He asks God which church he ought to join. God and Jesus appear to him and tell him not to join any church at all.

COLE PORTER arrives at the exclusive Worcester Academy, 1905. He furnishes his dorm room with oil paintings and a piano.

AHMET ERTEGUN is given a record-cutting machine by his mother, 1937.

RICHARD RODGERS is introduced to the twenty-one-year-old librettist Oscar Hammerstein II after a performance of the annual varsity show at Columbia University in New York, 1916.

ARETHA FRANKLIN makes her first recording, 1956. She's already a veteran of the gospel circuit.

WILT CHAMBERLAIN reaches his full height of seven foot one, 1950.

NOËL COWARD plays Slightly in *Peter Pan*, 1913.

HOWARD HUGHES learns to fly, 1919.

JOHN O'HARA steals his father's Buick, 1919.

BILL CODY is a rider for the Pony Express, 1860.

PAUL MCCARTNEY's father gives him a trumpet for his birthday, 1956. Paul takes it to a music shop and trades it for a guitar. In the fall his mother dies of breast cancer, two weeks after being diagnosed. Paul writes his first song, "I Lost My Little Girl."

HANS CHRISTIAN ANDERSEN runs away to Copenhagen, where he becomes an apprentice at the Royal Theater, 1819.

SALVADOR DALI smashes a fellow student's violin to demonstrate the superiority of painting over music, 1918.

When her father dies, GRETA GARBO leaves school and gets a job as a lather girl in a barbershop, 1919.

PHILO T. FARNSWORTH is tilling a potato field, back and forth, back and forth, on his family's farm in Idaho, when he gets the idea for transmitting pictures via radio waves, one line at a time, 1921.

BENEDICT ARNOLD is apprenticed to a druggist, 1755.

H. G. WELLS is working as an apprentice in a drapery store, 1880.

JAMES JOYCE visits his first prostitute, 1896.

SHERLOCK HOLMES travels to the south of France with his family, where he is enrolled in a fencing salon, 1868.

HANK WILLIAMS performs his original song "WPA Blues" in a talent contest at the Montgomery, Alabama, Empire Theater and wins, December 1937. He begins performing the song on WSFA radio.

ARCHIBALD LEACH joins the Pender troupe of comedic acrobats, lying about his age and forging his father's signature on a letter of introduction, 1918.

JOHN HUSTON quits school to become a boxer, 1920.

ANSEL ADAMS takes his first pictures of Yosemite with a Kodak Brownie, 1916.

ANNE FRANK is listening to the radio and hears the voice of General Eisenhower announcing the invasion of Europe, June 1944. She records the news in her diary: "I have the feeling that friends are approaching."

f i f t e e n

At fifteen one is first beginning to realize that everything isn't money and power in this world, and is casting about for joys that do not turn to dross in one's hands.

—ROBERT BENCHLEY, "The Boy Who Grew Up" (1924)

JACK LONDON is an oyster pirate, 1891.

GRAHAM GREENE is taken to London for psychoanalysis, 1920. He has been experimenting with various forms of suicide, including overdoses of aspirin, hair pomade, and deadly nightshade.

DICK FRANCIS quits school to become a jockey, 1936.

CHARLES RUDOLPH WALGREEN loses the tip of one of the fingers on his left hand in a stitching machine at the shoe factory where he is working, 1889. The doctor who treats the injury suggests he get a job as a druggist's apprentice.

LANA TURNER skips a typing class at Hollywood High and crosses Highland Avenue for a Coke at the Top Hat Café, 1937. A dark man in a nice suit and a mustache asks her if she'd like to be in movies.

After school and on weekends STEVE MARTIN has a job twirling lassos at Frontierland at Disneyland, 1960. He is promoted to a job doing magic tricks in Tomorrowland.

SUSAN SONTAG buys her first copy of *Partisan Review* at a newsstand on Hollywood Boulevard, 1948.

JIMI HENDRIX picks up the guitar, 1958.

LEONARD BERNSTEIN attends his first orchestra concert, 1934. At summer camp he stages a one-man performance of *Carmen*, wearing a wig and a black gown. The audience loves him.

LADY JANE GREY is Queen of England very briefly in July 1553. She doesn't want the crown, but her parents and her father-in-law do. She is removed from the throne after nine days by her cousin, Mary Tudor. Then she is removed to the Tower of London, where her head is removed from her shoulders shortly thereafter.

W. H. AUDEN decides to become a poet, 1922.

JACK LALANNE becomes a vegetarian and joins the Berkeley, California, YMCA, 1930.

MARY, QUEEN OF SCOTS is married to Francis, the heir to the French throne, 1558. Her French uncles make her sign a pre-nup that will make Scotland a duchy of France if she dies childless.

JOHNNY DEPP's family has moved thirty times, 1979.

JERRY GARCIA discovers the guitar, and marijuana, 1957.

SUN MYUNG MOON is visited by Jesus atop a mountain in Korea, 1935.

JESSE JAMES rides with Quantrill's Raiders in their attack on the abolitionist community of Lawrence, Kansas, 1863. One hundred fifty men, women, and children are murdered.

ALBERT EINSTEIN uses a note from a doctor to drop out of school, 1894. The next year he will fail the entrance examination to the Eidgenössische Technische Hochschule in Zurich.

EUBIE BLAKE is playing piano in a Baltimore brothel, 1902.

Diarist SAMUEL PEPYS is in the crowd assembled to see the beheading of Charles I, 1649.

ANNE FRANK writes the last entry in her diary, August 1, 1944. Three days later the Franks are arrested by the Gestapo, after Otto Frank's business partner informs on them. Anne Frank dies in the Bergen-Belsen concentration camp, a month before it is liberated by the Americans.

BILLIE HOLIDAY is performing in a Brooklyn nightclub, 1930.

BOBBY FISCHER becomes an international grand master at chess and drops out of school, 1958. His school records indicate he has an IQ of 180.

SAMMY DAVIS JR. meets Frank Sinatra in Detroit, 1941.

WALKER EVANS's father abandons the family, 1918. At around this time Evans receives his first camera, a Kodak Brownie, which he takes around Toledo, like a spy, catching people unaware.

Sophie Auguste Friedericke of Prussia marries sixteen-year-old Grand Duke Peter, 1744. Peter prefers playing with his toy soldiers to playing with her. She will have many affairs and pass the time reading Voltaire and Rousseau before becoming CATHERINE THE GREAT in 1762.

ANNIE OAKLEY challenges the famous marksman Frank Butler to a shooting match and beats him, 1875. She later marries him, and Irving Berlin will write a musical about it.

SIXTEEN

Perhaps having built a barricade when you're sixteen pro-
vides you with a sort of safety rail. If you've once taken part in
building one, even inadvertently, doesn't its usually latent
image reappear like a warning signal whenever you're tempted
to join the police, or support any manifestation of Law and
Order?

—JEAN GENET, *Prisoner of Love* (1986)

TAMMY WYNETTE marries Euple Byrd a month before graduating from high school, 1959.

ELIE WIESEL is freed from Buchenwald, 1945.

PYOTR ILICH TCHAIKOVSKY falls in love with schoolmate Sergei Kireev, 1856.

MARLON BRANDO is sent to military school in Faribault, Minnesota, 1940. He will eventually be expelled for insubordination.

BENJAMIN FRANKLIN becomes a vegetarian, 1721.

GEORGE S. KAUFMAN, future playwright and Algonquin Round Table wit, forms a pact with six of his pals to remain pure until marriage, 1905. They call it the Black and White Club. Kaufman will remain a virgin until he marries Beatrice Bakrow in 1917.

ALLEN STEWART KONIGSBERG changes his name to Woody Allen, 1952. He sees his first Bergman film, *Summer with Monika*.

JOHN D. ROCKEFELLER learns single- and double-entry bookkeeping and other practical business skills at Folsom Commercial College in Cleveland, 1855.

On a boat bound for India, SAMUEL COLT carves a model of a pistol with a single barrel and six revolving cylinders, 1830.

WERNHER VON BRAUN attaches six toy rockets to a wagon and sets it loose among the pedestrians on Tiergarten Allee in Berlin, 1928.

STEVEN SPIELBERG makes a two-hour film about space aliens, 1964. Budget: $500.

WENDY BECKETT enters the order of the Sisters of Notre Dame, where she will learn to appreciate art, 1946.

HENRY FORD drops out of school and walks to Detroit to find work, 1879.

LANA TURNER shaves her eyebrows for the part of a Eurasian handmaiden in the film *The Adventures of Marco Polo*, 1938. Most of her scenes in the movie are cut, and her eyebrows never grow back. She will have to draw them on for the rest of her life.

MIKE NICHOLS attends a production of *A Streetcar Named Desire* and decides he'd like to become a director, 1948.

LENA HORNE is making $25 a week as a chorus girl at the Cotton Club in Harlem, 1933.

GEOFFREY CHAUCER, having been captured by the French at the Battle of Rheims, is ransomed by Edward III for £16 in 1360.

AARON BURR graduates from Princeton, where he's been studying theology, 1772.

ALEXANDER HAMILTON arrives in New York from Nevis, West Indies, and enrolls at what is now Columbia University, 1773.

To improve himself, GEORGE WASHINGTON copies out a handbook of 110 rules for gentlemanly behavior, 1747. The fifty-third rule reads: "Run not in the Streets, neither go too slowly nor with Mouth open go not Shaking yr Arms kick not the earth with yr feet, go not upon the Toes, nor in a Dancing fashion."

ALBERT EINSTEIN visualizes what it would be like to travel alongside a beam of light, 1895. He begins to think that time and motion are relative.

GEORGES BIZET composes his Symphony in C but leaves explicit instructions that it never be performed, 1855. His wishes will be respected until 1935.

Jeanne-Antoinette Poisson, the future MADAME DE POMPADOUR, performs in a play by Voltaire at the château at Etiolles, 1737. The author is in the audience.

JOHN LENNON meets Paul McCartney for the first time at a church fete in Woolton, Liverpool, July 1957. He's grown his sideburns out and plays a Gallotone Champion guitar he bought for ten quid.

ARTIE SHAW switches from alto sax to clarinet, 1926.

NORMA JEANE BAKER marries twenty-one-year-old neighbor Jimmy Dougherty, 1942. They've been dating for six months.

MARY WOLLSTONECRAFT runs away to the Continent with the poet Percy Bysshe Shelley, 1814. He is already married. They have to wait until December 1816 for Shelley's first wife to drown herself before they can marry.

GIACOMO CASANOVA receives his doctorate from the University of Padua, 1742. Among his subjects: moral philosophy and medicine.

THOMAS LANIER WILLIAMS, not yet known as Tennessee, places third in a national essay contest sponsored by *Smart Set* magazine, 1927. The title of his essay is "Can a Good Wife Be a Good Sport?"

NERO is made Emperor of Rome on the death of Claudius, October 13, A.D. 54. According to Tacitus, Claudius was poisoned by Nero's mother Agrippina.

EDMUND HILLARY, a son of New Zealand beekeepers, sees snow for the first time on a school outing to Mount Ruapehu, 1935.

FRED ROGERS and Arnold Palmer are high school chums in Latrobe, Pennsylvania, 1944.

T. S. ELIOT attends the St. Louis World's Fair and writes some short stories about the native villages he sees there, 1904.

ABRAHAM LINCOLN borrows a copy of Parson Weems's *Life of Washington* from his neighbor, 1825. When the book becomes damaged, he works off the debt. The damaged volume becomes the first book he has ever owned.

Chess master BOBBY FISCHER takes some of his winnings and changes his look, trading in the jeans, the flannel shirts, and tennis shoes for bespoke suits, 1959.

SEVENTEEN

Joseph, being seventeen years old, was feeding the flock with his brethren; and the lad was with the sons of Bilhah, and with the sons of Zilpah, his father's wives: and Joseph brought unto his father their evil report.

Now Israel loved Joseph more than all his children, because he was the son of his old age: and he made him a coat of many colors.

—Genesis 37: 2–3

Having been voted "best dressed" and "least likely to succeed" by his graduating classmates at South Side High School in Fort Wayne, Indiana, BILL BLASS heads east to New York, 1939. He will go into the pants business.

JANE FONDA goes swimming in the Mediterranean with Greta Garbo, who tells her she should become an actress, 1955. Miss Garbo, fifty, is wearing a bathing cap but no bathing suit.

After many years at Disneyland, STEVE MARTIN leaves the Magic Kingdom for a job at Knott's Berry Farm, 1962. As he is leaving, he is asked not to exit via the front of Sleeping Beauty's Castle because there is a photographer taking a picture of it. The photographer is Diane Arbus.

CHARLES LUTWIDGE DODGSON develops a stammer, 1849.

CHARLES SCHULZ's cartoons are rejected by his high school yearbook, 1940.

CARSON MCCULLERS arrives in New York City, planning to attend Juilliard, but she loses her wallet and with it her tuition money, so she finds a job and begins going to classes at Columbia with the idea of becoming a writer, 1935.

IAN FLEMING receives seven blackballs when his brother Peter puts him up for membership in Pop, the exclusive Eton social club, 1925.

Debutante UNITY MITFORD brings her pet rat to a garden party at Buckingham Palace, 1932.

J. K. ROWLING is head girl at Wyedean Comprehensive in Tutshill, Gloucestershire, 1982.

Having fallen out of touch for years, MICK JAGGER bumps into Keith Richards again on a train between Dartford and London, 1960. Jagger is a student at the London School of Economics. The two chat about blues and rock 'n' roll.

HANS CHRISTIAN ANDERSEN enrolls in school and is placed in a class of eleven-year-olds, 1822.

Impoverished poet and literary forger THOMAS CHATTERTON takes poison and dies in his London garret, 1770.

JOSEPH CONRAD goes to sea, 1875. Already fluent in Polish and French, he begins learning English.

EDGAR ALLAN POE moves into room 13, West Range, at the University of Virginia, 1826. He will leave the university before year's end.

ELIZABETH TAYLOR is dating Howard Hughes, 1949.

Having fled Turkey the year before, ARISTOTLE ONASSIS leaves Greece for Argentina, penniless and alone, 1923. He gets a job as a dishwasher.

MARTHA Kostyra, later STEWART, graduates from Nutley High School in New Jersey, 1959. The motto in her senior yearbook is "I do what I please and I do it with ease."

MICKEY ROONEY portrays Andy Hardy, the all-American boy, in the first of fifteen films, 1937.

JOSEPH SMITH is visited by an angel named Moroni, 1823. The angel tells him about an ancient record of God's dealings with the former (presumably white) inhabitants of America, inscribed on thin golden plates.

ARTHUR C. CLARKE joins the British Interplanetary Society, 1935.

LINUS PAULING fails to receive a high school diploma after refusing to take a civics course. He insisted he didn't need to, having already read everything it taught, 1918.

ADOLF HITLER is refused admission to art school in Vienna, 1907.

NICCOLÒ PAGANINI pawns his violin to pay his gambling debts, 1799.

WILLIAM FAULKNER drops out of high school, 1915.

Rural southern boy TRUMAN CAPOTE finds New York life disorienting, drops out of school, and gets a job at *The New Yorker,* 1941. Some days he arrives at the magazine wearing an opera cape.

MARIA CALLAS debuts as Tosca in Athens, 1941.

In April 1429 JOAN OF ARC sets out at the head of a French army to rescue Orleans from the English armies that surround it. Joan's forces break the English siege in ten days. In July she stands beside Charles VII when he is crowned King of France. A month later she makes her triumphant entry into Paris.

KURT COBAIN leaves home and finds work as a hotel cleaner but is fired for sleeping in the rooms, 1984.

Eighteen

I was thrown out of N.Y.U. my freshman year . . . for cheating on my metaphysics final. You know, I looked within the soul of the boy sitting next to me.

—Woody Allen (1935–)

Philosopher David Hume decides he doesn't believe in God, 1729. Some thirty years earlier a college student was hanged in Edinburgh for saying the same thing in public.

Princess Elizabeth Alexandra Mary of York receives a corgi for her birthday, 1944. She names it Susan.

Ambulance driver Ernest Hemingway is wounded while rescuing an Italian soldier under fire and has more than two hundred pieces of shrapnel removed from his legs, 1918. He has a brief flirtation with his nurse, Agnes von Kurowsky.

Woody Allen gets a D in film production at NYU, 1953. He flunks out of school after one semester.

Quentin Tarantino has a job as an usher in a porn theater, 1981.

Billie Jean Moffitt is playing on the tennis team at California State University at Los Angeles, 1964. She can beat everybody on the men's team, which is no wonder because she's won two Wimbledon titles already. But because she's a woman, she doesn't rate a scholarship.

Judy Garland is making $150,000 a picture at MGM and seeing a psychiatrist, 1940.

Pocahontas is kidnapped by English colonist Captain Samuel Argall, with the idea of using her to ransom English captives held by her father, Chief Powhatan, 1613. While in captivity, Pocahontas will meet colonist John Rolfe and eventually marry him.

Franz Schubert is teaching primary school but also finds time to write two symphonies, four operas, two masses, and 150 songs, 1815.

Diane Nemerov marries Allan Arbus, 1941. He begins to teach her photography.

On a rainy September day in 1925 Frida Kahlo is riding a Mexico City bus when it collides with a streetcar. She is treated for a broken pelvis, a dislocated shoulder, two broken ribs, and shattered bones in her right leg and foot. A series of operations and painful convalescences follow. She puts aside her plans to attend medical school and begins to paint.

Anne Frank's diary is posthumously published in Amsterdam, 1947.

Arthur Rimbaud is shot in the wrist by his friend Paul Verlaine, July 10, 1873. Verlaine gets two years. Rimbaud writes *A Season in Hell*.

Percy Bysshe Shelley is expelled from Oxford, 1811.

King Tutankhamen dies, 1323 B.C.

Elvis Presley pays four dollars and cuts his first record at the Memphis Recording Service, 1953. On one side he sings "My Happiness," on the other "That's When Your Heartaches Begin." He gives the acetate recording to his mother.

Hunter S. Thompson is arrested for robbery and sentenced to sixty days in jail, 1956.

Allen Ginsberg meets beat novelist Jack Kerouac, June 1944.

W. H. Auden arrives at Christ Church, Oxford, 1925. He plans to study biology but changes his mind and studies English instead. He meets up with his old school friend Christopher Isherwood.

Joan of Arc is captured by the Burgundian rivals of King Charles VII and is handed over to the English, who try her as a witch, 1430.

Malcolm X gets a job as a waiter at Small's Paradise in Harlem, 1943.

Rudolph Valentino arrives in America, 1913. He gets a job as an undergardener to the millionaire Cornelius Bliss and begins to study the tastes and mannerisms of the rich.

Django Reinhardt loses two fingers from his left hand when his Gypsy caravan catches fire, 1928. He is forced to invent a new way to finger the notes on his guitar using his three remaining digits.

Mary Stuart, Queen of Scots, sets foot in Scotland for the first time, 1561. She is already the widow of the King of France.

On a rainy evening in June 1816, Mary Wollstonecraft is in Geneva with her lover, Percy Bysshe Shelley, Lord Byron, and Byron's friend John Polidori when Byron suggests that each of them write a ghost story. When the men can't think of any good ideas, Mary writes one about a creature made out of spare parts from dead bodies. Back in England, she begins to turn the story into a novel, titled *Frankenstein*, which will be published in March 1818.

Bruce Chatwin is working his way up from the lowly job of porter at Sotheby's, in London, 1958. By the time he leaves the firm in 1966, he will be the director of modern art. He has an eye for fakes.

Richard Nixon is offered scholarships to both Harvard and Yale, 1931. Because of the Depression, he has to attend local Whittier College instead, where he is elected freshman class president.

Prior to entering Christ Church at Oxford, Sherlock Holmes is tutored, briefly, by a Professor James Moriarty, 1872.

Blaise Pascal invents a mathematical device that he calls a calculator, 1641.

The first book using Louis Braille's system of six raised dots is published in 1827.

Billy the Kid has already been charged with twelve murders, 1878.

TY COBB is sold by the Augusta (Georgia) Tourists to the Detroit Tigers for $750, 1905.

ERIC CLAPTON is invited to join the Yardbirds, 1963.

DYLAN THOMAS begins writing poems in a notebook, 1932. He will later crib most of his best work entirely or in part from the poems he wrote when he was eighteen.

WINSTON CHURCHILL passes the entrance exam to Sandhurst on his third try, qualifying for the cavalry, which has lower intellectual standards, 1893. He receives a letter from his father deploring his "slovenly happy-go-lucky harum-skarum style of work." The letter goes on: "I am certain that if you cannot prevent yourself from leading the idle useless unprofitable life you have had during your schooldays & later months, you will become a mere social wastrel . . . and you will degenerate into a shabby unhappy & futile existence." Churchill's father will die two years later of syphilis.

RALPH WALDO EMERSON is a mediocre student at Harvard, 1821.

JAMES DEAN plays Grandpa Vanderhof in the Fairmount High School production of Kaufman and Hart's *You Can't Take It with You* in Fairmount, Indiana, 1949.

HOWARD HUGHES has declared that his goals in life are to become the world's best golfer, the world's best pilot, and the world's best movie producer; then he inherits the very profitable Hughes Tool Company, 1924.

JIMI HENDRIX enlists in the army, May 1961.

A new father, GANDHI sails from Bombay to England, alone, to study law, 1888.

Nineteen

Remember that as a teenager you are at the last stage in your life when you will be happy to hear that the phone is for you.

—Fran Lebowitz, "Tips for Teens,"
Social Studies (1981)

Poet John Berryman is on the track team at Columbia, 1934.

Robert Zimmerman is studying art at the University of Minnesota, in 1960, and performing folk music in coffeehouses in the Dinkytown neighborhood. He changes his name to Bob Dylan, after the poet Dylan Thomas, but his real inspiration is Woody Guthrie. In 1961 he will move to Greenwich Village, in New York, and visit Guthrie, who is dying in a New Jersey hospital.

Alice Waters transfers from the University of California at Santa Barbara to Berkeley, 1964.

Jean Genet escapes from reform school and joins the Foreign Legion, 1930. He soon deserts.

Doris Lessing is married to a civil servant and busy with the usual wifely duties of making tea and having babies, 1938.

Josephine Baker debuts at the Théâtre de Champs-Élysées in Paris, wearing only a skirt made of bananas, 1925.

Having left school after the eighth grade in 1891, Carl Sandburg delivers milk, harvests ice, threshes wheat, and shines shoes before setting off as a hobo in 1897. During his year on the road he will learn quite a few folksongs and become familiar with the contrasts between the lives of the rich and the poor in America.

ABRAHAM LINCOLN joins the crew of a flatboat carrying produce and travels down the Mississippi River, 1828. In New Orleans he sees a slave auction.

NORMAN ROCKWELL is the art director of *Boys' Life,* the magazine of the Boy Scouts of America, 1913.

ELVIS PRESLEY makes his first appearance on the *Grand Ole Opry,* 1954. One of the *Opry*'s people recommends that Elvis go back to driving a truck.

ARISTOTLE ONASSIS is enjoying the benefits of his new Argentine citizenship by trafficking in counterfeit cigarettes and perhaps opium, 1925.

STEVE JOBS has a job at Atari, 1974.

ANTHONY TROLLOPE goes to work in the post office, 1834. He will stay for thirty-three years.

Eric Blair leaves Eton after two years and goes to Burma to be a policeman, 1922. He will later change his name to GEORGE ORWELL.

ARTHUR RIMBAUD quits poetry, 1873. He will eventually find work as a gunrunner in Africa.

In what he will call "the most important year of my life," FEDERICO FELLINI travels around Italy with his friend, the comedian Aldo Fabrizi, as part of a vaudeville troupe, 1939. Fellini plays small parts, writes sketches, paints scenery, and fills the role of "company poet."

PETER MAYLE visits France for the first time, 1958.

Having been expelled from Columbia University, ALLEN GINSBERG joins the merchant marine, 1945. He experiments with marijuana for the first time with some Puerto Rican sailors.

HENRY DAVID THOREAU delivers an address at Harvard in which he says men should work one day a week and spend the rest of the time contemplating Nature, 1836.

GERTRUDE STEIN is one of the first students enrolled at Harvard's sister college, Radcliffe, 1893. One of her professors is the philosopher

William James, who suggests she try "automatic writing," simply writing down everything that comes into her head.

Zsa Zsa Gabor is chosen Miss Hungary of 1936.

David Lean is working as a tea boy at Gaumont Pictures, 1927.

Groucho Marx is performing as one of the Three Nightingales, 1909. In a year Harpo will make it the Four Nightingales.

Frank Sinatra gets his big break as one of the Hoboken Four on *Major Bowes Original Amateur Hour,* September 1935.

Jerry Lewis meets Dean Martin, at Broadway and 54th, March 1945.

Tom Stoppard stages *Rosencrantz and Guildenstern Are Dead,* 1966.

James Dean is paid $30 to sing "Pepsi Cola hits the spot" in a TV commercial, 1950.

In early 1964 Pete Townshend of The Who accidentally breaks the neck of his guitar on the low ceiling of a hall they are playing. The fans love it so much he makes it a regular part of the act. Keith Moon starts routinely smashing up his drumset. Townshend has already borrowed the windmill style of guitar playing from Keith Richards.

Diana Spencer is photographed being kissed by Prince Charles at Balmoral, 1980. The photograph winds up in the tabloids.

Joan of Arc is burned at the stake, May 30, 1431.

George Herman Ruth is signed to a professional contract by the Baltimore Orioles for $600 a season as a pitcher, 1914. He's given the name "Babe." In his first exhibition game he hits a home run so deep he walks around the bases. By midpoint in the season, his salary has tripled.

TWENTY

What is love? 'tis not hereafter;
Present mirth hath present laughter;
What's to come is still unsure;
In delay there lies no plenty;
Then come kiss me, sweet and twenty,
Youth's a stuff will not endure.

—WILLIAM SHAKESPEARE, *Twelfth Night* (1600)

BOB DYLAN writes "Blowin' in the Wind," 1962.

CLYDE BARROW meets Bonnie Parker, 1930.

NORMA Jeane Baker signs a $125-a-week contract with Twentieth Century–Fox, dyes her hair blond, and changes her name to MARILYN MONROE, 1946.

WHILE a student at Smith, SYLVIA PLATH takes an internship at *Mademoiselle* magazine, 1953. When she doesn't get into a writing seminar at Harvard, she has a nervous breakdown and attempts suicide.

RUDOLF NUREYEV is invited to join the Kirov Ballet, 1958.

FRÉDÉRIC CHOPIN leaves Warsaw for Vienna, never to return, 1830. In his luggage is a container of Polish soil that will be buried with him nineteen years later.

DAYS before his twenty-first birthday, the poet ROBERT GRAVES is serving on the Western Front with the Royal Welch Fusiliers, when he is gravely wounded by an exploding shell, July 1916. While he is recovering in the hospital, his parents are mistakenly informed of his death and receive his personal belongings. His obituary appears in the *Times* (of London).

STEPHEN KING sells his first story to·*Startling Mystery Stories* magazine, 1967.

EDWARD LEAR is invited by Lord Derby to paint the animals in his private zoo, 1832. He is charmed by the earl's grandchildren, and they by him, and he ends up spending much of his free time making up silly songs for them and drawing funny pictures. One of the songs is about an owl and a pussycat who go to sea in a beautiful pea green boat.

JERRY LEWIS and Dean Martin team up to fill in for another performer in Atlantic City, 1946. They are an instant sensation. Lewis's act has consisted of playing popular records and mocking them onstage. He switches to mocking Martin. Their salaries go from $350 to $5,000 a week.

On his twentieth birthday, while riding a train from London to Southampton, The Who guitarist PETE TOWNSHEND writes "My Generation," 1965. Its most memorable line is "Hope I die 'fore I get old."

ROBERT M. PARKER spends his Christmas break in France visiting his girlfriend and tastes wine for the first time, 1967. He likes it.

KURT COBAIN forms a band with high school friend Krist Novaselic, 1987. They decide to call the band Nirvana.

ELVIS PRESLEY signs with Colonel Tom Parker, August 15, 1955. In November Sun Studios sells his contract to RCA. "Heartbreak Hotel," his first song for RCA, will go to number one and stay there for eight weeks.

DJANGO REINHARDT meets Stephane Grappelli at the Croix du Sud in Montparnasse in Paris, 1930.

RALPH ELLISON gets into Tuskegee Institute on a trumpet scholarship, 1933. Short of funds, he hops a freight train to get from Oklahoma to Alabama.

JAMES ABBOTT MCNEILL WHISTLER flunks out of West Point after failing chemistry, 1854.

BILL GATES drops out of Harvard during his junior year, 1976, to devote more of his time to a small company he and his friend Paul Allen started the year before. The company is called Microsoft. He tells his teachers he will be a millionaire before he is thirty.

GENGHIS KHAN assumes the Mongol throne, 1185.

ALEXANDER (not yet the Great) becomes King of Macedonia, 336 B.C.

JAMES STEWART is a member of Princeton's Triangle Club, where he performs with his accordion, 1928.

CHARLES LINDBERGH quits the University of Wisconsin engineering school to become a show pilot at county fairs, 1922.

ORVILLE WRIGHT opens a bicycle shop in Dayton, Ohio, with his older brother Wilbur, 1892.

BILLY THE KID is shot dead by Sheriff Pat Garrett, 1881. Myth has it the young outlaw killed twenty-one men, one for every year of his life. He never reached twenty-one years and killed only nine men.

After graduating from Yale, SAMUEL F. B. MORSE studies in London with painter Benjamin West, 1811.

GRAHAM GREENE leaves Oxford to take a job on the night shift at a newspaper in Nottingham, 1925. His girlfriend is a Catholic and refuses to marry him unless he converts, which he agrees to do. He also offers her a celibate marriage because she is afraid of sex. Their secret code for "I love you" is 143. They will marry after two years.

PLATO becomes a disciple of Socrates, 407 B.C.

ALEXANDER GRAHAM BELL teaches a dog to say "How are you, Grandmama?" 1867.

IGOR SIKORSKY returns from Paris, where he has been a student, to Kiev, 1909. He brings with him a three-cylinder 25-horsepower Anzani motorcycle engine, which he uses to build a helicopter with coaxial twin-bladed rotors. It has a seat for the pilot and wires to adjust the blades, but it doesn't fly.

The poet WILLIAM WORDSWORTH goes on a walking tour of France, the Alps, and Italy, 1790.

CHARLES LAMB suffers a period of insanity, 1795. Madness runs in his family. The following year his sister takes a knife and stabs their parents. Their father survives, but their mother does not. When Mary is released from the asylum, it will be into her brother's custody.

CHARLES MANSON marries a waitress, 1955.

SIGMUND FREUD writes his first published article, on the sexual organs of eels, 1876.

The former art student ADOLF HITLER is penniless and wandering around Vienna, spending his days in bars and sleeping in flophouses and in homeless shelters, some of which are sponsored by the very Jews that he despises, 1909.

ALEKSANDR SOLZHENITSYN wants to be a writer but is studying mathematics and physics at Rostov University, 1939. It's his useful degree in math and physics that will keep him alive after he enters the gulag.

PICASSO begins his Blue Period, 1901.

P. G. WODEHOUSE is employed at the Hong Kong and Shanghai Bank in London, 1901.

JOHN GIELGUD plays Hamlet in London's West End, 1924. It is his first starring role.

FELIX MENDELSSOHN persuades an audience at the Berlin Academy of Music to listen to a mass by the unfashionable and mostly forgotten Johann Sebastian Bach, 1829. The performance of the century-old *St. Matthew's Passion* is a surprising success, renewing interest in the dead composer.

PRINCE REGENT HIROHITO becomes the first member of the Japanese royal family to set foot outside Japan, 1921. He spends six months touring Europe.

HELEN KELLER is told about the joys of romantic love by Alexander Graham Bell, who spells the words into her hand, 1900. She replies that marrying her would be like marrying a statue.

FRIDA KAHLO meets Diego Rivera, 1928.

Freedom Rider ANDREW GOODMAN is murdered by members of the Ku Klux Klan near Philadelphia, Mississippi, 1964.

TWENTY-ONE

We are students of words: we are shut up in schools, and colleges, and recitation-rooms, for ten or fifteen years, and come out at last with a bag of wind, a memory of words, and do not know a thing.

—RALPH WALDO EMERSON,
Amory Hall lecture (1884)

LANGSTON HUGHES quits Columbia University after one year and signs on to a steamship bound for the Canary Islands and Africa, 1923. Off Sandy Hook he takes his college books on deck and throws them into the ocean.

ZELDA FITZGERALD has a daughter, 1921. They name her Frances Scott Fitzgerald, after her father, but they will call her "Scottie." Zelda says, "I hope it's beautiful and a fool—a beautiful little fool." If not as brilliant as her parents, Scottie will have a great deal more sense.

Poet DYLAN THOMAS meets his muse, Caitlin Macnamara, on April 12, 1936. She is sitting on a bar stool in the Wheatsheaf, a pub in the Fitzrovia neighborhood of London. To ingratiate himself, he puts his head in her lap and tells her she's beautiful and that he's going to marry her.

ERIC CLAPTON joins with Jack Bruce and Ginger Baker to form the band Cream, 1966.

ENRICO CARUSO debuts in a small Neapolitan opera house, 1894.

FRÉDÉRIC CHOPIN arrives in Paris, where he develops a cough, 1831.

In January 1964, in a Paris hotel room, PAUL MCCARTNEY plays a new song for producer George Martin. He calls it "Scrambled Eggs." Six months later the Beatles record it at the Abbey Road Studio, four days before Paul's twenty-second birthday. By then the song has lyrics and a new title: "Yesterday."

HANK WILLIAMS is committed to a sanitarium in Prattville, Alabama, to dry out, May 1945. In June he publishes the songs "Honkey-Tonkey," "I'm Not Coming Home Anymore," and a few others.

The British aristocrat UNITY MITFORD falls in love with Hitler and arranges to meet him at a popular Italian restaurant in Munich, 1935. He finds her charming in a blond, Aryan kind of way and allows her to follow him around like a domestic pet.

JESSICA MITFORD is married to Esmond Romilly, Churchill's nephew, 1938. They are ardent Communists.

After undergoing electroconvulsive therapy and dyeing her hair blond, SYLVIA PLATH returns to Smith College midyear, in February 1954. She's very popular.

STEVE MARTIN performs his comedy act in Aspen, Colorado, March 1967. Late nights are spent discussing the Zeitgeist, something that is everywhere in 1967, especially Aspen.

HUMPHREY DAVY invents "laughing gas," 1799.

STEVE JOBS cofounds Apple Computers with Steve Wozniak on April Fool's Day, 1976.

The mime MARCEL MARCEAU is a member of the French Resistance during World War II, 1944.

PAUL SIMON sits down in his bathroom in Queens, with the water running and the lights off, and writes "Sounds of Silence," 1962.

In his senior year at Harvard, JOHN UPDIKE writes a paper on poet Wallace Stevens, 1954. He gets a C-plus.

WALLACE STEVENS covers the funeral of Stephen Crane for the *New York Tribune,* 1900.

ANDY WARHOL arrives in New York, 1949. He finds work drawing shoes for advertisements.

JANN WENNER publishes the first issue of a magazine called *Rolling Stone* in San Francisco, November 9, 1967.

THE Rolling Stones are on their third U.S. tour, May 1965. They are staying in a motel in Clearwater, Florida, when KEITH RICHARDS dreams the trademark riff of "(I Can't Get No) Satisfaction." He gets out of bed and records it then and there. Mick Jagger writes the lyrics in ten minutes beside the motel pool the following day.

ALICE WATERS visits France for the first time, 1965.

COLE PORTER graduates from Yale, having written the school's football song "Bulldog" and been voted "most entertaining" in his class, 1913.

TAMMY WYNETTE enrolls in a beauticians' school in Tupelo, Mississippi, 1963. She has two young daughters.

LOUIS ARMSTRONG is invited to Chicago to join King Oliver's band, 1922.

SAMUEL CLEMENS is learning how to be a steamboat pilot on the Mississippi, 1857.

JOHN D. ROCKEFELLER begins to look into the new business of oil, 1862.

T. E. LAWRENCE is a student at Jesus College, Oxford, 1910. He researches his thesis on Crusader castles by bicycling 2,400 miles through France and walking 1,100 miles through Syria.

FREDERIC, the apprentice pirate in *The Pirates of Penzance*, turns twenty-one and declares he isn't obligated to be a pirate anymore, but is reminded, in Act III, that since he was born on February 29, in a Leap Year, he has celebrated only five birthdays and is technically only five years old and therefore technically still a pirate, 1856.

MICKEY ROONEY marries Ava Gardner, 1942.

SHIRLEY TEMPLE is a divorcée and no longer working in pictures, 1949.

JOHANN WOLFGANG VON GOETHE begins work on *Faust,* 1770. He will finish it sixty-one years later, just before he dies.

AYN RAND celebrates her birthday in Berlin, February 1926. Later in the year she arrives in Los Angeles, where she gets a job as an extra in Cecil B. DeMille's *King of Kings.*

Among the soldiers on duty at the execution of the abolitionist John Brown, in December 1859, is a twenty-one-year-old sometime actor named JOHN WILKES BOOTH.

The emperor NERO murders his mother, Agrippina, A.D. 59.

BENJAMIN SPOCK wins a gold medal for rowing at the Olympics in Paris, 1924.

PHILO T. FARNSWORTH transmits the first television picture, 1927. It only goes from one room to another and is of a straight line drawn on a sheet of paper, which doesn't augur well for the future content of the medium.

DJANGO REINHARDT hears the jazz recordings of Louis Armstrong for the first time, 1931.

PRESTON STURGES invents kiss-proof lipstick, 1920.

MAX BEERBOHM writes "A Defence of Cosmetics," 1894.

WALT DISNEY leaves Kansas City for Hollywood with $40 in his pocket, 1923.

In 1916, playing in his first major league season as a pitcher for the Boston Red Sox, BABE RUTH wins twenty-three games, has a 1.75 ERA, and gives up no home runs in 324 innings pitched.

SAMUEL COLT patents the six-shooter, 1836.

JOHN DILLINGER robs a grocery store and is put away for nine years, 1924.

O. J. Simpson wins the Heisman Trophy, 1968.

Jane Austen begins writing *Sense and Sensibility*, November 1797. It will not be published for another fourteen years.

Paul Robeson delivers the valedictory address to his graduating class at Rutgers University, 1919. Despite the violent racism of his teammates he has earned fifteen varsity letters, in baseball, basketball, football, and track, and has been named a football All-American twice.

Young boxer Cassius Clay inspires poet Marianne Moore to write, "He is neat, spruce; debonair with manicure; his brow is high. If beaten he is still not 'beat.' He fights and he writes," 1963.

George Armstrong Custer graduates last in his class from the U.S. Military Academy but quickly distinguishes himself at the First Battle of Bull Run, 1861.

Robert Louis Stevenson quits the engineering profession in favor of a career as a writer, 1871. His father's firm builds lighthouses.

Jack London drops out of the University of California at Berkeley and joins the Klondike Gold Rush, 1897. He will return with $4.50 in gold dust and a few stories.

Norman Mailer is an army rifleman in a reconnaissance platoon in the Philippines, 1944. The experiences will form part of his first novel *The Naked and the Dead*, published in 1948.

Mathematician John Forbes Nash finishes his doctoral dissertation, 1950. The topic is "game theory." The paper lays the groundwork for what will be called "Nash's Equilibrium." But the balance of Nash's mind will soon come into question.

In his third year at Oxford, Stephen Hawking notices a sudden clumsiness in his movements. In 1963, shortly after his twenty-first birthday, he is referred to specialists who take muscle samples and run a series of tests. They don't know what he has but believe whatever it is will kill him in a few years. They prescribe vitamins. Hawking begins listening to Wagner.

TWENTY-TWO

All the world's a stage and most of us are desperately unrehearsed.

—SEAN O'CASEY (1880–1964)

In December 1944 KURT VONNEGUT is captured by German forces at the Battle of the Bulge and is sent to Dresden, where he and other POWs are put to work in a factory making vitamins. On February 14 and 15, 1945, Dresden is firebombed by 1,299 British and American aircraft.

JESSICA MITFORD has a job at Bloomingdale's, 1939.

LORD BYRON writes in a May 3, 1810, letter to Henry Drury: "This morning I swam from Sestos to Abydos . . . The current renders it hazardous;—so much so that I doubt whether Leander's conjugal affection must not have been a little chilled in his passage to Paradise. I crossed the 'broad Hellespont' in about an hour and ten minutes."

After her father dies, VIRGINIA STEPHEN has a nervous breakdown, 1904. The birds start singing in Greek, Edward VII swears at her from the shrubbery, and she tries to kill herself by jumping out of a window. She and her siblings move into a house at 46 Gordon Square, Bloomsbury, where she will meet her brother Thoby's Cambridge friends, including Leonard Woolf, whom she will later marry.

GORE VIDAL travels through Italy with Tennessee Williams, 1948. Vidal's novel *The City and the Pillar* is published in America. Critics are shocked to discover that it depicts homosexuals as if they are perfectly normal people. The *New York Times* will refuse to review his next five novels.

JASCHA HEIFETZ buys the 1742 "ex David del Gesu" Guarneri violin, 1923. It's the instrument that he will perform on for the next sixty-four years.

On November 12, 1912, DWIGHT EISENHOWER misses a crucial tackle on Jim Thorpe, and the Carlisle Indians go on to defeat sixth-ranked Army 27–7. Before the game the Carlisle coach Pop Warner had told his players to remember Wounded Knee.

On February 25, 1964, Cassius Clay wins the World Heavyweight title, beating Sonny Liston with a seventh-round TKO. Two days later he announces his conversion to the Nation of Islam and changes his name to MUHAMMAD ALI.

François-Marie Arouet is imprisoned in the Bastille for writing disrespectful verses, 1717. While in prison he begins to sign his works with the pen name VOLTAIRE.

WOODY ALLEN gets a job writing for Sid Caesar's television show, 1958.

The joke is going around Asia Minor that JULIUS CAESAR slept with Nicomedes, the King of Bithnya, A.D. 78.

SALVADOR DALI meets Picasso, 1926. Picasso tells him he was wise to visit him instead of the Louvre.

Painter WILLEM DE KOONING stows away on a ship bound for New York, 1926. He settles in Hoboken, New Jersey, where for the next decade he will earn a living as a housepainter.

J. D. SALINGER is dating Oona O'Neill, the daughter of the famous playwright, 1941. For a time he and a friend named Holden are employed as entertainers aboard the Caribbean cruise ship MS *Kungsholm*. Among their duties: arranging deck tennis competitions and being available to dance with unescorted ladies. In November, he sells his first story to *The New Yorker* magazine. It's a sad little Christmas story about a kid named Holden Caulfield. The magazine plans to run "Slight Rebellion off Madison" in late December, but when the

Japanese attack Pearl Harbor, the story suddenly seems trivial. Salinger is drafted into the army. Oona O'Neill breaks up with him and begins dating Charlie Chaplin.

HUNTER S. THOMPSON is the Caribbean correspondent for *Time* magazine and is writing for a bowling magazine called *El Sportivo*, 1959.

THEODOR SEUSS GEISEL adds the honorific "Dr." to his pen name Seuss, hoping his father won't know he's dropped out of school, 1926.

GLORIA STEINEM graduates magna cum laude from Smith College, 1956. Pregnant and engaged to be married, she realizes she doesn't want to be a housewife and mother. She obtains an abortion, breaks off the engagement, and accepts a two-year fellowship to study in India.

JOSEPH HELLER is discharged from the army in 1945. He flew sixty missions for the air corps as a bombardier while stationed in Italy.

ARTHUR CONAN DOYLE receives his bachelor of medicine in 1881 and signs on as ship's doctor on a West African steamship. He contracts a fever and nearly dies.

Poet ROBERT BROWNING visits Italy for the first time, 1834.

NORMAN ROCKWELL paints the first of his 321 covers for *The Saturday Evening Post*, 1916.

ERNEST HEMINGWAY arrives in Paris, 1921.

After two years flying as a barnstorming show pilot, CHARLES LINDBERGH enrolls in the army's pilot-training program to learn how to do it properly, 1924.

In his major league debut CASEY STENGEL goes four for four for the Brooklyn Dodgers and steals three bases, 1912.

CHARLES DICKENS is the most celebrated parliamentary reporter in England, 1834. He takes down the debates in shorthand and transcribes them in a cab, using his hat for a desk.

Thomas Pynchon moves to Seattle, where he goes to work for Boeing, writing technical documents on the Bomark guided missile, 1960. He begins work on his first novel, *V.* It will take him two years to finish.

Bob Dylan is dating Joan Baez and having his lyrics compared to Rimbaud and Keats, 1964.

Kurt Cobain and his band Nirvana release their first album, *Bleach*, in June 1989, produced at a cost of $606.17.

Buckminster Fuller is expelled from Harvard, 1917. He joins the navy, where he invents a winch for rescuing drowning sailors.

Pocahontas, now Rebecca Rolfe, dies in England, 1617. She is buried in St. George's churchyard in Gravesend.

Judy Garland stars in *Meet Me in St. Louis* and marries the film's director, Vincente Minnelli, 1945.

On April 6, 1327, Petrarch sees a beautiful woman in church to whom he will dedicate 366 poems, addressing them simply to Laura.

James Boswell meets Dr. Samuel Johnson in Davies's bookshop in London, May 16, 1763.

A week before his twenty-third birthday, the autodidact, poet, and wit Alexander Pope publishes the poem that will make him famous, 1711. The title isn't sexy, but *An Essay on Criticism* contains the memorable lines "A little learning is a dangerous thing," "To err is human, to forgive, divine," and "Fools rush in where angels fear to tread."

Frank Sinatra is arrested and booked for seduction and adultery by the Bergen County Sheriff's Department, November 1938. The charges are later dismissed when it is discovered that the woman was already married and therefore not a virgin.

Alexandre Dumas fights a duel in which his pants fall down, 1825.

"I grow old, I grow old / I will wear the bottoms of my trousers rolled." T. S. Eliot writes *The Love Song of J. Alfred Prufrock*, 1911.

CHARLES DARWIN sets sail aboard the *Beagle* for a five-year voyage to the South Seas and Australia, 1831.

JAMES JOYCE falls in love with Nora Barnacle, whom he has known for about a week, on June 16, 1904. This becomes "Bloomsday," the day in which the plot of *Ulysses* takes place. Joyce leaves Ireland for the Continent; Nora goes with him.

CARESSE CROSBY, a descendant of *Mayflower* bluestockings, patents the first brassiere, 1914.

CYRUS McCORMICK invents the McCormick reaper, 1831.

ALBERT EINSTEIN writes around to universities trying to get a teaching position, without success, 1901. His flat feet and varicose veins help him to avoid military service.

CHARLES STEWART ROLLS is arrested for reckless driving, 1899. The speed limit is four miles an hour in London, and Rolls had also failed to have a flagman walking in front of his car.

AMELIA EARHART enrolls in a premed program at Columbia University, 1919, but leaves after one semester. She moves to Los Angeles and starts flying lessons.

ROBERT E. LEE graduates second in his class from West Point, 1829. He had wanted to go to Harvard, but the family couldn't afford it. Late in life he will remark: "The greatest mistake of my life was receiving a military education."

Twenty-three

. . . she
Was married, charming, chaste, and twenty-three.

—Lord Byron, *Don Juan*, First Canto (1819)

Benjamin Franklin fathers an illegitimate child, 1729.

In December 1922 a suitcase containing all of Ernest Hemingway's early stories is stolen from a train between Paris and Switzerland. In the first week of July 1923 he runs with the bulls at the Feast of San Fermin in Pamplona, Spain.

Queen Victoria rides on a train for the first time, 1842.

Milton Bradley invents a board game called *The Checkered Game of Life*, 1860. Players try to reach Happy Old Age by landing on Honesty, Bravery, and Success, but often land on Idleness, Poverty, and Disgrace instead, leaving the game early by Ruin and Suicide. The reinvented *Game of Life* will be much sunnier in 1960.

In the summer of 1969 Neil Young joins Stephen Stills, David Crosby, and Graham Nash, to form Crosby, Stills, Nash and Young, which is not a law firm.

Joni Mitchell writes the song "Both Sides Now" and settles in the Chelsea neighborhood of New York City, 1967.

In one year, between September 1818 and September 1819, John Keats writes most of the poems that will ensure his immortality, including "Ode on a Grecian Urn," "Ode to a Nightingale," and "To Autumn."

On January 4, 1952, the Argentine medical student ERNESTO "CHE" GUEVARA DE LA SERNA sets out with Alberto Granado on a 1939 Norton 500cc motorcycle for a tour of South America.

JANE GOODALL visits a friend in Kenya, April 1957. It is her first trip to Africa.

While on tour with the Kirov Ballet in Paris in 1961, the dancer RUDOLF NUREYEV defects from the Soviet Union. To celebrate, he takes off his clothes and has his picture taken by Richard Avedon.

SAUL BELLOW is employed, in 1938, by the WPA Writers' Project in Chicago, where he has a small reputation for collaborating on a Yiddish translation of T. S. Eliot's very Gentile *The Love Song of J. Alfred Prufrock*.

JOHN UPDIKE gets a job at *The New Yorker,* 1955, and thus begins the slow, deliberate work of reverse nepotism that will see his mother's short stories finally accepted by the magazine in the late 1960s.

R. CRUMB moves to Haight-Ashbury in San Francisco, 1966. The neighborhood is ground zero of the hippie culture of the time. Here he will invent his cartoon characters Fritz the Cat and Mr. Natural.

FRANKLIN DELANO ROOSEVELT marries his cousin Eleanor, 1905.

After he is fired from his position with the art dealer Goupil & Cie, VINCENT VAN GOGH decides to become a preacher, 1876.

MALCOLM X converts to the Nation of Islam, 1948.

WILLIAM SHAKESPEARE leaves an unhappy marriage in Stratford-upon-Avon and moves to London to become an actor, 1587. He will become a playwright as well.

FREDERICK DOUGLASS meets the abolitionist leader William Lloyd Garrison at an antislavery convention on Nantucket, 1841. Douglass begins speaking widely about his slave experiences.

HENRI CARTIER-BRESSON is traveling in West Africa when he buys a secondhand camera, 1931. He finds he is good at photography. In

1932 he buys the 35mm Leica that will become his instrument of choice. He will use only available light, no flash, and will crop nothing—"editing in the camera," as he likes to say.

Herman Melville jumps ship and spends a few months living among the inhabitants of the Marquesas Islands, 1842. No clothes, free love, and cannibalism provide good material for a book.

George Washington shows no tactical flair but considerable coolness under fire, having four bullets shot through his coat and two horses killed under him while serving as an aide to General Braddock in the French and Indian War, 1755.

George III marries Princess Charlotte of Mecklenburg-Strelitz, who has an unfashionable nose and a thick German accent, 1761. During the trip from St. James Palace to Westminster, the large diamond falls out of his crown. Many later see this as an omen predicting his loss of the American colonies. Queen Charlotte will bear him fifteen children.

William Somerset Maugham, M.D., is working as an obstetrician in the London slums and writing a novel, 1897.

Monica Lewinsky decides not to have her blue Gap dress dry-cleaned and instead puts it in the back of her closet, 1997.

Marlon Brando is suggested by director Elia Kazan for the part of Stanley Kowalski in *A Streetcar Named Desire*, 1947.

Elvis Presley is drafted, March 1958. He is given number 53310761 and a GI haircut. In August his mother dies at age forty-six.

The fourteenth Dalai Lama escapes from Chinese-controlled Tibet and is given asylum in India, 1959. Eighty thousand Tibetans follow him into an exile that will last more than forty years.

Jerry Garcia's band, Warlock, becomes the house band for Ken Kesey's Acid Test series of concerts, December 1965. Later in the month they change their name to the Grateful Dead, after finding the phrase in a dictionary.

Plague and fire drive Isaac Newton out of London, 1666. He moves back in with his mother, in Woolthorpe, and begins prism experiments. He spends some of his time sitting under a tree in the orchard behind the house, where he begins to think about gravity. But the story about the apple is credited to Voltaire.

Red Sox outfielder Ted Williams bats .406 for the season in 1941. Nobody's done it since.

In 1926 Leslie McFarlane is working the hotel beat for a newspaper in Massachusetts when he receives a letter from Edward Stratemeyer, inviting him to write books for boys at $125 apiece: "They will be mystery stories, the doings of two lads, sons of a noted detective." McFarlane accepts and begins work on *The Tower Treasure*, featuring sleuths Frank and Joe Hardy. The first book appears in 1927 under the name Franklin W. Dixon.

Sylvia Plath meets Ted Hughes at a party in Cambridge, February 1956. They embrace in a bedroom. He takes off her earrings and her headband. She bites his cheek hard enough to make it bleed. Four months later, on June 16, Bloomsday, they are married at St. George the Martyr in London.

In 1566 Mary, Queen of Scots' second husband, Lord Darnley, puts a loaded pistol to her head, while his henchmen stab her secretary fifty-six times. Within the year, Darnley will be blown out of bed with gunpowder and strangled in his own nightshirt by the Earl of Bothwell. Mary, Queen of Scots will marry the Earl of Bothwell.

Annie Oakley has her picture taken with Chief Sitting Bull, 1884.

F. Scott Fitzgerald's first novel, *This Side of Paradise*, sells twenty thousand copies in one week in March 1920. Now a success, he marries rich girl Zelda Sayre in April.

Hart Crane is working as an advertising copywriter in Cleveland, 1923. Among his clients is the manufacturer of a fake leather product called Naugahyde.

In 1885 EDITH WHARTON marries a man she doesn't love. She will not be entirely faithful, but her one passionate affair will remain undiscovered until 1975, when it will put her stuffy old novels back into print. "Life is always a tightrope or a featherbed," she wrote. "Give me the tightrope."

ANDREW LLOYD WEBBER has his first hit show with *Jesus Christ Superstar* but is disappointed when he is unable to get John Lennon to play the lead role, 1971.

WHITTAKER CHAMBERS joins the Communist Party, 1925. He won't start spying for the Soviets until 1932.

TRUMAN CAPOTE writes *Other Voices, Other Rooms*, 1948.

VLADIMIR HOROWITZ makes a powerful impression on his first American audience when he finishes the Tchaikovsky Piano Concerto no. 1 several bars ahead of the orchestra, 1928.

CARSON MCCULLERS publishes her first novel, *The Heart Is a Lonely Hunter*, 1940. It is received well, but her marriage of three years breaks up, and she spends Thanksgiving in Brooklyn Heights with W. H. Auden, Louis MacNeice, Benjamin Britten, Peter Pears, and stripper-turned-novelist Gypsy Rose Lee.

TONY CURTIS is performing on the borscht circuit in the Catskills, 1948.

JAMES DEAN flies from New York to Los Angeles to star in the film *East of Eden*, 1954. It's his first plane ride. He carries his clothes in a brown paper bag.

JANE TAYLOR writes the most famous poem in the world, "Twinkle Twinkle Little Star," 1806.

ORSON WELLES spooks much of America with his Mercury Theater production of *The War of the Worlds* on Halloween night, 1938. He is courted by Hollywood.

MICKEY ROONEY is divorced by Ava Gardner, 1943.

In 1967 BILLIE JEAN KING defends her Wimbledon singles title and wins the U. S. Open title as well, bringing home some nice silverware but no money because championship tennis isn't open to professionals. Until recently she's spent time between tournaments making $100 a week as a playground instructor in Los Angeles.

WOODY ALLEN begins seeing a psychiatrist, 1959.

ALEXANDER HAMILTON is General George Washington's aide-de-camp, 1780. He has already outlined a model for the government of the United States, based on a strong central authority vested in a congress and a chief executive, perhaps even a king.

JACKIE ROBINSON is drafted into the army in 1942. While serving at Fort Hood, he is arrested and court-martialed for refusing an order to move to the back of the bus. He is acquitted.

CHRISTOPHER MARLOWE's *Tamburlaine* is staged in London, 1587. It is the only one of his plays to be staged in his lifetime. Marlowe is already working as a spy for Queen Elizabeth.

Twenty-*four*

Twenty-four is a prudent age for women to marry at.

—Samuel Richardson,
Sir Charles Grandison (1753–54)

Newlyweds Sylvia Plath and Ted Hughes purchase a Ouija board, autumn 1956.

On September 30, 1955, James Dean dies in a head-on collision while driving his Porsche Spyder to a race in Salinas, California. He has starred in three films, all made within the past year—*East of Eden, Rebel Without a Cause,* and *Giant*—for which he's received two Oscar nominations.

Ahmet Ertegun founds Atlantic Records with one partner and $10,000 borrowed from the family dentist, 1947. Their first office is in a condemned hotel on West 56th Street between Sixth and Broadway.

Martha Stewart quits her modeling career after the birth of her daughter Alexis, September 1965.

Betsy Ross sews the flag, 1776. She persuades her client, George Washington, to change the stars in his design from six points to five.

Jasper Johns paints the flag, 1954.

Johnny Cash meets June Carter for the first time backstage at the *Grand Ole Opry* in Nashville, 1956. As is so often true in country music, she is already married.

While finishing *Pet Sounds* in early 1966, Brian Wilson, the shy, depressive Beach Boy, writes a song describing the intangible something that animals can sense about people. "A dog would pick up vibrations from these people that you can't see but you can feel," Wilson would later say. The song is "Good Vibrations."

DOLORES HART, who played the "good girl" pursued by George Hamilton in *Where the Boys Are*, quits the movie business, jilts her fiancé, and enters a Benedictine convent, 1963.

ALEXANDER POPE writes *The Rape of the Lock*, 1712.

POL POT wins a scholarship to study radio electronics in Paris, 1949. He joins the French Communist Party.

TY COBB bats .420 and leads the league in hits, doubles, triples, runs scored, runs batted in, and stolen bases, 1911.

BOB DYLAN goes electric on the first side of his 1965 album *Bringing It All Back Home*. He is booed at the Newport Folk Festival.

Unhappily married and living in Hollywood, LILLIAN HELLMAN meets Dashiell Hammett at a restaurant, 1930. They hit it off.

JEANNE-ANTOINETTE POISSON D'ETIOLES meets King Louis XV at a masked ball celebrating the dauphin's wedding, February 1745. She goes to bed with him. Later in the year she and her cuckolded husband purchase the Marquisate of Pompadour.

The general store that ABRAHAM LINCOLN has been operating in New Salem, Illinois, fails after one year, 1833.

While teaching at Arnold House School in Wales, EVELYN WAUGH attempts suicide by swimming out to sea but turns back after being stung by a jellyfish, 1925.

MIGUEL DE CERVANTES suffers three harquebus wounds at the Battle of Lepanto, 1571.

GROUCHO MARX plays the Palace Theater for the first time, 1915.

JAMES STEWART is rooming with Henry Fonda in New York, where the two are trying to break into acting, 1932.

ADOLF HITLER flees Vienna for Munich to avoid military service, May 1913. He is arrested and taken back to Austria, where he is found to be unfit for service: "too weak, unable to bear arms."

BABE RUTH is sold by the Red Sox to the Yankees for $100,000, 1919. The Red Sox owner, Harry Frazee, uses the money to stage *No, No, Nanette* on Broadway. The transaction puts a curse on the Red Sox that won't be lifted until October 2004.

DANIEL DEFOE is selling hosiery in London, 1684.

JAMES JOYCE is working in a bank in Rome, 1906, and sleeping head to toe with Nora Barnacle in a bed in an apartment on the Via Frattina.

LOUIS ARMSTRONG makes his first recording with the Hot Five, November 12, 1925. "My Heart" is on the A-side of the 78; "Yes, I'm in the Barrel" is on the other.

MARILYN MONROE has small speaking parts in *The Asphalt Jungle* and *All About Eve*, 1950. Her gifts are noticeable. Truman Capote says of her, "She looked twelve years old, a pubescent virgin who had just been admitted to an orphanage and is grieving her plight."

BETTE DAVIS's career is going nowhere, so she dyes her hair platinum blonde, 1932.

CHRISTOPHER ROBIN MILNE is wounded in action near Sant'-Archangelo in northern Italy, 1944.

STEPHEN CRANE writes *The Red Badge of Courage*, a novel about the Civil War, 1895. Crane was born six years after the war's end but had read about it in a magazine.

J.R.R. TOLKIEN spends four months of 1916 fighting in the trenches at the Battle of the Somme, before being hospitalized for trench fever. While recuperating, he passes the time writing stories about elves and trolls and goblins.

Just out of the military, CLINT EASTWOOD drifts into Los Angeles and has a screen test with Universal Studios, 1954. The studio signs him to a contract for $75 a week. His first picture is *Revenge of the Creature*.

On March 16, 1968, LIEUTENANT WILLIAM CALLEY Jr. orders Company C to round up the villagers of My Lai, Vietnam. The company kills 347 men, women, and children, and burns the village to the ground.

PHAM XUAN AN is working as a spy for the Communists in Saigon, French Indochina, 1952. To avoid being drafted into the French colonial army, he gets a job as a press censor in the central post office. Among his duties is to black out the newspaper dispatches written by Graham Greene. He is taking English classes at the United States Information Service.

KEN KESEY, on a tip from fellow Stanford grad student Vik Lowry, enrolls in psychotomimetic drug experiments being conducted by the government at the Veterans Administration Hospital in Menlo Park, California, June 1960. He also signs on as an aide on the night shift in the psych ward. He will turn his experiences there into a novel titled *One Flew Over the Cuckoo's Nest,* which he will dedicate to Lowry.

MARCEL MARCEAU dons a striped jersey and a crumpled opera hat and creates the character Bip, 1947.

GARBO speaks, 1930. Her first sound movie is an adaptation of Eugene O'Neill's *Anna Christie.* Her line, delivered in a strong Swedish accent, is "Gimme a whiskey."

Print tycoon and socialite HENRY LUCE launches *Time* magazine with $86,000 of borrowed money, 1923. To start with, he pays himself a weekly salary of $40. Among the words coined by *Time* are *tycoon* and *socialite.* The poet Richard P. Blackmur will describe writing for the magazine as "a kind of fur-lined purgatory."

For three years TED TURNER has been selling billboard space at his father's company, Turner Advertising. When his father shoots himself, Ted becomes company president, 1963.

FRANK CAPRA is unemployed and living in San Francisco when he hears about a new motion picture company starting up in an abandoned gymnasium, 1922. He talks his way into a directing job. His first movie, a one-reeler, is based on a poem by Kipling.

ARETHA FRANKLIN signs with Atlantic Records, 1966. On February 1, 1967, she records "I Never Loved a Man (The Way I Love You)" at Rick Hall's Fame Studio in Muscle Shoals, Alabama. The song goes to number nine. In June, the song "Respect" will hit number one.

RICHARD NIXON graduates from Duke Law School, 1937, but is rejected by the elite East Coast law firms to which he has applied.

Security guard FRANK WILLS calls the Washington, D.C., police about a break-in at the Watergate Hotel, 1972.

ROBERT E. LEE marries the great-granddaughter of George Washington and moves into the Custis mansion across the river from the capital, in Arlington, 1831.

MICHAEL JACKSON performs the moonwalk in concert for the first time, 1983. The move was actually devised by mime Marcel Marceau.

LORD BYRON has a scandalous affair with Lady Caroline Lamb, another with the Countess of Oxford, and one with Lady Webster, 1812. He finds time to publish Cantos I and II of *Childe Harold's Pilgrimage*, and on March 10 he wakes up famous. It is Mrs. Lamb who will describe Byron as "mad, bad, and dangerous to know."

TWENTY-*five*

*I shall soon be six and twenty. Is there anything in the future
that can possibly console us for not being always twenty-five?*

—LORD BYRON (1813)

JOHN KEATS dies of consumption in a rented room near the Spanish
Steps in Rome, February 3, 1821. His epitaph reads: "Here lies One
Whose Name was writ in Water."

ERIC CLAPTON records the song "Layla" with his newest band, Derek
and the Dominos, 1970. The song is about Mrs. George Harrison,
with whom Clapton is in love. It will take two years for the song to be a
hit, five for Mrs. Harrison to get a divorce, and seven before she marries Eric Clapton.

With a little money that he's scraped together, JACK KEROUAC sets off
on the road from New York to Los Angeles, 1947. He plans to hitch-
hike, but it's raining and nobody stops to give him a ride, so he spends
most of his money on a bus ticket as far as Chicago. He will hitch the
rest of the way, eating mostly apple pie and ice cream. He sees his first
cowboy in Omaha.

BRUCE SPRINGSTEEN releases *Born to Run* in August 1975. With its
background of strings, glockenspiel, keyboards, and more than a dozen
guitar tracks arranged by Phil Spector, the song has taken three and a
half months to record.

CLYDE BARROW and Bonnie Parker die in an eighty-mile-an-hour
shootout on a Louisiana back road, 1934.

J. D. SALINGER lands in Normandy in the fifth hour of D-Day in 1944. A few weeks later he meets Ernest Hemingway in Paris. He will close out the year fighting in the Battle of the Bulge.

In July 1966 BOB DYLAN is seriously injured in a motorcycle accident near his home in Woodstock, New York. A few months later he and The Band rent a house they call Big Pink in West Saugerties and start recording tracks that are never released but will become coveted bootlegs in the late 1960s.

On November 14, 1943, LEONARD BERNSTEIN fills in for Bruno Walter, who is too sick to conduct the New York Philharmonic. The Sunday afternoon concert is broadcast on the radio and is reviewed on the front page of the *New York Times*. Favorably.

SAUL BELLOW is in Mexico City and has an appointment with Leon Trotsky on the morning of August 20, 1944, but the Communist leader is murdered before the two can meet.

WILLIAM F. BUCKLEY is recruited by the CIA, 1950. He is sent to Mexico City, where he learns his tradecraft from Howard Hunt, later to become famous for burgling the Democratic national headquarters at the Watergate Hotel.

J. EDGAR HOOVER becomes a Mason, 1920.

ORSON WELLES produces, cowrites, directs, and stars in the greatest motion picture ever made, 1941. It is called *Citizen Kane*. It is his first picture.

The steamship *Commodore*, bound for Cuba carrying writer STEPHEN CRANE to report on a civil war there, sinks off the coast of Florida, 1897. The writer survives four days in a dinghy with the captain, the ship's cook, and an oil man. The experience will form the nucleus of his famous story "The Open Boat," which begins, "None of them knew the color of the sky."

GEORGE GERSHWIN writes *Rhapsody in Blue*, 1924. When he premieres it at Aeolian Hall in front of an upper-crust audience, it causes a sensation. The conductor is Paul Whiteman. Because he hasn't written it down yet, Gershwin plays the piano part himself, extemporaneously.

PICASSO paints *Les Demoiselles d'Avignon*, 1907.

CHARLIE CHAPLIN, disgusted at the slipshod quality of the films being made in Hollywood, puts up $1,500 of his own money as security and becomes his own director, 1914. In six months he writes, directs, and stars in sixteen films and creates the character for which he will become world famous, "the Little Tramp."

SINCLAIR LEWIS sells Jack London nine story plots for $52.50, 1910.

In 1990, while sitting on a train delayed between Manchester and London, J. K. ROWLING has the idea for a story about a boy who discovers he is a wizard and is invited to attend an unusual private school. Seven years, one divorce, one child, periodic unemployment, and many rejections later, the story will be published as *Harry Potter and the Philosopher's Stone*.

ALEXIS DE TOCQUEVILLE arrives in America, May 1831. He travels around the country for eight months and collects enough insights to lard the after-dinner speeches of politicians for the next 175 years.

On March 2, 1962, WILTON NORMAN CHAMBERLAIN, "Wilt the Stilt," scores one hundred points in an NBA game in Hershey, Pennsylvania.

In a March 1966 interview with the *Evening Standard*, JOHN LENNON says, "We're more popular than Jesus now."

On September 3, 1939, an hour after the declaration of war, British upper-class Hitler-worshipper UNITY MITFORD sits down on a bench in Munich's Englischer Garden and shoots herself twice in the head. She doesn't die from it and lives out the war in a vague, childlike state at her parents' country house in Oxfordshire.

In the autumn of 1797 SAMUEL TAYLOR COLERIDGE is living in a farmhouse between Porlock and Linton, when he wakes from a reverie caused by two grains of opium and writes the famous poem "Kubla

Khan." The poem comes to him as a vision. Unfortunately, while he is writing it down a friend from Porlock drops by, interrupting him.

Vincent Van Gogh is fired from his pastoral position for being too enthusiastic and giving away all his belongings to the poor, 1878.

On Mother's Day 1973 high school teacher Stephen King figures that the paperback sale of his first novel will allow him to quit his job. The novel is called *Carrie* and is about a schoolgirl with issues.

Emily Dickinson's bread wins second prize at the county fair, 1856.

Marconi invents the radio, 1899.

Paul Robeson graduates from Columbia University Law School, 1923. He takes a job in a New York law firm but quits when a white secretary refuses to take dictation from him. He decides to go into the theater.

Lena Horne is working at MGM, 1942. Her contract stipulates she won't play stereotypical African-American roles. Max Factor invents a special makeup for her, to darken her up, which he calls "Little Egyptian." Her first role (uncredited) is as a nightclub singer in *Panama Hattie*.

Grace Kelly costars with Cary Grant in *To Catch a Thief*, in which she speaks the immortal line, "Would you like a breast or a thigh?" 1955. She enjoys being in Monaco, where the movie is filmed.

Coco Chanel has an affair with a cavalry officer and goes to live with him at his château, 1909.

Lester Young replaces Coleman Hawkins in Fletcher Henderson's band, 1934.

Kurt Cobain marries Courtney Love, 1992.

Stephen Foster writes "Old Folks at Home," 1851. In February 1852, he travels by steamboat to New Orleans. He is a pure Yankee, and this is his first and only visit to the Deep South, "Swanee River" notwithstanding.

At the height of the Vietnam War, MUHAMMAD ALI refuses induction into the U.S. Army, citing his religious beliefs. He is arrested, has his boxing license suspended, and is stripped of the heavyweight title. He will remain inactive from March 1967 to October 1970, probably his peak years.

GEORGE PLIMPTON launches *The Paris Review* with Peter Matthiessen, 1952. Having provided the two bottles of absinthe, Plimpton is named editor.

BING CROSBY is introduced to marijuana by Louis Armstrong, 1928.

Poet MARIANNE MOORE is teaching commercial subjects at the United States Indian School in Carlisle, Pennsylvania, 1913. Olympian Jim Thorpe is one of her students.

Illustrator EDWARD GOREY graduates from Harvard with a French major, 1950. Classmates remember him as the student who wore a cape and kept a gravestone in his campus apartment.

ANNE BOLEYN marries Henry VIII, 1533.

RICHARD BRINSLEY SHERIDAN stages *A School for Scandal*, 1777.

FRED ASTAIRE and his sister Adele open in George Gershwin's *Lady Be Good* at the Liberty Theatre on Broadway, December 1, 1924. The show will run for 330 performances. After the show the pair also perform at the Trocadero for $5,000 a week.

Oxford medical student ROGER BANNISTER is the first to run the mile in under four minutes, May 6, 1954. His time is 3:59.4. Within a month, his record will be broken by Australian John Landy. Bannister retires from athletics within the year.

TIGER WOODS has won the PGA, the U.S. Open, the British Open, and two Masters, 2001.

On May 20 and 21, 1927, CHARLES LINDBERGH flies solo across the Atlantic, winning a $25,000 prize and instant world fame.

WINNIE THE POOH embarks on a tour of America, 1947. He is insured for $50,000.

EVELYN WAUGH marries Evelyn Gardner, the daughter of a lord, 1928. They decide to get married one day when they become bored waiting for a bus. For a while they are known as "He-Evelyn and She-Evelyn" by all of London's "bright young things," but he goes off to the West Country to write a novel, she has an affair with a friend of his, and they are soon divorced.

TWENTY-SIX

If you have the household keys, throw them in the well and go away. Be free, be free as the wind. Believe what I say, Anya; believe what I say. I'm not thirty yet; I am still young, still a student; but what I have been through! I am hungry as the winter; I am sick, anxious, poor as a beggar. Fate has tossed me hither and thither; I have been everywhere, everywhere. But wherever I have been, every minute, day and night, my soul has been full of mysterious anticipations. I feel the approach of happiness, Anya; I see it coming . . .

—ANTON CHEKHOV, *The Cherry Orchard* (1904)

EVELYN WAUGH becomes a Catholic, 1930.

In late 1969 MICHAEL PALIN and Terry Jones (who is twenty-seven) write a song about a lumberjack who has very healthy self-esteem. Early the following year they collaborate on a comedy sketch in which a man and a woman trying to order breakfast in a small café are constantly interrupted by Vikings singing about processed meat. The television program is called *Monty Python's Flying Circus.*

ERNEST HEMINGWAY publishes *The Sun Also Rises*, 1926. When his mother's book club chooses the book, she refuses to read it.

JACK KEROUAC says, "You know, this is really a beat generation," 1948.

In December 1732 BENJAMIN FRANKLIN publishes the first edition of a miscellany of advice, tide tables, homilies, weather reports, and odd information under the name of Richard Saunders, who calls himself "Poor Richard."

HUGH HEFNER quits his job at *Esquire* and launches *Playboy* magazine with $600 of his own money, 1953. He lays out the first issue, which includes a nude centerfold of Marilyn Monroe, on his kitchen table. *The Playboy Philosophy*, which he writes, is arguably the most influential American document since the Bill of Rights.

Diplomat, courtier, and painter of fabulous nudes PETER PAUL RUBENS is sent as ambassador from the Duke of Mantua to Phillip III of Spain, 1603.

MARCEL DUCHAMP's cubist masterpiece *Nude Descending a Staircase, No. 2* causes a furor at New York's Armory Show, 1913.

SALVADOR DALI surrenders his virginity, 1930.

ANNA MARY ROBERTSON marries Thomas Salmon Moses, 1887. She will bear him ten children, five of whom will survive infancy. She supplements their farm income by making potato chips. She won't take up painting for another fifty years.

JOHN LENNON meets Yoko Ono on November 9, 1966. Her art is in a show at the Indica Gallery in London.

In October 1836, at a party at the apartment of Franz Liszt's mistress, FRÉDÉRIC CHOPIN meets George Sand. He takes an instant dislike to her.

CHARLES STEWART ROLLS meets Henry Royce in the Palm Court of the Midland Hotel in Manchester, in May 1904.

GRACE KELLY marries Prince Rainier of Monaco, 1956.

MARIE SKLODOWSKA meets Pierre Curie, 1894.

GIUSEPPE BONANNO, "Joe Bananas," becomes a don, 1931. He starts diversifying the family business, moving into clothing, cheese-making, and funeral homes. It is in the funeral home business where he invents the "double coffin" for easy disposal of inconvenient bodies.

NERO is actually out of town when Rome catches fire on July 1, A.D. 64. Despite subsequent accounts that he played his fiddle while it burned, he actually rushed back to the city and led efforts to put the fire out. Anyway, he never played the fiddle; it was the lyre.

HANK WILLIAMS sets fire to his bed in the Tulane Hotel in Nashville, where he is staying after a fight with his wife, Audrey, in May 1950. His songs "Long Gone Lonesome Blues" and "Why Don't You Love Me (Like You Used to Do)" hit number one.

WALTER RALEIGH makes his first voyage to the New World, 1578. He takes up smoking.

On August 3, 1943, JOHN F. KENNEDY's PT boat is cut in half by a Japanese destroyer. Despite his own injuries, Lieutenant Kennedy manages to save the lives of most of his crew.

Sitting in his Harlem apartment, ALLEN GINSBERG has a vision of the poet William Blake, 1948. He feels "a sense of cosmic consciousness, vibrations, understanding, awe, and wonder and surprise." But being a poet won't pay the rent. He gets a job at an advertising agency located in the Empire State Building, writing ads for Ipana toothpaste.

JIMI HENDRIX plays "The Star-Spangled Banner" at Woodstock, August 18, 1969.

WALT DISNEY does the voice for Mickey Mouse in the first sound cartoon, *Steamboat Willie*, which premieres at the Colony Theater on November 13, 1928.

FRED ROGERS helps launch a new program called *The Children's Hour* on WQED in Pittsburgh, 1954. He made the puppets—Daniel Striped Tiger, King Friday XIII, and Curious X the Owl—himself, and does the voices, but he never appears on camera.

MICKEY ROONEY plays teenager Andy Hardy for the last time, 1947.

AL CAPONE is the King of Chicago, running the brothels, the speakeasies, a chain of breweries, and gambling houses, not to mention most of Chicago's politicians and police, from suburban Cicero, 1926.

Millionaire playboy HOWARD HUGHES produces *Scarface*, 1932. The storyline is loosely based on Chicago gangster Al Capone.

Bluesman Robert Johnson records forty-one songs in two recording sessions in 1937. They are the only recordings he will ever make. He will die the following year, at age twenty-seven, at a bar he is playing in Greenwood, Mississippi. Johnson often plays with his back to the audience to prevent other guitarists from stealing his technique, which he learned from the devil in exchange for his soul.

In 1968 Tammy Wynette divorces Don Chapel after being married a year. Without any sense of irony, she records "Stand By Your Man" and "D-I-V-O-R-C-E." Both songs hit number one. She marries George Jones in 1969.

Otis Redding is a hit at the Monterey Pop Festival, June 1967. Afterward, while staying on a friend's houseboat, he writes a song. "Sittin' on the Dock of the Bay" makes it to number one on the pop charts six months later, but by this time Redding is dead, along with four members of his band, in a plane crash.

Daniel Ellsberg leaves the Marine Corps after three years of service in a rifle company, 1957. He becomes a junior fellow at Harvard; his doctoral thesis will be titled *Risk, Ambiguity and Decision*.

Samuel Taylor Coleridge's new poem, *The Rime of the Ancient Mariner*, is about a sailor who shoots an albatross and is doomed to sail the seas forever, 1798.

Herman Melville finishes *Typee*, 1846. It is his first book. Despite the title, Melville's manuscript is handwritten.

Thomas Pynchon begins writing *Gravity's Rainbow*, 1963.

In October 1962, at the height of the Cuban Missile Crisis, lounge pianist Vaughn Meader records an album called *The First Family* featuring his imitation of President Kennedy. It sells 200,000 copies in its first week, sells 7.5 million in a year, and wins the Grammy for album of the year. JFK, supposedly, sends a hundred copies as Christmas gifts. Meader appears on *The Ed Sullivan Show*. Then, on November 22, 1963, Kennedy is assassinated, and it's all over. Comedian Lenny Bruce sighs and says, "Vaughn Meader is screwed." Meader will live another forty-one years.

PAUL GAUGUIN is a successful Paris stockbroker and art collector when he meets Camile Pissarro and some of the other impressionist painters, 1874. He decides to take up painting as a hobby, but doesn't quit stockbroking.

EDNA ST. VINCENT MILLAY graduates from Vassar and moves to Greenwich Village, 1918.

DR. MARTIN LUTHER KING JR. is a young pastor at the Dexter Avenue Baptist Church in Montgomery, Alabama, December 1955. When Rosa Parks is arrested for refusing to give up her seat on the bus to a white man, King organizes a boycott of the city bus service.

HO CHI MINH is working as a pastry cook at the Carlton Hotel in London, 1916. Years later Mae West will allude to a romantic encounter with the protorevolutionary.

E. M. FORSTER's first novel, *Where Angels Fear to Tread*, is published in 1905.

THOMAS GRAY begins his "Elegy Written in a Country Churchyard," 1742. It will take him nine years to finish it. Many consider it the most beautiful poem in the English language.

While staying with the Bigg family at Manydown in Hampshire, JANE AUSTEN is proposed to by Harris Bigg-Wither, 1802. She accepts but changes her mind overnight and asks to be driven to Bath.

On January 1, 1660, SAMUEL PEPYS begins his famous diary with this first entry: "This morning (we lying lately in the garret) I rose, put on my suit with great skirts, having not lately worn any other clothes but them." The diary will continue for eight and a half years, ruining his eyesight.

MICHELANGELO begins work on his statue of David, 1501. It will take him three years.

ALBERT EINSTEIN proposes his Special Theory of Relativity, June 1905. In three papers, written in March, April–May, and June, he has completely rewritten the laws of physics and proved that time is a fiction created by our own perceptions. It's the March 1905 paper on the photoelectric effect that will win him the Nobel Prize, but not for another sixteen years.

KATHARINE HEPBURN'S stage performance in *The Lake* "ran the gamut of emotions from A to B," or so says Dorothy Parker, 1933.

BILL CODY, famous buffalo hunter for the railroads and Indian scout for the U.S. Cavalry, takes the advice of dime novelist Ned Buntline and goes on the stage, creating the buckskin character Buffalo Bill, 1872.

NATHANIEL HAWTHORNE adds the W to his last name, 1830.

D. H. LAWRENCE elopes with Mrs. Frieda von Richtofen Weekley and is arrested by the police in Metz, Germany, 1912. They believe he is a spy.

COLE PORTER flops on Broadway, sails for Paris, and joins the Foreign Legion, but only informally, 1917.

Six years after joining the Fourth Hussars, WINSTON CHURCHILL still owes his tailor for the uniforms he had made, 1901.

NELSON MANDELA joins the African National Congress, 1944.

MERIWETHER LEWIS is employed as private secretary to President Thomas Jefferson, an old family friend, 1801.

GEORGES SIMENON has already published many novels under many names. But in 1929, he buys a boat and embarks on a canal tour of Holland, during which he writes the first novel featuring Inspector Maigret. This time he signs his own name. One hundred Maigret novels follow, eight within the first year. Eventually they will be translated into more than forty languages.

JOHN LENNON meets Maharishi Mahesh Yogi at the Hilton Hotel in London on August 8, 1967.

Twenty-seven

It was about then that I wrote a line which certain people will not let me forget: "She was a faded but still lovely woman of twenty-seven."

—F. Scott Fitzgerald, "Early Success" (1937)

Michael Jackson has plastic surgery, 1985.

Salvador Dali paints a painting of melted watches hung from trees, 1931.

Johnny Depp plays an adolescent who has scissors instead of hands, 1990.

Joni Mitchell's third album, *Ladies of the Canyon*, is a hit in 1970. It includes songs about her relationship with Graham Nash, about paving paradise to put up a parking lot, and about Woodstock, which she didn't actually attend.

Johnny Mercer writes the song "Hooray for Hollywood," 1937.

In April 1924, rich, successful, chic, bored, wasteful, alcoholic, irresponsible F. Scott Fitzgerald writes *How to Live on $36,000 a Year* (which is a lot of money in 1924). He, Zelda, and daughter Scottie sail for France. They visit Paris, then settle into a house on the Riviera, where they meet Gerald and Sara Murphy, and Zelda has an affair with a French aviator. Scott writes to Maxwell Perkins recommending a young writer named Hemingway, whom he hasn't met. He also writes a novel he decides at the last minute to call *The Great Gatsby*.

George Washington marries a rich widow, 1759.

On July 8, 1955, Che Guevara meets Fidel Castro. The two talk the entire night, and by morning Che has decided to join the "26th of July Movement," which hopes to overthrow the Batista government of Cuba.

Sherlock Holmes is introduced to Dr. John H. Watson at St. Bartholomew's Hospital in London, 1881. "You have been in Afghanistan, I perceive," says Holmes.

George S. Patton is the best swordsman in the U. S. Cavalry, 1913.

To attract customers to his Moses Lake, Washington, motorcycle shop, Evel Knievel announces he will jump his motorcycle forty feet through the air over parked cars and a box of rattlesnakes, 1966. He lands on the rattlesnakes. A thousand people are awestruck.

Samuel Clemens adopts the pen name Mark Twain, 1863. It's a term from his days as a steamboat pilot. "Mark Twain" is the boundary between safe water and dangerous water.

Martha Stewart gets her stockbroker's license and goes to work for Perlberg, Monness, Williams and Sidel, August 1968.

Patricia Highsmith is working in the toy department at Bloomingdale's, 1948. An attractive blond woman comes in to buy a doll for her daughter, and Highsmith falls immediately in love. She never sees the woman again, but two years later she will travel to the address she left and stand for two hours outside her house.

Stephen Crane has settled in England with his new wife, Cora Taylor, an author and former owner of a Jacksonville, Florida, whorehouse, 1898. In 1899 he sails for Cuba to cover the Spanish-American War and sees the Battle of San Juan Hill.

Walker Evans's first published photographs are of the Brooklyn Bridge in a book of poems by Hart Crane, 1930. He prefers to take pictures of ordinary things, people on the subway who don't know they are being observed, the bedrooms of working men, empty houses.

Between jobs in banking and stockbroking, IAN FLEMING spends a leisurely few weeks traveling around France with the wife of a friend, 1935. Afterward he sends the friend a polite note to thank him.

JIMI HENDRIX dies from an overdose of barbiturates and alcohol in London, 1970.

In October 1969 a rumor races around the world that PAUL MCCART-NEY is dead. The main evidence is the message heard by teenage fans who play a certain song track backward.

On August 28, 1971, ALICE WATERS opens a restaurant called Chez Panisse in Berkeley, California. The set menu that first night is pâté en croûte followed by duck with olives, a salad, and an almond tart; $3.95. The kitchen isn't finished yet, and they run out of silverware. Berkeley is charmed.

EDGAR ALLAN Poe marries his cousin Virginia, who is thirteen years old, 1836. Soon afterward Poe learns that his wife has tuberculosis, the disease that killed both of his parents. His writing is rather morbid already.

On October 2, 1950, CHARLES SCHULZ debuts his comic strip *Peanuts* in seven newspapers. The syndicate is paying him $90 a month.

EDWARD GEORGE BULWER-LYTTON begins his novel *Paul Clifford* with the immortal words "It was a dark and stormy night," 1830.

OSCAR WILDE arrives in New York, January 3, 1882. Asked if he has anything to declare, he replies: "Nothing but my genius."

Poet EDMUND SPENSER begins writing *The Faerie Queen*, 1579.

Novelist KEN KESEY's bungalow in the bohemian neighborhood of Menlo Park, California, is torn down by developers, 1963. He moves to a place deep among the redwoods in nearby La Honda, where it's said that marijuana grows like a weed. On September 1, 1963, he forms the Merry Pranksters.

JACK LONDON writes *The Call of the Wild*, 1903.

KURT VONNEGUT quits his public relations job at General Electric, 1950.

MARILYN MONROE marries Joe DiMaggio at San Francisco's city hall, January 1954. During the honeymoon in Japan, Marilyn performs for thousands of adoring GIs, which makes Joe very jealous. The marriage lasts nine months.

BENNETT CERF buys a small publishing house called Modern Library and decides to publish a few other titles "on the side, at random," 1925.

In March 1994 KURT COBAIN is in a coma for twenty hours after over-dosing on Rohypnol and champagne. A month later he is found dead from a self-inflicted shotgun wound at his home in Seattle. Grieving widow Courtney Love reads from his suicide note at a memorial service that is attended by five thousand people.

WILLIAM FAULKNER is a very disorganized postmaster at the University of Mississippi. He ignores the customers, doesn't deliver their mail, throws letters out with the trash, and reads their magazines; he turns the mailroom into a reading room and card parlor but spends much of his workday writing. In December 1924 a postal inspector summarizes these charges and fires him.

GEORGE SAND leaves her husband and two children and returns to Paris, where she begins to write for *Le Figaro*, 1831. She begins to wear men's clothes.

While living with a friend in Sonoma, California, HUNTER S. THOMPSON sends in $25 for a mail-order doctorate, 1965.

GEORGE BERNARD SHAW has written five novels over the past five years; all of them have been rejected by publishers, 1883. He thinks about writing a play.

TWENTY-EIGHT

He had just reached the time of life at which "young" is ceas-
ing to be the prefix of "man" in speaking of one. He was at the
brightest period of masculine growth, for his intellect and his
emotions were clearly separated: he had passed the time during
which the influence of youth indiscriminately mingles them in
the character of impulse, and he had not yet arrived at the
stage wherein they become united again, in the character of
prejudice, by the influence of a wife and family. In short, he
was twenty-eight, and a bachelor.

—THOMAS HARDY, *Far from the Madding Crowd* (1874)

CALVIN TRILLIN meets Alice Stewart at a party, December 1963.

CHARLES SCHULZ's marriage proposal is rejected by a red-haired girl named Donna Mae Johnson, July 1950.

KAHLIL GIBRAN moves from Boston to Greenwich Village, 1911. A female admirer pays the rent.

FRANK SINATRA reports to the New Jersey draft office but is rated 4F for being undernourished, 1943.

KATHARINE HEPBURN dresses as a boy in the 1935 film *Sylvia Scarlett*.

CHARLES RUDOLPH WALGREEN buys the drugstore where he works, when his employer retires, 1902. He will buy his second store in 1909.

MIGUEL DE CERVANTES is captured by pirates, 1575. He'll spend the next five years imprisoned in Algiers.

Saul Bellow is dismissed from a film-reviewing job at *Time* magazine by fellow-traveler Whittaker Chambers, June 1943. It's said that Chambers dislikes Bellow's assessment of the poet Wordsworth. Bellow takes a job at *Encyclopaedia Britannica*.

Arthur Conan Doyle introduces Sherlock Holmes to the public in *A Study in Scarlet*, 1887. It is his first novel.

Buster Keaton breaks his neck during the filming of *Sherlock Jr.*, 1924. The fracture won't be diagnosed until years later.

Jazz cornetist Bix Beiderbecke dies of drink, 1931.

Stephen Crane dies, 1900. In a four-year span he published five novels, two volumes of poetry, three story collections, and two books of war writing. It didn't pay much. Crane once told a friend that he couldn't afford a typewriter.

Thomas Edison invents an electric pen, 1875. He also discovers radio waves, but nobody believes him.

While young poet Ezra Pound is working as secretary to famous poet W. B. Yeats, he begins a correspondence with an unknown writer named James Joyce, 1913. Pound will write articles about him, collect money for him, get him published in magazines, send him clothes, and be his champion. In 1914 Pound marries Dorothy Shakespear. (No relation.)

Montgomery Ward sends out his first mail-order catalogue; it is one page long and contains 162 items, 1872.

Hank Williams buys the baby blue Cadillac he will eventually die in, August 15, 1952. On August 16 "Jambalaya" hits number one.

Paul Harvey starts using the phrase "that's the rest of the story" to end the special in-depth reports he broadcasts on WENR radio in Chicago, 1946.

Cleopatra is introduced to Marc Antony, by mutual friends, 41 B.C. He follows her from Tarsus to Egypt.

FRANK WILLS, the security guard who discovered the Watergate burglary, plays himself in the movie *All the President's Men*, 1976.

Activist JERRY RUBIN says, "Never trust anyone over thirty," 1966.

Alcoholic and addicted to pills, JUDY GARLAND is fired by MGM during the filming of *Annie Get Your Gun*, 1950.

SAMMY DAVIS JR. loses his left eye in an automobile accident, 1954.

DUKE ELLINGTON plays New York's Cotton Club for the first time, December 1927. The gig will last three years.

ANDREW CARNEGIE is drafted into the Union Army and pays a poorer man $850 to take his place, 1864.

Rabbit, Run, JOHN UPDIKE's second published novel, is his best yet, 1960. When the lawyers at Alfred A. Knopf ask him to come to New York to go over the "obscene parts" of the book, he says he can't because he has to teach Sunday school.

MARIE SKLODOWSKA marries fellow physicist Pierre Curie (age thirty-five), 1895. They set up housekeeping in a three-room apartment at 4 Rue de la Glacière in Paris. The decoration is minimal: two chairs, a table, bookcases, a bed, and nothing on the walls.

JOHN ADAMS marries Abigail Smith on October 25, 1764.

A year after dropping some weights from the top of the Leaning Tower of Pisa to prove a point about gravity, GALILEO is granted the chair of mathematics at the University of Padua, 1592.

T. E. LAWRENCE takes part in the Arab Revolt against the Ottoman Turks, joining Sharif Faisal, 1916.

LORD BYRON leaves for the Continent, 1816. His marriage is on the rocks, the bailiffs are after him, and he has made his half-sister pregnant. He will never see England again.

Novelist THOMAS WOLFE meets editor deluxe Maxwell Perkins, January 1929. Perkins is reminded of the poet Shelley.

FRÉDÉRIC CHOPIN vacations with George Sand in Majorca, 1838. But the place they're staying in is cold and drafty, and Chopin has to put up with a lousy rented piano. Even though he is sick most of the time, he manages to compose twenty-four preludes.

In 1869 the *New York Herald* sends HENRY MORTON STANLEY to Africa to find Dr. David Livingstone. He sets out from Zanzibar with two hundred native porters. Reliable accounts describe him as a brutal and violent employer.

CECIL RHODES, who will one day establish the Rhodes Scholarships, finally graduates from Oxford after nine and a half years, 1881.

Playwright HAROLD PINTER writes *The Birthday Party.* It opens on May 19, 1958, at the Lyric in Hammersmith, London. The critics hate it, they express sympathy for the actors in it, and the play closes after a week.

ALEXANDER GRAHAM BELL invents the telephone, 1876.

MALCOLM X is under surveillance by the FBI, 1953.

JACKIE ROBINSON debuts with the Brooklyn Dodgers on April 15, 1947.

AUDREY HEPBURN is romanced by Fred Astaire in *Funny Face* and by Gary Cooper in *Love in the Afternoon*, 1957. Astaire is fifty-eight, Cooper fifty-six.

In 1962 JANE GOODALL is criticized by her Ph.D. advisers at Cambridge for naming the chimpanzees she is studying. They suggest she give them numbers instead.

ADOLF EICHMANN has been working as a file clerk cataloging Freemasons for the Nazi Party but is happier after being transferred to the cataloging of Jews, 1934.

SHIRLEY JACKSON writes a story about a woman, much like herself, who lives in a New England village just as she does. *The New Yorker* publishes "The Lottery" on June 26, 1948. Many who read the story expect the heroine to win a washer-dryer and are upset by how the story turns out and angry with Jackson for writing it.

THOMAS LANIER WILLIAMS moves to New Orleans and formally adopts his college nickname of Tennessee, 1939.

ARTIE SHAW records "Begin the Beguine" for the Bluebird label, in July 1938, and is soon annoyed when concert audiences request it over and over and over and over and over. Within a year he will be making $60,000 a week. He quits the music business and moves to Mexico.

Outnumbered ten to one by the French, and without the speech Shakespeare will write for him in 1599, HENRY V of England wins the Battle of Agincourt, 1415.

JULIE ANDREWS is passed over to play Eliza Doolittle in the film version of *My Fair Lady.* She plays Mary Poppins instead and wins the Oscar for best actress, beating Audrey Hepburn, who played Eliza Doolittle, 1964.

ANTHONY TROLLOPE has a safe job in the post office but decides to try writing a novel, 1843.

TWENTY-NINE

There is a difference between twenty-nine and thirty. When you are twenty-nine it can be the beginning of everything. When you are thirty it can be the end of everything.

—GERTRUDE STEIN, *Mrs. Reynolds* (1940–43)

GERTRUDE STEIN moves to Paris, 1903. She and her brother Leo take an apartment at 27 Rue de Fleurus, on the Left Bank. Their apartment soon becomes a salon for artists and writers, including Guillaume Apollinaire, Pablo Picasso, Henri Matisse, and Ezra Pound. Stein will live in Paris for the next thirty years.

JAMES FENIMORE COOPER moves to Scarsdale, 1818.

ALEXANDER THE GREAT reaches India, 327 B.C.

ON November 6, 1952, CHARLES SCHULZ draws a strip in which Lucy holds a football and invites Charlie Brown to kick it.

EVEL KNIEVEL jumps a motorcycle 151 feet over the fountains at Caesars Palace in Las Vegas, Nevada, New Year's Eve 1967. He crashes on landing and spends twenty-nine days in the hospital. On his release he announces plans to jump the Grand Canyon.

GERONIMO goes to war against Mexico and the United States after the massacre of his wife and family near Janos, Mexico, 1858. Wounded many times, he will gain a reputation for being impervious to bullets.

GORE VIDAL signs a five-year contract to write scripts for MGM and moves into the Château Marmont, 1955. He becomes friends with Paul Newman and Joanne Woodward.

QUEEN VICTORIA takes a lease on Balmoral, a fairy-tale castle in Scotland, 1848. She meets a young stablehand named Brown.

GEORGIA O'KEEFFE visits New Mexico for the first time, 1917.

In June 1972 BOB WOODWARD, assigned to the police beat at the *Washington Post*, writes a brief story about a second-rate burglary at the Watergate Hotel.

STEVE MARTIN's hair is gray, 1974. He starts wearing a white suit.

Art critic JOHN RUSKIN marries Euphemia Gray, 1848. The marriage is never consummated and is eventually annulled. Gossip has it that Ruskin is so revolted to discover that his bride has pubic hair that he refuses to go to bed with her.

GLORIA STEINEM gets a job as a Playboy bunny and writes a book about it, 1963.

ERNEST HEMINGWAY gets beat up by fellow writer Morley Callaghan in a boxing match at the American Club in Paris, June 1929. F. Scott Fitzgerald stands in as timekeeper, a role usually filled by Spanish surrealist painter Joan Miró. Hemingway, who is a half-foot taller than Callaghan, blames Scott for not paying attention to the clock.

THEODORE DREISER's novel *Sister Carrie* is published, 1900. It is ahead of its time and sells only five hundred copies. Dreiser considers suicide.

JESSE JAMES tries to rob the First National Bank in Northfield, Minnesota, 1876. The townspeople chase his gang out of town, killing two bandits and wounding several others.

MERIWETHER LEWIS sets out with William Clark on their journey up the Missouri River toward the Pacific Ocean, two mountain ranges away, 1804. They will survive on boiled beef, eggs, vegetables, horsemeat, and the kindness of strangers.

EZRA POUND writes to the editors of *Poetry* magazine telling them he'll resign as foreign editor if they don't print a new poem he's just read.

The poet, a young banker living in London, is a complete unknown. *The Love Song of J. Alfred Prufrock* by T. S. Eliot is published in the June 1915 issue.

EMILY BRONTË publishes *Wuthering Heights*, 1847. Her editors believe she's a man.

JANE AUSTEN's father dies, leaving her and her sisters and mother in serious financial straits, 1805. On holiday in the West Country, she falls in love, but the young man dies suddenly.

The playwright CHRISTOPHER MARLOWE dies in a tavern brawl, stabbed through the eye, 1593.

In 1896, already wealthy and lacking any particular ambition, JOHN GALSWORTHY decides to be a writer, on the suggestion of a merchant seaman he met on a ship two years earlier. The merchant seaman was Joseph Conrad.

On his way from Montgomery, Alabama, to Charleston, West Virginia, HANK WILLIAMS is found dead in the backseat of his car, on New Year's Day 1953. In February, "Your Cheatin' Heart" hits number one.

O. J. SIMPSON does a TV commercial for Hertz Rent-A-Car, 1976.

The poet PERCY BYSSHE SHELLEY goes sailing near Spezzia, in Italy. A storm comes up, the boat capsizes, and he drowns, 1822. He is given a Viking's funeral on the beach by Lord Byron and Leigh Hunt.

The novelist STENDHAL is with Napoleon at the burning of Moscow, 1812.

HANNIBAL marches his army over the Alps, 216 B.C.

By 1751 MADAME DE POMPADOUR has stopped sleeping with the king, but they remain "very good friends." She is made a duchess.

H. G. WELLS writes *The Time Machine*, 1895.

CARY GRANT is sharing a house in Hollywood with Randolph Scott, but no one thinks anything of it, 1933.

GRAHAM GREENE has discovered that you can get soup, a large plate of roast or boiled beef, roast lamb, or pork, magnificent celery, and a dessert, for one and ninepence, at the Salisbury in St. Martin's Lane, London, 1933.

BOBBY FISCHER defeats Boris Spassky in twenty-one games to become the world chess champion, 1972. He is miffed at not being invited to the White House and will not play publicly for another twenty years.

THOMAS WOLFE's manuscript for *Look Homeward, Angel* is rumored to contain between a quarter and a half-million words and fills several suitcases, 1929.

ELEANOR OF AQUITAINE divorces Louis VII of France and marries Henry II of England, taking half of France with her, 1152.

FRIDA KAHLO has an affair with Leon Trotsky, 1937. The famous Communist and his wife are houseguests of Kahlo and her husband, Diego Rivera, in Mexico City.

SONNY ROLLINS stops performing, 1959. His wife, Lucille, takes a secretarial job in the physics department at NYU. Sonny practices his saxophone on the Williamsburg Bridge but will remain off the stage for two years.

A few months after *Bridge Over Troubled Water* wins Album of the Year, Record of the Year, and Song of the Year at the 1971 Grammy Awards, SIMON AND GARFUNKEL decide to break up the act.

JOHNNY DEPP breaks up with Winona Ryder, 1993. He alters his tattoo to read "Wino Forever."

OSCAR WILDE is married at St. James Church, in Bayswater, London, May 29, 1884. He designs the bride's dress; also the bridesmaids'.

In April 1951 JACK KEROUAC writes *On the Road* in twenty days on a continuous roll of paper, which he cranks through his typewriter to avoid interruptions. When it is published six years later, Truman Capote will remark, famously, "That isn't writing, it's typing."

EDVARD MUNCH paints *The Scream*, 1893.

ALLEN GINSBERG reads "Howl" to an audience at the Six Gallery in San Francisco, on October 7, 1955. Living in North Berkeley at the time, he and houseguest Jack Kerouac ride the bus across the Bay Bridge and then bum a ride in Lawrence Ferlinghetti's Aston Martin to the gallery near Fillmore and Union. The fifth poet on the program, Ginsberg begins with the famous line: "I saw the best minds of my generation destroyed by madness." Afterward Ginsberg, Kerouac, and a few others go out for Chinese.

FELIX HOFFMANN, working with Arthur Eichengrün, synthesizes heroin for the first time, 1897. The pair had invented aspirin a few weeks before. For many years aspirin will be available only by prescription while heroin can be purchased over the counter.

DUSTIN HOFFMAN plays twenty-one-year-old Benjamin Braddock in *The Graduate*, 1967. In the film Hoffman is seduced by his girlfriend's mother, Mrs. Robinson, played by Anne Bancroft who, at thirty-five, is old enough to be his sister.

T HIRTY

*Thirty —the promise of a decade of loneliness, a thinning list
of single men to know, a thinning brief-case of enthusiasm,
thinning hair.*

—F. Scott Fitzgerald, *The Great Gatsby* (1925)

Saul of Tarsus has a change of heart on the road to Damascus, A.D. 35.
He sets out from Jerusalem with orders from the high priest to arrest
the Christians living in Damascus, but along the way God speaks to
him out of a thunderstorm. Saul becomes a Christian and changes his
name to Paul.

Mathematician John Forbes Nash begins experiencing "mental disturbances," 1959. He will resign his faculty position at MIT, spend
fifty days as a patient at the McLean Hospital, and travel to Europe to
seek refugee status there.

Joni Mitchell's "Help Me" climbs to number seven on the American pop charts, 1974.

Benjamin Franklin organizes a volunteer fire department, 1736.

After touring Europe as principal dancer in *Porgy and Bess*, Maya
Angelou is working in Hollywood as a nightclub singer and living in
Laurel Canyon, 1958. In June, Billie Holiday is a houseguest for most
of a week.

Che Guevara has his picture taken by Cuban photographer Alberto
Korda, 1960. After Guevara's death in 1967, the photograph will
become an icon, appearing on millions of T-shirts around the world.

William F. Buckley Jr. founds a magazine, which he names *The National Review*, 1955.

Jann Wenner moves from San Francisco to New York, taking *Rolling Stone* magazine with him, 1976.

While on an unofficial espionage mission, Ian Fleming is caught trying to smuggle condoms out of the Soviet Union, 1939. His idea was to have the artificial latex analyzed to determine the state of the Soviet rubber industry. His cunning and initiative win him an important, very hush-hush job in wartime Naval Intelligence.

Woody Allen takes the 1964 Japanese film *Kokusai Himitsu Keisatsu: Kagi No Kagi* and rewrites the subtitles into a storyline about a stolen egg salad recipe. The resulting film is called *What's Up, Tiger Lily?*, 1966.

Giacomo Casanova is imprisoned for impiety and magic in Venice, 1755, but after a year in the Doge's prison he will make a daring escape across the rooftops.

John Dillinger is paroled from state prison in Michigan City, Indiana, 1933. Carrying out plans made while inside, he springs a few of his pals and forms the first Dillinger Gang. Four months later he's back in jail again, in Lima, Ohio. This time his gang springs him. He is captured again in Tucson and sent back to Indiana. He breaks out of the escape-proof jail in Crowne Point, Indiana, using a wooden gun blackened with shoe polish, and escapes in the sheriff's Ford V-8.

Jerry Lewis breaks up with Dean Martin at the end of their tenth anniversary show at the Copacabana, July 25, 1956.

Mozart premieres *The Marriage of Figaro* in May 1786. He is constantly in debt and forced to give music lessons to keep his wife in frocks. The greatest of all Mozart operas closes in Vienna after only nine performances but is a hit in Prague.

On March 1, 1932, the twenty-month-old son of aviator Charles Lindbergh is kidnapped from the upstairs nursery of the Lindberghs' home in rural New Jersey. A ransom is paid. The child's body is found ten weeks later.

AGATHA CHRISTIE introduces the Belgian detective Hercule Poirot in *The Mysterious Affair at Styles*, 1920.

ADOLF HITLER grows a mustache, a small, compact model, of a size that will fit neatly inside a gas mask, 1919.

PAUL MCCARTNEY grows a mullet, 1972.

NAPOLEON assumes control of the government of France, 1799.

RICHARD NIXON wins more than $10,000 playing poker with fellow sailors in the Pacific, 1943. He will use the money to finance his first congressional bid in 1946.

In 1967, ABBIE HOFFMAN leads a group of demonstrators into the New York Stock Exchange, where they rain dollar bills from the gallery onto the trading floor. A riot erupts as traders scramble for the money. Later in the year Hoffman will organize an exorcism of the Pentagon. Fifty thousand people will converge on the building and attempt to levitate it with their combined psychic energy.

EDGAR ALLAN POE writes "The Fall of the House of Usher," 1839.

MARIE CURIE has a daughter and discovers radium, 1898. Her husband plays a part in both.

Julia McWilliams, who will become better known as JULIA CHILD, begins her job at the OSS, the World War II forerunner of the CIA, in August 1942. She lives in a tiny two-room apartment in the Brighton Hotel in Washington, where she makes do with a two-burner hotplate set on top of the refrigerator in her living room. She isn't famous for her cooking.

GEORGE BURNS marries Gracie Allen, in 1926, after courting her for four years.

Xerox inventor CHESTER CARLSON is enrolled in law school, partly as a way to escape the unhappiness of married life, 1936. He can't afford law books, so he copies them in longhand at the New York Public

Library. The writer's cramp he gets from this effort makes him think there has to be a better way of copying existing documents.

MAN O' WAR, the greatest Thoroughbred of all time, dies in November 1947. Thousands of mourners come to see him lying in state.

Not yet a national hero, HORATIO NELSON is unemployed and living in Norfolk, England, 1788.

T. E. LAWRENCE attends the Paris Peace Conference, 1919, and sees the British betray the promises made to the Arab allies during the war. He begins writing *The Seven Pillars of Wisdom* about his war experiences. An American reporter, Lowell Thomas, begins a lecture tour immortalizing him as "Lawrence of Arabia."

Oxford don Charles Dodgson (aka LEWIS CARROLL) takes ten-year-old Alice Liddell and her sister on a picnic along the river and tells them a story about Alice falling down a rabbit hole, 1862.

In December 1962, SYLVIA PLATH takes a five-year lease on a London house where Yeats once lived. Then on a Monday morning in February 1963 she puts her head in the oven, leaving 230 poems, two books of short stories, one novel (*The Bell Jar*), and two small children.

MARILYN MONROE marries brainy leftist playwright Arthur Miller, 1956. At the time Miller is being hounded by the House Un-American Activities Committee. Monroe is gutsy enough to defend him in public.

Novelist E. M. FORSTER finally learns about the mechanics of sexual intercourse, 1909.

ALEKSANDR PUSHKIN falls in love with sixteen-year-old Natalya Nikolayevna Goncharova, who is almost as aristocratic and impoverished as he is, 1829. They will marry in another two years, when she is old enough.

JAMES JOYCE visits Ireland for the last time, 1912.

RAY CHARLES's recording of "Georgia on My Mind" hits number one, November 1960.

THOMAS EDISON invents the phonograph, 1877.

PAUL THEROUX has quit teaching to be a writer full time and is finally making enough to afford his first telephone, 1971.

Environmentalist JOHN MUIR settles in Yosemite, 1868. He will stay for six years.

MARCEL DUCHAMP creates his readymade masterpiece *Fountain* from a porcelain urinal, 1917. The original, sadly, has since been lost.

ELVIS PRESLEY receives a visit from the Beatles at Graceland, August 1965. Because he can't tell them apart and doesn't know their names, he addresses each of them individually as "Beatle."

WILLIAM S. BURROUGHS becomes addicted to heroin and meets Allen Ginsberg and Jack Kerouac, 1944. He has held a number of jobs, as a private detective, a factory hand, a copywriter, an exterminator, and a bartender.

EDWARD ALBEE quits his job as a Western Union messenger, which he has held for three years, and sits down at his kitchen table to write a play as a thirtieth birthday present to himself, 1958. He titles it *The Zoo Story.*

THIRTY-ONE

To think, when one is no longer young, when one is not yet old, that one is no longer young, that one is not yet old, that is perhaps something.

—SAMUEL BECKETT, *Watt* (1953)

JOHN D. ROCKEFELLER devises a plan for gaining complete control of the American oil market, 1871.

TY COBB invests in Coca-Cola, 1918.

Humorist ROBERT BENCHLEY has his first drink, at Jack and Charlie's Puncheon Club, a speakeasy located where Rockefeller Center now stands, 1920. An Orange Blossom.

CHARLES SCHULZ gives Linus a security blanket, June 1954.

MARY QUANT invents the miniskirt, 1965. She will receive an OBE for this important achievement in the following year.

GALILEO, who is writing a theory of tides, decides Copernicus is probably right and that the earth really does revolve around the sun and not the other way around, 1595.

In the summer of 1913 VIRGINIA WOOLF finishes *The Voyage Out*, her first novel, and has a nervous breakdown that will last most of the next two years.

CLARE BOOTHE lets boyfriend Henry Luce "go all the way" on a secret trip to Florida, January 1935. She admires his strong hands and long fingers.

HERMAN MELVILLE writes *Moby-Dick*, 1851.

CARL JUNG meets Sigmund Freud (age fifty) for the first time, in Vienna, 1907. Their initial conversation lasts over thirteen hours. It's about word association.

RAY CHARLES does a country-western album, 1962.

SUSAN SONTAG is screen-tested by Andy Warhol, 1964. Her essay "Notes on Camp" appears in *Partisan Review.* In it, she argues that even bad art can be appreciated.

ELIZABETH TAYLOR is paid $1 million to play Cleopatra, 1963. During filming she sleeps with her costar, Richard Burton. The public affair breaks up her marriage to Eddie Fisher, whose marriage to Debbie Reynolds she had broken up just a few years before.

JOSEPHINE BAKER gets married, converts to Judaism, and becomes a French citizen, 1937.

CHARLES DICKENS publishes *A Christmas Carol,* 1843.

CHRISTOPHER ROBIN MILNE has married his cousin and moved to Devon, 1951. The two of them open a bookstore. He receives no royalties from the books his father wrote and must make a go of it on his own, which he does.

PETE TOWNSHEND suffers hearing loss after a Who concert at Charlton Football Ground, London, in May 1976.

On September 7, 1911, the poet GUILLAUME APOLLINAIRE is arrested on suspicion of masterminding the theft of the *Mona Lisa.* A friend of his, a painter named Pablo Picasso, is also arrested but is released after a few hours. Apollinaire is held for a week. The painting won't be recovered for another two years, during which time eight forgeries will be painted and sold.

ABBIE HOFFMAN is arrested for protesting outside the Democratic National Convention in Chicago, 1968. He will be arraigned as one of the Chicago Seven and become a national folk hero for insulting the judge.

Poet ARTHUR RIMBAUD writes to his mother from Ethiopia, telling her he's giving up coffee-trading in favor of gun-running, October 22, 1885.

JAMES BROWN records "Papa's Got a Brand New Bag," 1965.

QUEEN VICTORIA is prescribed a monthly dose of marijuana by her physician, for the relief of menstrual cramps, 1850.

In the midst of the Great Depression, WALKER EVANS embarks on an odyssey across the southern states, taking pictures of the lives and faces of ordinary people, 1935. The photographs will accompany the words of James Agee in the book *Let Us Now Praise Famous Men*, but the people in the photos are not famous and are not being praised, simply immortalized.

HARPER LEE quits her job as a reservations clerk for Eastern Airlines in New York City in order to write short stories about life in the South where she grew up, 1957. An editor suggests she turn the stories into a novel.

CHARLOTTE BRONTË publishes *Jane Eyre*, 1847, giving her astonished audience the famous phrase: "Reader, I married him."

DAPHNE DU MAURIER writes *Rebecca*, 1938.

LOUIS LUMIÈRE launches the motion picture business, 1895. The notable event occurs in France, not in California. Lumière sees no real future in the medium.

BILL GATES takes Microsoft public, 1986. Suddenly he's a billionaire.

JULIA MCWILLIAMS meets fellow spy Paul Child on the veranda of a tea plantation in Ceylon, 1944. He is forty-two.

MIKE NICHOLS changes careers, leaving his very successful comedy partnership with Elaine May to become a stage director. His first play is *Barefoot in the Park*, for which he wins the first of his five Tony awards, 1963.

Film sheik RUDOLPH VALENTINO dies, 1931. Thousands attend the funeral in the rain.

FRANZ SCHUBERT dies of typhus, contracted from the bad plumbing in the Vienna suburbs where he had gone to recover from the symptoms of syphilis, 1828. He is mourned by few.

AVA GARDNER is sleeping with a bullfighter, 1954.

ALICE WATERS's restaurant Chez Panisse gets a rave review in the October 1975 issue of *Gourmet* magazine, and suddenly everything changes. Foodies begin to camp outside the restaurant. People start calling from other time zones asking for a reservation.

CLAUDE MONET paints *Impression, Sunrise*, giving a name to impressionism, 1872. The critics hate it.

KATHARINE HEPBURN is declared box office poison by a trade magazine distributed to theater owners, 1938.

HOWARD HUGHES sets a new speed record flying from Los Angeles to New York in seven hours, twenty-eight minutes, and twenty-five seconds, 1937.

RALPH NADER writes *Unsafe at Any Speed*, 1965, creating the consumer safety movement.

BABE RUTH promises Johnny Sylvester, a sick kid in a St. Louis hospital, that he'll hit a home run for him in game four of the World Series against the Cardinals, 1926. He hits three.

ROBERT THE BRUCE, outlawed and exiled to Ireland, takes inspiration from a spider, 1306.

CECIL B. DEMILLE directs *The Squaw Man* in a small town in southern California, 1913.

JOHN DILLINGER is gunned down by G-men outside the Biograph Theater on the north side of Chicago, 1934.

HARRY HOUDINI buys a seven-acre farm in Connecticut, 1905. A little place to escape to.

PHILIP II of Spain wishes to marry Elizabeth I of England, but she puts him off, 1558. He begins to build boats.

THIRTY-TWO

Bill's thirty-two. He looks thirty-two. He looked it five years ago, he'll look it twenty years from now. I hate men.

—BETTE DAVIS, *All About Eve* (1950)

NOËL COWARD's play *Private Lives* is running on Broadway, 1931. He wrote the book and lyrics and stars in it himself, opposite Gertrude Lawrence.

ROBERT BROWNING sends a chaste love note to Elizabeth Barrett, January 10, 1845. The two poets begin to correspond.

RUDYARD KIPLING is living in England but writing about India, 1898. George Orwell, when he is thirty-two, will write of him, "I worshipped Kipling at 13, loathed him at 17, enjoyed him at 20, despised him at 25, and now again rather admire him."

DAVID Cornwell's third novel is successful enough to allow him to quit his job and become a writer full time, 1963. The novel is *The Spy Who Came In from the Cold*, written under the name JOHN LE CARRÉ. The day job was with British intelligence. In Le Carré's opinion all writers are spies.

IN 1921, CHARLIE CHAPLIN visits London for the first time since he left it as a minor stage comedian eleven years earlier. When he arrives, he is lifted on the shoulders of the crowd at Waterloo Station and cheered by thousands along the three-mile cab ride to the Ritz Hotel.

ALEXANDER THE GREAT dies of appendicitis in what is now Afghanistan, 323 B.C., having conquered most of the known world and had thirteen cities named after him. His empire will last for another twelve years.

With investment capital from an heir to the Fleischman's Yeast fortune, HAROLD ROSS founds *The New Yorker* magazine on February 21, 1925. The magazine will lose about $8,000 a week for the first year.

NORMAN MAILER is one of the founders of *The Village Voice*, 1955.

BUCKMINSTER FULLER, bankrupt and jobless, contemplates suicide in the icy waters of Lake Michigan, 1927, but decides to "commit egocide" instead. He calls himself Guinea Pig B (for Bucky) and begins his "experiment to discover what the little, penniless, unknown individual might be able to do effectively on behalf of all humanity." The experiment will consume the next fifty-four years.

ANTON CHEKHOV has a medical degree but seldom practices medicine, although he is busy during the cholera epidemic of 1892–93. He says, "Medicine is my lawful wife and literature my mistress. When I get tired of one, I spend the night with the other."

EUDORA WELTY confides to Katherine Anne Porter that she's still a virgin, and Porter replies that she always will be, 1941. Welty's just sold her first book.

ROSA PARKS tries to register to vote in Montgomery, Alabama, where she lives, 1945. She is prevented from doing so twice by white officials but finally succeeds.

SAMMY DAVIS JR. is dating Kim Novak, 1958. Harry Cohn, the studio boss who owns her movie contract, forces them to break it off.

TED TURNER buys Channel 17, an independent TV station in Atlanta, 1970.

In 1938, architect PHILIP JOHNSON attends the Nazi Parteitag in Germany, giddily describing the Nuremberg rallies as "even more staggering than Wagner's *Ring*."

MILLARD KAUFMAN cocreates the bumbling, nearsighted cartoon character Mr. Magoo, 1949.

ROSE MARY WOODS is hired to be Richard Nixon's secretary after he is elected to the Senate in 1950.

William Blake publishes *Songs of Innocence*, 1789.

Saint Augustine is baptized by Saint Ambrose on the day before Easter, 387. Of course, neither of them is a saint yet, just saintly.

One evening in September 1931, C. S. Lewis has a late-night discussion about Christianity with his Oxford chums J.R.R. Tolkien and Hugo Dyson. The next day he and his brother motorcycle to the zoo. Lewis will later recount that when he started off for the zoo, "I did not believe that Jesus Christ was the Son of God, and when we reached the zoo I did."

Thomas Edison invents the lightbulb, 1879.

Richard Francis Burton makes his famous pilgrimage to Mecca, 1853. Traveling in disguise, he is the first European ever to visit the holy city.

Meriwether Lewis and William Clark arrive back in Washington from their trip to the Pacific on September 23, 1806. They have been gone two years.

Frank Sinatra and his new doll Ava Gardner get loaded and shoot up the desert town of Indio, California, 1948.

Steve Martin announces that he is a "wild and crazy guy" on live network television, September 24, 1977.

Tennessee Williams is writing screenplays in Hollywood but gets fired for putting too many big words into a script for Lana Turner, 1943. He continues to collect his $250 a week paycheck anyway.

Thor Heyerdahl sets sail in the *Kon-Tiki* to prove that Polynesia could have been settled by South Americans, 1947.

Fridtjof Nansen sails the ship *Fram* into the drifting arctic ice with the aim of floating up over the North Pole in three years, 1893. His plan very nearly succeeds.

Joseph Conrad takes command of a small steamship traveling down the Congo River from Stanley Falls to Leopoldville, 1890. Twelve years later the experience will provide the germ of his novel *Heart of Darkness*.

HART CRANE sails for Mexico, hoping to write a poem about Cortés's conquest, but he soon gives it up and embarks from Vera Cruz for New York. On a day in April 1932, after a night of drinking, he jumps from the ship into the ocean and drowns. Crane's father was a wealthy Cleveland candymaker and the inventor of the Life Saver mint.

In October 1976, ALICE WATERS's restaurant Chez Panisse starts listing where the ingredients came from right on the menu. "Preserved California geese from Sebastopol." "Big Sur Garrapata Creek smoked trout steamed over California bay leaves." It will get to the point where you feel like you're eating animals and plants Ms. Waters knew personally.

EDWARD GOREY begins his twenty-five-year run of perfect attendance at performances of the New York City Ballet, 1957.

FIDEL CASTRO overthrows the Batista government in Cuba, 1959.

J. D. SALINGER publishes *A Catcher in the Rye*, July 1951.

ALEXANDER CALDER invents a new kind of sculpture, 1932. Marcel Duchamp calls it a mobile.

GERTRUDE STEIN sits to have her portrait painted by Pablo Picasso, 1906. It requires eighty sessions. Picasso finally wipes the face clean in frustration. Later, after viewing an exhibition of primitive art at the Louvre, he repaints the face. When Stein complains that she looks nothing like the portrait, Picasso replies, "You will."

SYLVIA BEACH opens her bookshop, Shakespeare and Company, in the Left Bank in Paris, 1919.

WILLIAM FAULKNER buys a run-down antebellum mansion in Oxford, Mississippi, 1930. He names it Rowan Oak. He will live and write there, off and on, for the rest of his life and never pay off the mortgage.

Treasury Secretary ALEXANDER HAMILTON introduces the national debt, which becomes the wellspring of the new American economy, suggesting confidence in endless continuity and prosperity, 1790.

JAMES THURBER meets E. B. White at a party in New York, 1927. White introduces him to Harold Ross, who immediately hires him to work at a new magazine called *The New Yorker.* "I'll hire anybody," Ross is heard to say.

Librettist WILLIAM SCHWENCK GILBERT meets composer Arthur Sullivan, 1869.

DEWITT WALLACE and his new wife, Lila, publish a new magazine made up of condensed articles selected from other magazines, February 1922. They decide to call it *Reader's Digest.*

EMILY POST divorces her husband, 1905. She decides to write for a living, fiction to begin with, then comedies of manners, magazine stories, a novel, and a humorous travelogue of a trip she took with her son to California.

FRED ASTAIRE becomes a solo act on the day before his thirty-third birthday, when his sister Adele quits show business to marry the future Duke of Devonshire, 1932.

THIRTY-THREE

Through life's road so dim and dirty,
I have dragged to three and thirty.
What have these years left to me?
Nothing except thirty-three.

—LORD BYRON (1821)

EDMUND HILLARY and Tenzing Norgay (age thirty-nine) reach the summit of Mount Everest at eleven-thirty on the morning of May 29, 1953, a few days before Queen Elizabeth II's coronation.

BRUCE CHATWIN has become a nomad, 1933. He pays for his travels writing articles for London's *Sunday Times Magazine*, but his friends notice he's also something of a professional houseguest.

Three years after the death of his ex-wife, TED HUGHES burns the last volume of Sylvia Plath's journals, 1963.

HUNTER S. THOMPSON runs for sheriff of Pitkin County, Colorado, 1970. His platform includes legalization of drugs and renaming the town of Aspen "Fat City." When he comes in second, he appoints himself executive director of the Woody Creek Rod and Gun Club.

Bank teller WILLIAM SYDNEY PORTER "borrows" some money from the till and invests it in a magazine he's started called *The Rolling Stone*, 1899. When he is released from prison three years later, he will change his name to O. Henry and move to New York. He will not trademark the name of the magazine.

LIZZIE BORDEN is found not guilty of giving her mother and father forty and forty-one whacks, respectively, 1893.

As a favor to his friend Dalton Trumbo, who is blacklisted, MILLARD KAUFMAN puts his name on the script for the 1950 film *Gun Crazy.*

HARPER LEE meets her old friend Truman Capote at Grand Central Terminal for a trip to Garden City, Kansas, where Truman is to write about a murder case, December 1959.

On October 5, 1949, HELENE HANFF writes a letter to Marks and Co., a London bookstore located at 84 Charing Cross Road.

GERTRUDE STEIN meets Alice B. Toklas, 1907.

WALTER CRONKITE joins CBS, 1950.

MAYA ANGELOU is the associate editor of *The Arab Observer*, in Cairo, the only English-language newsweekly in the Middle East, 1962.

MICHELANGELO is hired to paint the ceiling of the Sistine Chapel, 1508.

GORE VIDAL writes the script for *Ben-Hur* and introduces Tennessee Williams to Jack and Jackie Kennedy, 1958.

DR. SEUSS's *And to Think That I Saw It on Mulberry Street* is published by Random House, 1937. It was rejected by twenty eight publishers. Bennett Cerf, the publisher of William Faulkner and John O'Hara among others, remarks that he has only one genius on his list, and his name is Dr. Seuss.

MRS. BEETON's cookery advice first appears in *The Englishwoman's Domestic Magazine*, 1859.

CLAES OLDENBURG sculpts *Giant Ice Cream Cone* and *Giant Hamburger*, 1962.

In September 1666 the diarist SAMUEL PEPYS digs a hole in his back garden to bury his wine and his best cheese and hopefully save them from the Great Fire of London, which is burning closer by the day.

In September 1945 the German scientist WERNHER VON BRAUN, architect of the V-2 rocket program that has been blowing large holes in London, surrenders to the Americans instead of the Soviets. Which is why people on the moon speak English today instead of Russian.

Rand Corporation analyst DANIEL ELLSBERG joins a colleague at a 1964 matinee of Stanley Kubrick's *Dr. Strangelove, or How I Learned to Stop Worrying and Love the Bomb.* Leaving the theater, Ellsberg declares that the film was a documentary.

CLARE BOOTHE LUCE is too nervous to attend the Broadway opening of her play *The Women,* December 1936. She spends the evening at the observation deck atop the Empire State Building.

HANS CHRISTIAN ANDERSEN's feelings are hurt by a scathing review written by a twenty-five-year-old part-time journalist named Søren Kierkegaard, 1838.

Karen Blixen is growing coffee in Africa, where she meets Englishman Denys Finch Hatton, 1918. She will later change her name to ISAK DINESEN.

INGMAR BERGMAN directs nine soap commercials for Swedish television, 1951.

LILLIAN HELLMAN takes the profits from her play *The Little Foxes* and buys Hardscrabble Farm in Pennsylvania, May 1939.

WALTER RALEIGH establishes an English settlement on Roanoke Island off the coast of North Carolina, 1585. It quickly fails, but by then Raleigh is back in England. He'll try and fail again in 1587, and the queen will make him a knight.

Charles Dodgson, a mathematics tutor at Oxford, publishes *Alice's Adventures in Wonderland* under the name LEWIS CARROLL, 1865.

MARTIN LUTHER composes a ninety-five-point complaint against the Catholic Church and nails it to the door of his church in Wittenberg on October 31, 1517. He is especially angry that the church charges people to see holy relics and sells "indulgences" in exchange for fewer years in purgatory.

Edgar Allan Poe publishes "The Raven" in the *New York Evening Mirror*, 1845.

George Plimpton pitches to sixteen major league ballplayers in a 1960 exhibition game and is completely humiliated, although he does get Willie Mays to pop up. He will describe his experience in the book *Out of My League* (1961).

Robert Louis Stevenson spends the winter in Davos, Switzerland, writing *Treasure Island*, 1882.

Ho Chi Minh arrives in Moscow, where he will study to be a revolutionary, 1923.

Voltaire and a mathematician friend of his figure out that a French lottery has better odds than its sponsors planned, 1728. They form a syndicate and win enough money to become major international moneylenders.

Andrew Carnegie figures that in two years he will have enough money to retire and have $50,000 a year to live on, 1868.

Father Damien arrives on the island of Molokai in Hawaii as parish priest to the leper colony there, 1873. He will live with them and eat with them and dress their wounds, help build their homes and dig their graves, eventually dying there, of leprosy, in 1889.

Botticelli paints *Primavera*, 1477.

Andy Warhol paints *Campbell's Soup Cans*, 1962. Thirty-two in all, one for each flavor of soup.

Groucho Marx paints a mustache on for the first time during the run of *I'll Say She Is!*, 1924.

Jesus begins preaching in public, beginning in Nazareth, A.D. 27. The people of his hometown aren't persuaded. He begins to gather a few apostles and performs his first miracle by turning water into wine.

THIRTY-*four*

Stella this day is thirty-four
(We shan't dispute a year or more)—
However, Stella, be not troubled,
Although thy size and years are doubled,
Since first I saw thee at sixteen,
The brightest virgin on the green,
So little is thy form declined,
Made up so largely in thy mind.
Oh, would it please the gods, to split
Thy beauty, size, and years, and wit,
No age could furnish out a pair
Of nymphs so graceful, wise, and fair.

—JONATHAN SWIFT, "Stella's Birthday" (1719)

VIRGINIA WOOLF and her husband, Leonard, have moved to Hogarth House next door to the North Surrey Squash Rackets Club, in suburban Richmond, near London, 1916.

ELIZABETH TAYLOR stars in the film of *Who's Afraid of Virginia Woolf,* directed by Mike Nichols, 1966. The role wins her her second Oscar. She marries husband number five Richard Burton.

JOHN MILTON writes *The Doctrine and Discipline of Divorce,* published in 1643. Besides writing *Paradise Lost* and *Paradise Regained,* he will marry three times, not very happily.

After eight years of playing a cowboy on American television, CLINT EASTWOOD goes to Italy to play a cowboy for Sergio Leone, 1964.

JACK KEROUAC, author of *On the Road*, learns to drive, 1956. He will never have a driver's license.

HERNAN CORTÉS enters Mexico City, 1519.

Playwright JAMES BARRIE buys his wife a St. Bernard for a wedding present, 1894.

JAMES THURBER publishes his first book, *Is Sex Necessary?*, written with E. B. White, 1929.

ALFRED NOBEL patents a new invention called dynamite, 1867.

PELHAM GRENVILLE WODEHOUSE invents the quintessential valet Jeeves, 1915. Jeeves's employer, Bertie Wooster, will never age beyond thirty.

CARAVAGGIO paints *The Death of the Virgin* and murders Ranuccio Tomassoni, 1606.

Playwright ARTHUR MILLER wins a Pulitzer Prize for *Death of a Salesman*, 1949.

OSKAR SCHINDLER witnesses a Nazi raid on the Jewish ghetto in Krakow and sees hundreds of innocent men, women, and children herded onto rail cars to the death camps, 1942.

HAROLD PINTER's new play, *The Homecoming*, begins with the words, "What have you done with the scissors?" 1964.

NELSON MANDELA opens the first black law firm in South Africa, 1952. He wears smart suits, drives a large Oldsmobile, and refuses to act like a black man in a white man's court.

T. E. LAWRENCE enlists in the Royal Air Force under the name J. H. Ross, 1922, but is dismissed from the ranks when his cover is blown in the press. He enlists in the Tank Corps as T. E. Shaw but finds that he liked the RAF better. He finishes writing *The Seven Pillars of Wisdom*.

GEORGE PLIMPTON appears as a Bedouin extra in the film *Lawrence of Arabia*, 1961.

KATHARINE HEPBURN pairs with Spencer Tracy in *Woman of the Year*, the first of nine films they will make together, 1942. She will always give him first billing.

GUSTAVE FLAUBERT writes *Madame Bovary*, 1856.

EZRA POUND submits a poem to a contest sponsored by Newark, New Jersey, on the occasion of its 250th anniversary and wins one of ten fourth prizes, 1916. He is awarded $50.

Grief-stricken on the death of his wife, poet and painter DANTE GABRIEL ROSSETTI buries many of his unpublished poems with her at London's Highgate Cemetery, 1862. He will later change his mind and dig them up, publishing them in 1870.

The comments on FRED ASTAIRE's 1933 screen test for David O. Selznick say: "Can't act. Slightly bald. Also dances." On the set of *Flying Down to Rio*, he meets Ginger Rogers.

The light-skinned African-American singer LENA HORNE is a victim of racial discrimination when she is passed over for the part of Julie, the light-skinned mulatto heroine who is a victim of racial discrimination, in MGM's lavish 1951 filming of *Showboat*. The part is given to dark-skinned Caucasian actress Ava Gardner. The two are friends.

HARPER LEE's novel *To Kill a Mockingbird* is published, 1960. It is a best seller, wins the Pulitzer Prize, and is made into a movie starring Gregory Peck. In 1962 Lee tells an interviewer she is writing another novel, but slowly, only a page or two a day.

JOHN ADAMS defends the British soldiers charged in the Boston Massacre trials, 1770. He wins acquittals or reduced sentences for all the defendants.

JANE FONDA travels to North Vietnam and broadcasts a statement opposing the war on Radio Hanoi, 1972.

In February 1953, with his F-9 Panther in flames over North Korea, TED WILLIAMS decides that ejecting might break his legs or his spine, so instead he pilots his crippled plane to a crash landing at the air base in South Korea. This is his second war. He will survive to win batting titles for the Red Sox in 1957 and 1958.

ERNEST HEMINGWAY goes on his first African safari with second wife Pauline and a friend from Key West, 1933. He bags a lion and a case of dysentery.

ARTHUR CONAN DOYLE visits Reichenbach Falls in Switzerland and decides it is as good a place as any to kill Sherlock Holmes. "The Final Problem" appears in *The Strand Magazine* in December 1893. Twenty thousand people cancel their subscriptions.

Jazz saxophonist CHARLIE PARKER dies after years of drug addiction, 1955. The physician who examines the body guesses that Parker was sixty years old.

ALEKSANDR SOLZHENITSYN is released from the Soviet gulag after eight years and will be exiled to southern Kazakhstan for three more years, 1953. He had criticized Stalin in a letter to a friend.

T. S. ELIOT publishes *The Waste Land*, 1922.

Songwriter JOHNNY MERCER is seeing an analyst several times a week, 1944. While driving home one afternoon, he turns his doctor's advice into a lyric. He titles it "Ac-cent-uate the Positive." Harold Arlen writes the melody.

SIGMUND FREUD is given a couch by a grateful patient, 1890.

CHARLES MANSON buys a copy of the Beatles' *White Album*, 1968.

JESSE JAMES is shot and killed by Bob Ford, 1882.

MARIA CALLAS meets Aristotle Onassis at a party in Venice, 1957.

HORATIO NELSON meets Sir William Hamilton in Naples, who introduces him to his wife, Emma, 1793. The famous affair won't commence for another four years.

TENNESSEE WILLIAMS's *The Glass Menagerie* opens at the Playhouse Theatre in New York, March 31, 1945.

LIBERACE plays Carnegie Hall, 1953.

THIRTY-*five*

~~

Thirty-five is a very attractive age. London society is full of women of the highest birth who have, of their own free choice, remained thirty-five for years.

—OSCAR WILDE, *The Importance of Being Earnest* (1895)

MARTHA STEWART starts a catering business, 1976.

PAUL CÉZANNE paints a dish of apples, 1875.

DYLAN THOMAS arrives in New York City and has a drink at the White Horse Tavern on Hudson Street, 1950.

Rolling Stone editor JANN WENNER listens to Bob Pittman explain his idea for a cable channel devoted to videos of musicians performing their own music, 1981. Jann tells Bob that MTV is a stupid idea and refuses to invest in it.

MUDDY WATERS records his first single for Chess Records, 1950. The song is "Rolling Stone."

JOHN HUSTON writes and directs *The Maltese Falcon*, from the Dashiell Hammett novel, 1941. The movie makes Humphrey Bogart a star.

STEVEN SPIELBERG buys Rosebud, the famous sled from Orson Welles's *Citizen Kane*, at Sotheby's for $60,000, 1982.

JACK NICHOLSON buys courtside season tickets to the Los Angeles Lakers games, 1972.

In 1932, WILLIAM FAULKNER is making so little money from his novels that he goes to Hollywood to make a little more. He dislikes writing in the cramped writers' quarters at the studio, so he asks if he can write at home. Several weeks later his employers discover that "home" meant Mississippi.

SAINT AUGUSTINE returns to Africa, 389.

JOHN WAYNE plays a courageous airman in *Flying Tigers*, 1942.

Colonel JAMES STEWART is flying bombers over Germany, 1943. He will earn the Air Medal, two Distinguished Flying Crosses, the Croix de Guerre, and seven battle stars.

FREDERICK LAW OLMSTED takes a job as superintendent of New York's Central Park, 1857. It's neither central nor a park, just an empty tract of land on the edge of the city.

FREDERICK THE GREAT invites Johann Sebastian Bach to dinner, May 1747.

GERALD MURPHY and his wife, Sara, purchase a little house in Cap d'Antibes that they christen Villa America, 1923.

VINCENT VAN GOGH moves to the south of France, to a yellow house in Arles, 1888. He invites Paul Gauguin to move in with him. During a psychotic episode in December, Van Gogh cuts off his ear with a razor.

MERIWETHER LEWIS commits suicide in 1809. It's likely that he was driven insane by the mercury compound that the expedition's members took for constipation.

Poet and painter DANTE GABRIEL ROSSETTI has his picture taken by mathemetician, photographer, and author Lewis Carroll, 1863.

NAPOLEON crowns himself emperor, 1804.

The Who guitarist PETE TOWNSHEND nearly dies of a drug overdose at the Club for Heroes in London, 1985.

ROBERT LOUIS STEVENSON writes *The Strange Case of Dr. Jekyll and Mr. Hyde*, which is about a nice man who turns into a selfish creep after drinking a mysterious compound, 1886.

MARTIN LUTHER KING JR. wins the Nobel Peace Prize, 1964.

PAUL ROBESON stars in a film adaptation of Eugene O'Neill's *The Emperor Jones*, a role he played on the London stage, 1933.

HORATIO ALGER publishes "Ragged Dick," an inspiring story about a street urchin who, through hard work and positive thoughts, becomes a member of the middle class, 1867. He will write the same novel 135 times, with slight variations.

FRANK WILLS is sentenced to a year in prison for shoplifting a pair of shoes, 1983. Wills had left his job at the Watergate Hotel shortly after discovering the famous break-in and was unable to find other work as a security guard. "I don't know if they are being told not to hire me or if they are just afraid to hire me," he told a *Washington Post* reporter. (Charles Colson, who authorized the Watergate burglary that Wills uncovered, was sentenced to only seven months for his crimes.)

JOHNNY CASH plays a concert at Folsom State Prison in California, 1968.

ERNEST HEMINGWAY orders a boat from the Wheeler Shipyards of Brooklyn, New York, 1934. The thirty-eight-foot cabin cruiser has extra tankage for long days fishing, an auxiliary inboard motor, a lower transom with a wooden roller for landing big fish, and a live fish well. He names her the *Pilar*.

GRAHAM GREENE's London house is destroyed by a direct hit during the Blitz, 1940. Luckily he is sleeping at his mistress's flat at the time. "His life was saved because of his infidelity," his wife says afterward.

In the midst of the Depression, WALT DISNEY spends a million and a half dollars to make a feature-length cartoon about a young woman living with seven men, 1937.

MICHAEL JACKSON marries Lisa Marie Presley, 1994.

With the publication of *Main Street*, SINCLAIR LEWIS becomes famous around the world and is sincerely hated in the small Minnesota town where he grew up, 1920.

THE FBI has a three-hundred-page file on DR. JONAS SALK, itemizing his liberal sympathies, 1950. The material nearly derails his career. He has just begun work on his polio vaccine. In order to continue his research, he decides to avoid any involvement in politics.

JACKSON POLLOCK begins painting by the drip method, 1947.

LORD BYRON sets sail for Greece to join the revolution against the Turks. In his entourage are four friends, two servants, a gondolier, five horses, and a bulldog. He arrives in Missolonghi in early 1824.

MAURICE SENDAK publishes *Where the Wild Things Are*, 1963.

PAUL GAUGUIN decides to quit the stockbroking business altogether and be a painter full time, 1883.

AMELIA EARHART is the first woman and the second person to fly solo across the Atlantic and the first person to fly across it twice, 1932.

MOZART dies and is buried in an unmarked grave along with several other people who die the same day, 1791. He composed 41 symphonies, 29 piano concertos, 20 operas, 23 string quartets, and 35 piano sonatas, as well as numerous serenades, divertimenti, and the Requiem.

J. K. ROWLING makes more money in 2000 than any other woman in Britain, even the queen. Twenty million quid.

GORE VIDAL runs for Congress as a Democrat in very Republican Dutchess County, New York, and loses, 1960.

IN December 1933 GEORGE GERSHWIN begins composing the music that will become *Porgy and Bess.* He begins with "Summertime." When the show opens in 1935, it will run for 124 performances and lose its investors every penny.

LOU GEHRIG retires from baseball, eight games into the 1939 season. He hasn't missed a game in fifteen years. He will die in 1941 from what is now known as Lou Gehrig's disease.

THIRTY-SIX

Why are we here, that is the question. And we are blessed in this, that we happen to know the answer. Yes, in this immense confusion one thing alone is clear. We are waiting for Godot to come.

—SAMUEL BECKETT, *Waiting for Godot* (1953)

GRETA GARBO retires from motion pictures and moves to New York City to become a famous recluse, 1941.

JESUS goes to Jerusalem, tells everyone he is the Son of God, delivers an antiauthoritarian sermon endorsing shared wealth and pacifism, and is arrested after being betrayed by one of his disciples, A.D. 30. The rest of his disciples deny knowing him, and he is crucified on a hill outside the city. Several of the disciples begin writing their memoirs.

CHARLES SCHULZ draws a strip in which Linus awaits the coming of the Great Pumpkin, 1959.

In July 1941 GRAHAM GREENE becomes a spy. He is given the number 59200. He will give the same number to Wormold, the vacuum cleaner salesman and spy in his 1958 satire *Our Man in Havana*.

CHESTER CARLSON receives patent number 2,297,691 for a process he will later call Xerography, 1942.

PABLO PICASSO marries a ballerina, 1918. Surrealist Jean Cocteau, painter Max Jacob, and poet Guillaume Apollinaire are witnesses.

NORMAN ROCKWELL gets a divorce, 1930.

On April 9, 1824, LORD BYRON catches cold after being out in the rain. Ten days later he is dead. Despite his specific instructions, his body is shipped from Missolonghi back to England and is buried in June in Hucknall Torkard Church, near Newstead Abbey, where he once lived. His memoirs, which he had meant to publish, are burned by a group of his friends. He never finished writing *Don Juan*.

Navy seaman JAMES MICHENER is called to active duty and sent to the South Pacific, 1943.

Gonzo journalist HUNTER S. THOMPSON provides the model for the character of Uncle Duke in the *Doonesbury* comic strip, 1974.

WALT WHITMAN publishes *Leaves of Grass*, 1855.

Shortly after being inducted into the Order of the Knights of Malta, the painter CARAVAGGIO is expelled for wounding another knight in a brawl, 1608. He paints *The Beheading of Saint John the Baptist*.

ROBESPIERRE is executed by guillotine, 1794.

VINCENT VAN GOGH commits himself to the insane asylum in Saint-Rémy, 1889. He converts the adjacent cell into a workroom, where he paints 150 paintings. During one relapse, he tries to poison himself by swallowing paint.

SHERWOOD ANDERSON is running a mail-order paint company in Elyria, Ohio, 1912. One day, without explanation, he walks away from the office. He's found four days later in Cleveland. The diagnosis is a nervous breakdown, but it seems all he wanted to do was escape his humdrum job. He and his wife move to Chicago, and he begins to write.

MUHAMMAD ALI wins the world heavyweight title for the third time, 1978.

ANDY WARHOL announces his retirement from painting, May 1965.

JACK LALANNE begins exercising on television, 1951. His program will run for the next thirty years.

HELEN KELLER attempts an elopement with Annie Sullivan's secretary, 1916. Her mother intervenes.

Depressed after the critical and box office failure of his opera *Carmen*, GEORGES BIZET dies on June 3, 1875. After his death *Carmen* quickly becomes a fixture of the operatic repertoire.

Surprised by a much larger force of Cheyenne and Sioux warriors, GEORGE ARMSTRONG CUSTER dies with all of his men at the Battle of the Little Big Horn, June 25, 1876. The scene is soon immortalized as Custer's Last Stand in a lithograph that will replace murals of voluptuous nudes over saloon bars all across America.

Steeplechase jockey DICK FRANCIS suffers a serious fall and retires from racing, 1957.

JOSEPH CONRAD has been a merchant seaman for twenty years when he leaves the sea to settle in England, 1894. His plan is to write novels.

BENEDICT ARNOLD wins a decisive battle at Saratoga, but his superior takes the credit, 1777. When Arnold is passed over for promotion, General Washington has to talk him out of leaving the army.

PYOTR ILICH TCHAIKOVSKY attends the premiere of Wagner's *Ring Cycle* at Bayreuth, August 1876.

ADOLF HITLER's *Mein Kampf* is published on July 1, 1925. It gets bad reviews and sells poorly.

On September 6, 1946, Jesus speaks to MOTHER TERESA on the train to Darjeeling. It is their first conversation.

CHARLES LINDBERGH accepts a medal from Nazi Germany's Reichsmarschall and Luftwaffe chief Hermann Goering, 1938. Soon thereafter Lindbergh begins making speeches urging America to stay out of the looming war in Europe.

Marilyn Monroe dies in her Brentwood, California, home of an overdose of barbiturates, 1962. She has made thirty films.

Diana, Princess of Wales, dies in a car accident in Paris, 1997.

Wilkie Collins writes *The Woman in White*, 1860.

In the April 25, 1953, issue of the journal *Nature*, Francis Crick and James Watson (age twenty-five) write: "We wish to suggest a structure for the salt of deoxoribose nucleic acid." They have discovered the double helix structure of the DNA molecule that defines life.

Johnny Carson hosts *The Tonight Show* for the first time on October 2, 1962, taking over from Jack Paar. His first guest is Groucho Marx.

Che Guevara addresses the UN General Assembly, 1964. While he is in town, he has dinner at the Rockefellers'. A few months later he drops from sight. He'd spoken about becoming a global revolutionary, but his whereabouts will remain a mystery for two years.

Lech Walesa leads the strike in the Lenin Shipyard in Gdansk that begins the toppling of Communism, 1980.

Anton Chekhov sees *The Seagull* premiered in St. Petersburg, 1896. The play is so badly received that he vows to give up writing plays.

Agatha Christie's husband, the former war hero Colonel Archibald Christie, leaves her for a younger woman named Nancy Neele, 1926. Distressed, the mystery novelist disappears, setting off a much-publicized search across the length and breadth of England. When she is discovered some weeks later, she is living in a hotel in the spa town of Harrogate under the name of Mrs. Neele. She remembers nothing.

In 1918 James Joyce begins to publish bits and pieces of a long story he's been working on about one day in Dublin in 1904.

In 1964 the spy Pham Xuan An is secretly advising the South Vietnamese on how to deal with the Americans, the Communists on how to deal with the South Vietnamese and the Americans, and the Americans on how to deal with the Communists and the South Vietnamese. In his spare time he is reporting for *Time* magazine.

EINSTEIN completes his General Theory of Relativity, 1915.

JERRY LEWIS's film *The Nutty Professor* earns respectful notices in the influential French journal *Cahiers du cinéma*, 1962.

SAMUEL JOHNSON begins his *Dictionary*, 1746. It will be published in 1755.

JAMES FRAZER begins work on *The Golden Bough*, his comprehensive mythology, 1890. When he finishes it in twenty-five years, he will be Sir James Frazer.

On May 30, 1669, SAMUEL PEPYS writes the last entry in his famous diary: "And thus ends all that I doubt I shall ever be able to do with my own eyes in the keeping of my journal." He believes he is going blind, which sets his mind upon his own mortality. After a few months his eyesight improves, but he doesn't resume the diary. He will live another thirty-three years.

ERIC CLAPTON enters rehab in rural Minnesota, 1982.

ENRICO CARUSO sings in the first live opera broadcast on January 13, 1910, performing *Pagliacci* from the Metropolitan Opera House in New York City.

DANTE ALIGHIERI is exiled from Florence, never to return, 1302.

PETRARCH is crowned laureate in Rome, 1341.

JULIA CHILD arrives in France for the first time, in November 1948. Along the route from Le Havre to Paris, she has her first French meal in a restaurant: oysters, sole meunière, salad, cheese, coffee.

Poet WALLACE STEVENS is working for the Hartford Accident and Indemnity Company when he wins $100 from *Poetry Magazine* for the play "Three Travelers Watch a Sunrise," 1916.

THIRTY-SEVEN

I lean and loaf at my ease observing a spear of summer grass.
My tongue, every atom of my blood, form'd from this soil, this
*   air,*
Born here of parents born here from parents the same, and
*   their parents the same,*
I, now thirty-seven years old in perfect health begin,
Hoping to cease not till death.

—WALT WHITMAN, "Song of Myself,"
Leaves of Grass (1855)

LIBERACE is performing in London when the *Daily Mirror* describes him as a "deadly, winking, sniggering, snuggling, chromium-plated, scent-impregnated, luminous, quivering, giggling, fruit-flavored, mincing, ice-covered heap of mother love," 1956. The pianist sues. Three years later the newspaper will have to dish out a $22,400 libel judgment, and Liberace will cry all the way to the bank.

COCO CHANEL introduces the perfume Chanel no. 5, 1921.

WILLIAM WORDSWORTH writes a poem about daffodils, 1807.

JEAN GENET is convicted of burglary for the tenth time and receives a mandatory life sentence, 1948. But Jean-Paul Sartre, Jean Cocteau, and André Gide petition the president for his release. This being France, the petition is granted. To express his gratitude, Genet writes a poem about the importance of criminals.

Beat novelist WILLIAM S. BURROUGHS accidentally shoots and kills his wife while performing a William Tell trick, 1951. He flees Mexico, where they had been living, for Tangiers in North Africa.

Norman Mailer stabs his wife, Adele, with a penknife and is briefly committed to the Bellevue mental hospital, 1960.

To cover up his homosexuality, Pyotr Ilich Tchaikovsky marries one of his students, 1877. Unfortunately she is a nymphomaniac. The marriage lasts two months, and Tchaikovsky tries to drown himself in a river. He begins a safer relationship with a rich widow.

Richard Nixon wins election to the U.S. Senate by implying that New Dealer Helen Gahagan Douglas wears pink underwear, 1950.

On February 27, 1860, Mathew Brady takes his first photograph of Abraham Lincoln. The presidential candidate is in New York to deliver an antislavery speech at Cooper Union. Lincoln will claim afterward that it was this photo and this speech that won him the election.

Mary Ann Evans begins using the pen name George Eliot, 1857.

Jack London writes letters to Winston Churchill, George Bernard Shaw, and H. G. Wells, asking them how much they get paid for their writing, 1913.

Charles Dickens begins the monthly serialization of a new novel called *David Copperfield*, May 1849. In it he describes the young narrator's despair when his bankrupt father forces him to go to work in a shoe-blacking factory. It is an experience from the author's own childhood, which he has never told anyone before. His own children believe it is fiction.

After four years lying on his back, Michelangelo finishes painting the Sistine Chapel ceiling, 1512.

James Abbott McNeill Whistler paints his mother but calls the picture *Arrangement in Grey and Black, No. 1*, 1871.

Anton Chekhov contracts the tuberculosis that will eventually kill him, 1897. His best work is still ahead of him.

Sherwood Anderson publishes *Winesburg, Ohio*, 1919.

HOWARD HUGHES designs a special cantilevered brassiere to show off Jane Russell's cleavage in the film *The Outlaw*, 1943. In places where the film isn't banned, it is quite popular.

WHILE driving between Mexico City and Acapulco in January 1965, GABRIEL GARCÍA MÁRQUEZ is seized with an idea that will become the opening chapter of his famous novel *One Hundred Years of Solitude*. A year and a half later he will pawn his wife's hair dryer and the heater for their apartment to mail the twelve-hundred-page manuscript to publishers.

BRUCE CHATWIN publishes *In Patagonia*, his terse, allusive half-fiction about his six months roaming the tip of South America, 1977.

THE great imperial novelist and poet RUDYARD KIPLING refuses a knighthood for the second time in five years, 1903.

JOHN STEINBECK's novel *The Grapes of Wrath* is published, in April 1939. By May it will be selling ten thousand copies a week.

MARIE ANTOINETTE is guillotined on October 16, 1793, after four years of imprisonment. The charges are high treason and illicit sexual practices, but most of the resentment is over how much she spent on jewelry.

ELIZABETH TAYLOR receives a very large diamond from Richard Burton, for which he paid over a million dollars, 1969. He is her fifth husband.

SONGWRITER STEPHEN FOSTER, the inventor of American popular song, dies in the charity ward of Bellevue Hospital, 1864. He has thirty-eight cents in his pocket, and a piece of paper with the words "dear friends and gentle hearts" written on it.

IN 1953 FRANK SINATRA has been dropped by Universal Pictures, Columbia Records, and CBS Television, and ditched by Ava Gardner and by his agent. But he finagles the part of Angelo Maggio in *From Here to Eternity*. He plays the part for a paltry $8,000 and wins an Academy Award.

BILL CODY forms the official *Buffalo Bill's Wild West Show*, 1883. Annie Oakley joins the show in 1884. The extravaganza of genuine cowboys and Indians will tour the United States and Europe for years.

JAMES FENIMORE COOPER writes *The Last of the Mohicans*, 1826.

WASHINGTON IRVING publishes *Rip Van Winkle* and *The Legend of Sleepy Hollow*, 1820.

The painter RAPHAEL dies, 1520.

WILLIAM MAKEPEACE THACKERAY writes the great nineteenth-century novel about the corruption of society. He titles it *Vanity Fair*, 1848.

HENRY DAVID THOREAU writes the great nineteenth-century memoir about the purity of the hermit's life. He titles it *Walden*, 1854.

THOMAS PYNCHON wins the National Book Award for his novel *Gravity's Rainbow*, 1974. It is also a unanimous choice of the judges for the Pulitzer Prize, but their decision is overruled by the Pulitzer Advisory Board, which calls the book "unreadable," "turgid," "overwritten," and "obscene." No Pulitzer is awarded for 1974. Years later Pynchon says of his own book: "I was so fucked up while I was writing it . . . that now I go back over some of those sequences and I can't figure out what I could have meant."

On April 16, 1943, while conducting research on lysergic acid, ALBERT HOFMANN accidentally gets some of the alkaloid on his finger-tips and notices its strange sensory effects. The compound is better known today as LSD. Three days later he ingests a much larger amount, experimentally, and experiences the first acid trip. Believing he's ill, he bicycles home from the lab. Druggies have remembered April 19 as "Bicycle Day" ever since.

In early January 1909 PROUST takes a bite of a madeleine and begins *À la Recherche du Temps Perdu*. The first draft will take him four years to write. A madeleine is a bit like a Twinkie, but without the crème filling.

In the early hours of July 18, 1969, EDWARD KENNEDY, surviving brother of the late president, drives his mother's 1967 Oldsmobile Delmont '88 off a narrow bridge on Chappaquiddick Island near Martha's Vineyard. A young woman, Mary Jo Kopechne, drowns.

SHERLOCK HOLMES struggles with Professor Moriarty at the Reichenbach Falls in Switzerland, May 1891. Both men apparently plunge to their deaths.

CARL JUNG breaks with Sigmund Freud (age fifty-six), 1912.

JAMES BARRIE meets the Llewellyn-Davis boys in Kensington Gardens, 1897. Peter is still in a pram. Barrie begins telling them a story about a boy who escapes from his mother and never grows up.

VAN GOGH shoots himself in a wheat field, 1890. He has sold only one painting in his life.

GIACOMO PUCCINI produces *La Bohème*, 1896.

In November 1924 GEORGIA O'KEEFFE moves into Alfred Stieglitz's Upper East Side apartment in New York.

BOB HOPE pairs with Bing Crosby in the first of their seven "road pictures," *The Road to Singapore*, 1940. His performance doesn't win an Academy Award.

THIRTY-EIGHT

Experience is not a matter of having actually swum the Hellespont, or danced with the dervishes, or slept in a doss-house. It is a matter of sensibility and intuition, of seeing and hearing the significant things, of paying attention at the right moments, of understanding and co-ordinating. Experience is not what happens to a man; it is what a man does with what happens to him.

—ALDOUS HUXLEY, *Texts and Pretexts* (1932)

GEORGE PLIMPTON is Caroline Kennedy's date at her eighth birthday party, November 27, 1965. Jackie's date is the Duke of Marlborough.

JAMES I attends the first performance of Shakespeare's new play, *Othello*, 1604. He also commissions the translation of the Bible into English. The resulting King James Bible won't be published for another seven years.

WILLIAM, DUKE OF NORMANDY, defeats Harold, the last of the Saxon kings of England, at the Battle of Hastings, on October 14, 1066. The decisive moment comes when William pretends to withdraw his force, luring the Saxons out of their defensive position.

MALCOLM X vacations with Muhammad Ali in Miami, 1964. He meets Martin Luther King Jr.

Novelist HENRY MILLER moves to Paris, where he meets Anaïs Nin, 1930.

TITIAN paints *Sacred and Profane Love*, 1515.

D. H. LAWRENCE buys a 160-acre ranch outside Taos, New Mexico, 1924. He pays for it with the manuscript of his novel *Sons and Lovers*.

ROBERT FROST moves to a spot in Buckinghamshire, England, a mile or two from where John Milton wrote *Paradise Lost* and near the place where the poet Thomas Gray is buried, 1912. Here he will write such famous New Hampshire poems as "Mending Wall" and "Birches."

EZRA POUND moves to Italy, where he will fall deeply in love with Vivaldi and fascism, 1924.

PETE TOWNSHEND announces the end of The Who at a press conference in December 1983. He takes a job at the publisher Faber & Faber.

A private plane piloted by JOHN F. KENNEDY JR. crashes into the Atlantic off Martha's Vineyard, July 16, 1999. There are no survivors.

BOB DYLAN announces he is a born-again Christian, 1979.

For his January 1973 television special, broadcast from Hawaii, ELVIS PRESLEY commissions a special patriotic jumpsuit with a sequined eagle embroidered on it.

MICHAEL JACKSON is a father, 1997. His plastic surgeon advises against any more work on his nose.

IAN FLEMING is sleeping with the wife of a rival newspaper magnate, smoking seventy cigarettes and drinking a bottle of gin a day, 1946. He begins building a house in Jamaica, which he names Goldeneye.

PAUL REVERE dresses up like an Indian and takes part in the Boston Tea Party, 1773.

JOSEPH SMITH, the founder of the Mormon Church, is murdered by a mob in Carthage, Illinois, 1844. In his short life he produced many volumes of scripture and eleven children.

Since 1757 THOMAS PAINE has worked as a corset maker, an excise man, a schoolteacher, a tobacconist, a grocer, and a tax collector. He holds a European patent for a single-span bridge and is the inventor of a smokeless candle. He is also bankrupt. He lost his most recent job, as a journalist, in 1775, for writing that the American colonies should declare independence. In January 1776 he publishes *Common Sense*, which sells more than a half million copies. Six months later the American colonies declare independence. It is Paine's idea to name the new nation the United States of America.

Ralph Ellison's new novel is about being black, educated, well dressed, and invisible, 1952. Since he began writing *Invisible Man* in 1945, he has earned a living by writing for magazines and by building and installing hi-fi's.

James Stewart plays a disappointed everyman named George Bailey in *It's a Wonderful Life*, 1946. The movie does poorly at the box office and won't be widely seen for another twenty-eight years.

Harry Truman's Kansas City, Missouri, clothing store fails after three years in business, 1922.

Albert Einstein is divorced from his first wife, Mileva, on the grounds of infidelity, 1919. The divorce settlement includes the Nobel Prize money, which he has yet to win.

Bill Gates rents one of the Hawaiian Islands and marries one very special employee on New Year's Day, 1994.

L. Ron Hubbard, future founder of the Church of Scientology, is having some success as a science fiction writer, but in the spring of 1949 he tells a science fiction convention: "Writing for a penny a word is ridiculous. If a man really wanted to make a million dollars, the best way to do it would be to start his own religion."

Anton Chekhov retracts his vow to quit the theater and restages *The Seagull* in Moscow, 1898. This time the play is a great success, but poor health forces him to move to the south.

Ingmar Bergman directs *The Seventh Seal*, which features a black-garbed figure of Death that likes to play chess, 1956.

Having survived the Black Death of 1348, the Italian storyteller Boccaccio begins writing *The Decameron*, 1351.

SIGMUND FREUD tries to give up smoking, 1894. After seven weeks he goes back to smoking twenty cigars a day.

ALEKSANDR PUSHKIN is killed in a duel with his wife's brother-in-law, 1837. Rumors had spread that his wife was sleeping with her sister's husband, Baron George d'Anthes. Pushkin was the author of *Eugene Onegin, Boris Godunov,* and more than eight hundred lyric and narrative poems. He claimed to have had 113 lovers.

On his third New York trip in as many years, DYLAN THOMAS falls down a staircase while drunk and breaks his arm, 1953.

GEORGE GERSHWIN goes to Hollywood to recoup his losses after the failure of *Porgy and Bess.* Sam Goldwyn asks him why he doesn't stick to writing hits like Irving Berlin does. Gershwin begins experiencing violent headaches and mood swings, which doctors attribute to stress and disappointment. Then on July 9, 1937, he falls into a coma. He dies two days later of a brain tumor.

DOROTHY L. SAYERS has fallen in love with her fictional detective Lord Peter Wimsey, 1932.

MICK JAGGER buys a French château for two million francs, 1981.

The painter CARAVAGGIO dies, 1610.

JEAN GENET writes his memoirs, choosing the instructive title *The Thief's Journal,* 1949. In it he describes his life of stealing and begging and the charming world of opium trafficking and prostitution. He calls larceny a holy vocation.

Bored with grading papers, Oxford English professor J.R.R. TOLKIEN writes: "In a hole in the ground there lived a hobbit." The novel begun in 1930 will take him seven years to write.

HO CHI MINH is living in Siam disguised as a Buddhist monk, 1928.

CHARLOTTE BRONTË dies at the parsonage in Haworth, Yorkshire, on Easter Sunday 1855. She was expecting a child.

In May 1981 former world chess champion Bobby Fischer is arrested on the streets of Pasadena. Unshaven and dressed in rags, he answers the description of a drifter wanted for bank robbery. He recently turned down $3 million to play in a tournament in the Philippines.

Joseph Heller is a promotion manager for *McCall's* magazine when his first novel is published, 1961. The title, *Catch-22*, will in time become a metaphor for the illogic of war and of the people who write the rules.

THIRTY-NINE

Years ago we discovered the exact point, the dead center of middle age. It occurs when you are too young to take up golf and too old to rush up to the net.

—FRANKLIN P. ADAMS (1944)

IAN FLEMING vacations in Jamaica with the wife of a friend, 1948. While there he purchases a copy of the 1947 *Macmillan Field Guide to the Birds of the West Indies* by the ornithologist James Bond.

SARA MURPHY is painted into four of Picasso's paintings of 1923, *Femme assise les bras croisés, Portrait de Sarah Murphy, Buste de femme (Sara Murphy)*, and *Femme assise en bleu et rose*. In 1934 she and Gerald will be immortalized as Dick and Nicole Diver in F. Scott Fitzgerald's *Tender Is the Night*.

GRANT WOOD paints *American Gothic*, the iconic portrait of a farmer and his daughter in front of a whitewashed Iowa farmhouse, 1930.

SHIRLEY TEMPLE'S is one of the faces on the album cover of *Sgt. Pepper's Lonely Hearts Club Band*, along with Bob Dylan, Lenny Bruce, Karl Marx, Edgar Allan Poe, and Oscar Wilde, 1967.

MUHAMMAD ALI retires from the ring, 1981. He won fifty-six professional fights in all, thirty-seven by knockout, and is the most famous person in the world.

DUKE ELLINGTON meets a seventeen-year-old composer named Billy Strayhorn, December 1938.

The Norwegian ROALD AMUNDSEN reaches the South Pole, 1911. He is a couple of weeks ahead of the Englishman Robert Falcon Scott, who becomes a much bigger international celebrity after freezing to death.

BING CROSBY records the song "White Christmas" for Decca Records on May 29, 1942, backed by the Kim Darby Singers and the John Scott Trotter Orchestra. The Hollywood recording session lasts eighteen minutes. The temperature outside the studio is seventy degrees, with sunny skies.

JOHN HANCOCK signs his name extra large on the Declaration of Independence, July 4, 1776.

On December 23, 1776, THOMAS PAINE publishes the first of several tracts, titled *The Crisis*. It begins with the words "These are the times that try men's souls." George Washington has it read to the troops at Valley Forge.

On the evening of April 3, 1968, MARTIN LUTHER KING JR. is in Memphis, Tennessee, in support of a strike by sanitation workers. He says to his supporters: "I've seen the promised land. I may not get there with you. But I want you to know tonight that we, as a people, will get to the promised land." The following morning he is shot and killed on the balcony outside his room at the Lorraine Motel.

After thirteen years working for *The New Yorker* magazine, E. B. WHITE moves to a farm in North Brooklin, Maine, 1939. He starts writing a column for *Harper's* titled "One Man's Meat." He also begins work on a story about a mouse.

Tonight Show host JOHNNY CARSON receives instruction on throwing a tomahawk from Ed Ames, April 29, 1965.

WILLIAM CALLEY JR., formerly a lieutenant in the U.S. Army, has a job in merchandising and is living quietly with his wife in Georgia, 1983.

RICHARD NIXON is selected as Dwight Eisenhower's vice-presidential running mate, 1952. When he is accused of spending money from a secret campaign slush fund, he makes a famous televised plea to remain on the ticket. He tells America that his wife, Pat, wears a "Republican cloth coat," not a mink, and that he has decided to keep the dog Checkers because his daughters Tricia and Julie love it.

JOHN O'HARA has started carrying a walking stick, 1944. Hemingway (age forty-four) sees him in a New York bar and asks him, "When did you start carrying a walking stick?" O'Hara informs him it's the best blackthorn walking stick in New York. Hemingway says it isn't and offers to break it with his bare hands. O'Hara bets him $50 he can't. Hemingway takes the bet and breaks the blackthorn walking stick. Over his head.

EMILY DICKINSON receives a first visit from her friend Thomas Wentworth Higginson, 1870. She greets him with daylilies and tells him, "If I read a book [and] it makes my whole body so cold no fire ever can warm me, I know that is poetry. If I feel physically as if the top of my head were taken off, I know that is poetry."

ON November 9, 1953, two weeks after his thirty-ninth birthday, DYLAN THOMAS dies of asthma, smoking, pneumonia, a half-grain of morphine, cortisone, Benzedrine, two beers, and thirteen whiskies consumed the day before at the White Horse Tavern on Hudson Street, New York City. He had often expressed a wish to die before he was forty.

HENRI CARTIER-BRESSON meets Gandhi on the afternoon of January 30, 1948. He shows him a catalog of his Museum of Modern Art exhibition from the previous year. Gandhi pauses at a photograph of a man gazing at a hearse and asks the photographer what it means. Cartier-Bresson explains, "That's Paul Claudel, a Catholic poet very much concerned with the spiritual issues of life and death." Gandhi thinks for a few moments and then says: "Death. Death. Death." Fifteen minutes after the photographer leaves, Gandhi is assassinated.

GERTRUDE STEIN attends the second performance of Stravinsky's *Le Sacre du printemps*, 1913, narrowly missing the riot that broke out at the premiere the night before.

GOBULO WAN RONG, the last empress of China, dies in prison, 1946.

In 1844 HANS CHRISTIAN ANDERSEN begins a story: "As you know, the emperor of China is Chinese, and everyone around him is Chinese . . . The emperor's palace was the most beautiful in the world. It was built entirely of porcelain." The title of the story is "The Nightingale."

FLORENCE NIGHTINGALE publishes a 136-page book titled *Notes on Nursing*, 1859. It will sell millions of copies worldwide.

THEODORE ROOSEVELT leads his Rough Riders up a hill in Cuba and becomes a war hero, 1898.

Former soldier ULYSSES S. GRANT has failed at potato farming, cutting and selling ice, and storekeeping, so when the Civil War begins in early 1861, he writes letters trying to get a command in the Union Army, with little success.

CHE GUEVARA is leading a small group of revolutionaries in a remote valley in Bolivia when he is captured by government forces on October 8, 1967. As the soldiers move in, he shouts "Do not shoot! I am Che Guevara and worth more to you alive than dead." He is executed early the next afternoon. The CIA agent who had been hunting for him takes Guevara's Rolex for a souvenir.

Despite vaguely stated Nazi sympathies and his earlier opposition to American involvement in World War II, CHARLES LINDBERGH tries to enlist in the air force after Pearl Harbor is attacked on December 7, 1941. He is refused. He will fly more than fifty combat missions over the Pacific, as a civilian pilot.

WILLIAM F. BUCKLEY JR. suggests decriminalizing marijuana on libertarian grounds, 1965.

DAVE BRUBECK's "Take Five" tops the *Billboard* charts, 1960.

In the early morning hours of February 14, 1965, MALCOLM X's house is firebombed. He survives, but seven days later, just as he is beginning an address at the Audubon Ballroom in New York City, he is shot several times and is pronounced dead on arrival at Columbia Presbyterian Hospital.

On September 19, 1981, Paul Simon and Art Garfunkel reunite for a free concert in Central Park, New York. A half million people attend. Millions more watch the concert on television.

Chopin dies in Paris, 1849. He asks that his heart be removed and buried in Poland.

Between February and April 1936 F. Scott Fitzgerald publishes a series of essays titled *The Crack-Up* in *Esquire* magazine. He writes: "A writer can spin on about his adventures after thirty, after forty, after fifty, but the criteria by which these adventures are weighed and valued are irrevocably settled at the age of twenty-five." Zelda is hospitalized again in Asheville, North Carolina.

Dorothy Parker rents a house in Beverly Hills, 1933.

Giuseppe Verdi goes home after the 1853 premiere of his new opera at La Fenice and writes a bitter note to his publisher. "I am sorry that I must give sad news but I cannot conceal the truth from you. Let's not investigate the reason. It happened. Goodbye, goodbye." The opera that opened so badly is *La Traviata*.

Cleopatra and Marc Antony (fifty-three) kill themselves, 30 B.C. She uses an asp, which is a kind of snake. The date on the death certificate is said to be August 30, but that is doubtful because the month's namesake, Caesar Augustus, hadn't renamed it yet.

Peter Sellers stars in the films *Dr. Strangelove, A Shot in the Dark, The Pink Panther,* and *The World of Henry Orient,* works with a young actor named Woody Allen in *What's New, Pussycat?,* marries Britt Ekland, has a vision of heaven while experiencing a heart attack, and is the first man to appear on the cover of *Playboy* magazine, 1964.

John Galsworthy begins book one of what will eventually become *The Forsyte Saga,* 1906. He will end it in 1930 after ten volumes and more than a million copies sold.

Sir Leslie Stephen writes *The Playground of Europe,* 1871, which isn't about playgrounds but about climbers in the Alps. His daughter, Virginia Woolf, won't be born for another eleven years.

While attempting to fly around the world, aviatrix AMELIA EARHART disappears over the Pacific, 1937. On July 2 she and copilot Fred Noonan take off from New Guinea headed for Howland Island and are never seen again.

STONEWALL JACKSON dies at Chancellorsville after being accidentally shot by his own troops, 1863. Jackson's last words are "Let us cross over the river, and rest under the shade of the trees." Robert E. Lee says, "I have lost my right arm."

HORATIO NELSON is made a Knight of the Bath after he loses his right arm at Tenerife, 1797.

BENEDICT ARNOLD betrays the revolutionary cause, offering to surrender the strategic fort at West Point, 1780. When the plot is discovered, Arnold escapes and joins the British. But he receives very little reward for his effort—a low rank and small change. He later asks a captured officer what his former compatriots would do to him if they met again. He's told, "Cut off your right leg, bury it with full military honors, and then hang the rest of you on a gibbet." It was Arnold's right leg that was grievously wounded in his brilliant victory at Saratoga.

FRANKLIN ROOSEVELT contracts polio, 1921. He will never walk unassisted again.

*f*ORTY

I am in my prime.

—Muriel Spark, *The Prime of Miss Jean Brodie* (1961)

On December 8, 1980, John Lennon has a session with *Rolling Stone* photographer Annie Leibovitz. The most famous image is of John nude and in the fetal position embracing Yoko, who is fully clothed. That evening, as he is leaving the Dakota Apartments, he is shot dead by a deranged fan.

Andy Warhol predicts, "In the future everybody will be world famous for fifteen minutes," 1968.

Kahlil Gibran writes *The Prophet*, 1923.

After his father's death in 1896, Sigmund Freud begins collecting knickknacks. The small statues, totems, and fetishes soon cover the top of his desk and begin accumulating on the shelves and walls of his office.

Charles Schulz's book of *Peanuts* platitudes, *Happiness Is a Warm Puppy*, tops the best-seller list in 1963. Another Schulz book is number two. A JFK biography is third.

William F. Buckley starts his long-running interview program *Firing Line* on WOR-TV in New York, 1966. The object is to invite liberal intellectuals on and subject them to the slow torture of long words and batted eyelids.

Josephine Baker receives a medal for her work with the French Resistance, 1946.

LEO TOLSTOY finishes his masterpiece, *War and Peace*, 1868. His wife has copied out the fourteen hundred pages four times, carefully deciphering his crabbed handwriting and inserting his corrections every day. Most Russians are still living as serfs; Mrs. Tolstoy is no exception.

In April 1955 DR. JONAS SALK announces that he has perfected a vaccine against polio, the dreaded, paralyzing, often fatal disease that has terrorized America for several years. He doesn't patent it. Surprisingly, he never wins the Nobel Prize for medicine, despite what some call the most notable achievement of the century.

During the summer of 1960 DR. TIMOTHY LEARY visits Mexico and discovers the interesting hallucinogenic effects of mushrooms. In the fall he sets up the Harvard Psychedelic Project and has lunch with Aldous Huxley at the Harvard Faculty Club.

EDWARD HOPPER has sold only one painting, 1922.

ROBERT BENCHLEY becomes the drama critic at *The New Yorker* magazine, 1929. He says: "It took me fifteen years to discover that I had no talent for writing, but I couldn't give it up because by that time I was too famous."

D. W. GRIFFITH makes *Birth of a Nation*, 1915, inventing the grammar of modern filmmaking and also causing a great resurgence in the membership and power of the Ku Klux Klan.

Defying the Red Scare gripping Hollywood, KATHARINE HEPBURN delivers a speech endorsing Progressive candidate Henry Wallace for president, 1947. To underline her politics, she wears a red dress.

In the early hours of April 19, 1775, PAUL REVERE sets out to ride from Boston to Lexington and Concord. He reaches Lexington "at one by the village clock" but is waylaid on the road to Concord, and so it is Samuel Prescott who warns the Minutemen that the British are coming, even though Longfellow's poem gives Revere the credit.

Deciding the *Titanic* is too expensive, novelist THEODORE DREISER returns from Europe aboard the *Kroonland*, April 1912.

ELEANOR ROOSEVELT lobbies for equal pay for women and against child labor and is investigated by the FBI, 1924.

On his fortieth birthday JAMES JOYCE sees *Ulysses* into print, 1922. The publisher is Sylvia Beach's Shakespeare and Company. The novel contains a vocabulary of more than 33,000 words, half of which are used only once.

WILLIAM SOMERSET MAUGHAM is attached to a Red Cross ambulance unit in France in 1914, where he meets an American named Gerald Haxton. The two will remain inseparable until Haxton's death in 1944.

OSCAR WILDE's *The Importance of Being Earnest* opens at the St. James Theatre in London on Valentine's Day 1895. Three months later the playwright is convicted of "gross indecency" over his homosexual relationship with Lord Alfred Douglas and is sentenced to two years' hard labor.

JACK LONDON dies at "Beauty Ranch," in Glen Ellen, California, 1916.

VIRGINIA WOOLF reads Marcel Proust for the first time, 1922. The experience opens her eyes. She writes in her diary: "There's no doubt in my mind, that I have found out how to begin (at 40) to say something in my own voice." She begins work on *Mrs. Dalloway.* She also meets and has a brief love affair with Vita Sackville-West.

GEORGIA O'KEEFFE sells six paintings of calla lilies for $25,000 at the Intimate Gallery, owned by Alfred Stieglitz, 1928.

Playwright ALAN BENNETT lets an old woman move her van into the narrow space in front of his house in Camden Town, London, 1974. The van is Miss Shepard's home, and she will live in it, amid the detritus of plastic bags and half-eaten food, in Bennett's front garden for the next fifteen years.

While meditating in a cave on Mount Hira, the prophet MUHAMMAD has a vision that the angel Gabriel has called him to proclaim God's message to his people, 610.

SIR EDMUND HILLARY, who conquered Everest in 1953, sets out to discover the Abominable Snowman, 1960.

SHERLOCK HOLMES, long believed dead, returns to 221b Baker Street, London, 1894. He has spent the previous three years exploring the Himalayas disguised as Sigurssen, a Norwegian.

GEORGE MACDONALD FRASER purchases the miscellaneous papers of Harry Paget Flashman at a country house sale in Leicestershire, 1966.

MAO ZEDONG begins the Long March from Juichin, Kiangsi, to Yan'an, Shensi, a distance of six thousand miles, 1934. He reaches Shensi in October 1935.

EDGAR ALLAN POE dies, 1849.

Discouraged by lack of work, DJANGO REINHARDT hangs up his guitar, 1950. A few months later he hears Charlie Parker's recording of "KoKo" and begins playing again.

In July 1937 F. SCOTT FITZGERALD, broke and in debt, travels to Hollywood on a six-month contract with MGM for a thousand dollars a week. He lives at the Garden of Allah, where he takes up with gossip columnist Sheila Graham.

PLATO visits Italy, 387 B.C. He also founds his Academy in a sacred grove near Athens. Aristotle is a pupil.

HENRI MATISSE paints *The Dance*, 1910.

ELIZABETH BARRETT marries Robert Browning, 1846. Because her father has forbidden her to marry, the two run away to Italy first.

MAYA ANGELOU's autobiography *I Know Why the Caged Bird Sings* is nominated for the National Book Award, 1969.

CLIFF HILLEGASS borrows $4,000 and writes his first *CliffsNotes*, for Shakespeare's *Hamlet*, in the basement of his home in Lincoln, Nebraska, 1958.

Harriet Beecher Stowe publishes *Uncle Tom's Cabin*, the most influential book in American history and the first novel to sell a million copies, 1852.

Harland Sanders begins selling fried chicken at his Corbin, Kentucky, filling station, 1930. He will spend the next nine years perfecting his secret recipe of eleven herbs and spices.

Miguel de Cervantes has a job as a provisioner for the Spanish Armada, 1587.

Winston Churchill is fired from the Admiralty after the disastrous Dardanelles campaign, May 1915. He retreats to the country and takes up painting.

Having changed his mind about the Vietnam War, Daniel Ellsberg leaks the Pentagon's secret history of the conflict, which he helped write, to the *New York Times,* the *Washington Post*, and seventeen other newspapers, 1971. The first job of Nixon's "plumbers unit" is to ransack Ellsberg's psychiatrist's office looking for dirt.

British novelist and postal worker Anthony Trollope introduces the idea of the public mailbox to London, 1855. The short red pillar-boxes are his own design.

Like so many successful executives before and since, Napoleon divorces his first love to marry up; he trades in lovely but middle-class Josephine for the aristocratic Marie Louise of Austria, 1810.

Richard Wagner begins composing his *Ring Cycle,* 1853. He will finish it seventeen years later.

After the death of Lorenz Hart, Richard Rodgers and new partner Oscar Hammerstein II reinvent the American musical and call it *Oklahoma!,* 1943.

Henry Ford forms the Ford Motor Company, 1903.

John Glenn becomes the first American to orbit the earth, February 20, 1962.

LYNDON JOHNSON is elected to the U.S. Senate from the state of Texas with an eighty-seven-vote margin, 1948. Years later he shows reporters a photograph of 1948 campaign staffers in possession of a stolen ballot box. Johnson will become the most powerful congressional politician of the century.

HELEN GURLEY BROWN publishes her manifesto, *Sex and the Single Girl*, 1962. In it she instructs women to "be smart, be charming, and be good in bed."

ƒORTY-ONE

For more than forty years I've been speaking in prose without even knowing it!

—Molière, *Le Bourgeois Gentilhomme* (1670)

Robert Frost's poem "The Road Not Taken" is published in the August 1915 issue of *The Atlantic Monthly.*

Duke Ellington records "Take the A Train," February 1941.

Arch-conservative William F. Buckley Jr. meets arch-liberal John Kenneth Galbraith in an elevator taking them upstairs to Truman Capote's famous Black and White Ball at the Plaza Hotel in November 1966. Buckley tries to dislike Galbraith but fails.

On February 9, 1950, Wisconsin senator Joe McCarthy delivers a speech in Wheeling, West Virginia, during which he waves a piece of paper he claims holds the names of known Communists working for the State Department. There aren't any names on the piece of paper, but the Red Scare begins, and McCarthy has an era named after him.

Ralph Waldo Emerson lets Henry David Thoreau build a cabin in some woods he owns near Walden Pond, which Thoreau proceeds to set fire to accidentally, 1845.

Ingmar Bergman directs *The Virgin Spring*, 1960.

The poet A. E. Housman is vacationing in Venice and falls in love with a gondolier, 1900.

On June 27, 1928, Sylvia Beach gives a dinner party so she can introduce F. Scott Fitzgerald to James Joyce. Fitzgerald goes down on one knee and kisses Joyce's hand.

Descartes comes to the realization that "*Cogito ergo sum*," 1637.

Enrico Fermi perfects the first working nuclear reactor under the bleachers of Stagg Field at the University of Chicago, 1942. On the morning he conducts his first successful nuclear reaction, the State Department announces that two million Jews have been murdered by the Nazis.

At five-thirty A.M., Mountain War Time, on July 16, 1945, J. Robert Oppenheimer witnesses the explosion of the first atomic bomb, the creation of which he has supervised. He is reminded of a line from the sacred Hindu epic the *Bhagavad-Gita:* "I am become Death, the shatterer of worlds."

Cigarette tycoon Aristotle Onassis sleeps with Evita Perón, 1947.

Columbus sails the ocean blue, 1492.

Botticelli paints *The Birth of Venus*, 1485.

Children's book author and illustrator Maurice Sendak upsets parents all over America by putting a penis on the little boy in his book *In the Night Kitchen*, 1970. The book is banned in many places.

Salman Rushdie goes into hiding after the Ayatollah Khomeini issues a fatwa against his book *The Satanic Verses*, February 1989. Partly as a result of the fatwa, Rushdie's book becomes an international best seller.

Jane Austen dies, an old maid and mostly unknown, in the early hours of July 18, 1817, and is buried in Winchester Cathedral. She has published four novels; two others will be published within the year: all anonymously.

In December 1940 Ernest Hemingway and his new wife, Martha Gellhorn, pay $18,500 for Finca Vigia, a fifteen-acre estate located a few miles outside Havana, Cuba. They've been renting the place for $100 a month.

George Plimpton is in the kitchen of the Ambassador Hotel in Los Angeles when Sirhan Sirhan shoots Robert Kennedy, 1968. Plimpton helps wrestle the assassin to the floor, shouting, "Grab his thumbs! Get his thumbs!"

Clint Eastwood invents the quietly spoken police detective with the large gun in *Dirty Harry*, 1971. Americans begin asking each other, "Do you feel lucky?"

Retired jockey Dick Francis writes his first novel, *Dead Cert*, 1962. It is a crime novel about horse racing. He tells his publisher he'll write a book a year if the publisher will keep all of them in print. Both promises are kept.

During the editing process Woody Allen rethinks his new film from a murder mystery into a romantic comedy. He names it *Annie Hall* after the Diane Keaton character. The movie wins the Best Picture Oscar for 1977.

Dante begins his *Divine Comedy*, 1306.

Frank Sinatra inherits the chairmanship of the Rat Pack on the death of the original chairman, Humphrey Bogart, 1957. Members include Dean Martin, Peter Lawford, Sammy Davis Jr., Shirley MacLaine, and Joey Bishop.

Economist Thorstein Veblen introduces the concept of "conspicuous consumption" in *The Theory of the Leisure Class*, 1899.

Edward Gibbon finishes *The Decline and Fall of the Roman Empire* in the summerhouse in his garden in Lausanne, Switzerland, just before midnight on June 27, 1878. The writing has consumed fifteen years, producing 1.5 million words in six volumes, with eight thousand footnotes.

Samuel F. B. Morse becomes a professor of painting and sculpture at the University of the City of New York, 1832. In his diary he theorizes that it might be possible to transmit intelligence across great distances using electricity.

HERNANDO DE SOTO discovers the Mississippi River, 1541. The famous riddle soon begins to circulate around the Spanish court.

TY COBB retires from baseball, 1928. He owns most of the batting records, but more important he owns a lot of Coca-Cola stock, which has made him a millionaire.

FRANK CAPRA wins his third Oscar in five years for *You Can't Take It with You*, 1938.

*f*ORTY-TWO

Twenty years of romance makes a woman look like a ruin; but twenty years of marriage makes her look like a public building.

—OSCAR WILDE, *A Woman of No Importance* (1893)

MADAME TUSSAUD opens a wax museum in London, 1802.

Queen Victoria's husband, PRINCE ALBERT, dies suddenly of typhoid fever, 1861. She will wear black until she dies in 1901.

CHRISTIAN DIOR creates the New Look, 1947.

MARLON BRANDO buys a ninety-nine-year lease on the Tahitian atoll of Tetiaroa, 1966.

WILLIAM SOMERSET MAUGHAM makes his first trip to the South Seas, the setting for many of his stories and novels, 1916. On his way home he stops in New Jersey to marry Syrie Wellcome. She is very rich.

In 1947 GRAHAM GREENE begins his fifteen-year adultery with Catherine Walston, whom Evelyn Waugh describes as "unaffected to the verge of insanity." She is married, but her husband doesn't seem to mind. The resulting guilt is grist for the novelist's mill. Greene and Walston's code word for scx is "onions," which turns up in the novel *The End of the Affair.*

ALEXIS DE TOCQUEVILLE predicts a revolution in France, and a revolution takes place. In February 1848 King Louis-Philippe abdicates. In April de Tocqueville is elected to the Constituent Assembly. In May he is asked to help write a new constitution.

F. Scott Fitzgerald's contract isn't renewed at MGM, but he works briefly on the script for *Gone with the Wind*, January 1939.

Adolf Hitler becomes a vegetarian, 1931.

Truman Capote publishes *In Cold Blood* and becomes a huge celebrity, 1966. To celebrate the book's success, he throws what many consider the most legendary New York party ever, the Black and White Ball. Capote says he feels just like a debutante.

J. Edgar Hoover is the subject of a profile in *The New Yorker*, 1937. Apparently the FBI director is still living with his mother.

In the film *Harvey* James Stewart plays a man whose best friend is a six-foot invisible rabbit, 1950.

Preston Sturges wins the 1941 Best Screenplay Oscar for *The Great McGinty*, which he also directed. Before the year is out, he also writes and directs *Sullivan's Travels* and *The Palm Beach Story*.

Ted Turner launches CNN, the Cable News Network, 1980. With the taking of American hostages in Iran, it is a good moment for instant, nonstop news.

Cecil B. DeMille produces *The Ten Commandments* at the astonishing cost of $1.4 million, 1923. It makes money anyway.

Samuel Taylor Coleridge moves in with his doctor, 1816.

Elvis Presley dies on the floor of his bathroom on August 16, 1977.

Vladimir Nabokov, a recent immigrant, is struggling to make ends meet as a writer in Cambridge, Massachusetts, 1941. He decides to quit writing in Russian and write in English instead.

In two years' time, from 1844 to 1845, Alexandre Dumas writes both *The Three Musketeers* and *The Count of Monte Cristo*. They are both very, very long books containing lots of long sentences full of long words, all in French.

Novelist E. M. Forster takes the post of secretary to Tukoji Rao Puar III, the Maharaja of Dewas, 1921.

Anthony Burgess is married and teaching school in Brunei. He's already written a string of insignificant novels. But in 1959 he begins to suffer from terrible headaches, so he returns to England, where a doctor diagnoses a brain tumor and gives him a year to live. He writes five novels in that year. None of these is particularly successful either. The next one will be. It is titled *A Clockwork Orange*.

Joseph Conrad writes *Lord Jim*, 1900. The novel is about a young man who behaves badly in a moment of crisis and spends the rest of his life paying for it.

Edward VIII abdicates the English throne in order to marry Mrs. Wallis Simpson, 1936. The king's last moments before addressing the nation are spent having his toenails done.

Charles Dickens writes *Hard Times*, 1854.

Mathematician John Forbes Nash decides to stop taking his antipsychotic medication, 1970. He is called the Phantom of Fine Hall by the students at Princeton, where he is sometimes seen writing his equations on blackboards late into the night.

Albert Einstein wins the 1921 Nobel Prize in physics.

Ted Williams hits .316 for the season in 1960, then retires to go fishing. He hits his 521st home run in his last at-bat.

On December 1, 1955, Rosa Parks is arrested by Montgomery, Alabama, police for refusing to give up her seat on a bus to a white man.

To protest Nazism, Martha Graham refuses to dance at the 1936 Olympics in Berlin.

Abraham Lincoln skips his father's funeral, 1851. When his mother died, Lincoln's father left the children alone in their one-room cabin for six months to travel to another state to court a new wife. Lincoln never forgot this abandonment.

By 1748 BENJAMIN FRANKLIN has made enough money to retire, but retirement is a relative term. He writes, "A life of leisure and a life of laziness are two things. There will be sleeping enough in the grave."

ƒORTY-THREE

Grown-ups never understand anything for themselves, and it is tiresome for children to be always and forever explaining things to them.

—Antoine de Saint-Exupéry,
The Little Prince (1943)

Charles Schulz's *Peanuts* characters explain the true meaning of the holiday on *A Charlie Brown Christmas*, 1965. In the half-hour program Charlie Brown consults a psychologist about his depression, buys a tree because it looks lonely, quits the Christmas pageant, and mourns the fact that even his dog has gone commercial. There is no laugh track.

Clement Clark Moore, emeritus professor of Oriental and Greek literature at New York's General Theological Seminary, writes a poem about how Santa Claus flies in a sleigh drawn by reindeer and arrives down people's chimneys on Christmas Eve, 1822.

Sigmund Freud publishes *The Interpretation of Dreams*, 1899.

Adolf Hitler is appointed Chancellor of Germany, 1933.

Arms manufacturer Alfred Nobel places an ad in several newspapers, 1876: "Wealthy, highly-educated elderly gentleman seeks lady of mature age, versed in languages, as secretary and supervisor of household." The most qualified applicant is an Austrian pacifist, Countess Bertha Kinsky.

Robert Stephenson Smyth Baden-Powell organizes the defense of Mafeking, in the Boer War, 1900. The greatly outnumbered British garrison manages to survive a siege of 217 days before being relieved.

Baden-Powell returns to England to discover that his modest pamphlet *Aids to Scouting* has become a best seller.

JOHN F. KENNEDY is the youngest American president ever when he is inaugurated in January 1961, but much of the healthy glow is a mirage. He's suffered secretly for years from Addison's disease, a disorder of the adrenal glands, as well as from a bad back and other complaints. Some of his apparent vigor is due to prescribed steroid injections.

On August 7, 2007, BARRY BONDS breaks Hank Aaron's record of 756 career home runs. Bonds has been playing under a cloud ever since it was reported that he'd used performance-enhancing steroids beginning in 1998.

Retired baseball player WILLIE MAYS poses on a golf cart for an Interwoven socks advertisement, 1974.

While vacationing at Goldeneye, his house in Jamaica, IAN FLEMING invents James Bond, 1951. The first novel, titled *Casino Royale*, begins with a description of the atmosphere of nausea that pervades the gaming rooms. Fleming will write thirteen more Bond novels over the next eleven years.

ISAAC NEWTON finishes his *Principia*, 1686.

DOROTHY L. SAYERS gives up writing detective fiction to devote herself to writing about God, 1936.

COCO CHANEL introduces her signature "little black dress," 1926.

FEDERICO FELLINI directs his autobiographical film *8½*, 1963.

Senator JOSEPH MCCARTHY, a confirmed bachelor, is outed as a homosexual by a reporter for the *Las Vegas Sun*, 1952. He will marry his secretary within the year.

DR. ALFRED KINSEY begins teaching sex education at Indiana University, 1938. He takes the first of more than eighteen thousand sexual histories.

Dr. Benjamin Spock publishes *The Commonsense Book of Baby and Child Care*, 1946. Because it is a paperback, it quickly becomes ubiquitous. A woman can fit it in her purse or a drawer next to the bed. It begins with the ominous words: "You know more than you think you do."

George Eliot and George Henry Lewes buy a house at 21 North Bank, Regents Park, London, 1863. The two have been living together for several years. Lewes already has a wife and family.

Susan Sontag is diagnosed with breast cancer and given two years to live, 1976. She sits down to write *Illness as Metaphor*, which will be published in 1978.

Louis XIV moves the French court to the Paris suburb of Versailles, 1682.

For his master's thesis in architecture, Philip Johnson designs his famous Glass House, which he builds on a piece of property he owns in Connecticut, 1949. It is called one of the most beautiful houses in the world—and the least functional. The roof leaks.

Leslie McFarlane mails his last Hardy Boys manuscript, *The Phantom Freighter*, to the Stratemeyer Syndicate, 1946. He has written more than two million words under the name Franklin W. Dixon, twenty-one books read by millions of boys, but owns none of the copyrights.

William Golding publishes a first novel, titled *The Lord of the Flies*, 1954.

Charles Ingalls moves the family to a farm on the shores of Silver Lake in the Dakota Territory, 1879. He has settled, farmed, failed, and resettled nine times in eleven years. His daughter Laura will write a series of books about the experience.

George Washington is put in command of the Continental Army, 1775. His prudent strategy is to avoid direct engagement with the British and instead to retreat slowly and strike when least expected.

In September 1932 T. S. ELIOT moves out of the London apartment he's shared with his wife, Vivien. They have been married for almost twenty years, but her mental illness has made her increasingly difficult to live with. She has taken to biting visitors.

D. H. LAWRENCE publishes *Lady Chatterley's Lover* in Italy, 1928. It won't appear in England until 1960.

JAMES ABBOTT MCNEILL WHISTLER files a lawsuit after the critic John Ruskin writes a savage review of his *Nocturne in Black and Gold: The Falling Rocket*, 1877. He wins the case but is given only a farthing in damages, which becomes a comment on his reputation. The cost of bringing the suit ruins him. He loses his house and his famous collection of blue and white porcelain.

GROUCHO MARX appears in the film *Duck Soup*, with brothers Chico, Harpo, and Zeppo, 1933.

GEORGE SAND breaks up with Chopin when she suspects him of falling in love with her daughter, Solange, 1847.

*f*ORTY-*f*OUR

Say the woman is forty-four.
Say she is five seven-and-a-half.
Say her hair is stick color.
Say her eyes are chameleon.
Would you put her in a sack and bury her,
suck her down into the dumb dirt?

—ANNE SEXTON, "Hurry Up Please It's Time" (1974)

MARY, QUEEN OF SCOTS is executed by order of her cousin Good Queen Bess, 1587. The two have never met.

CHARLES DICKENS buys Gad's Hill Place, a large house in Kent, 1856. His father had said to him many times when the two of them were out walking in the neighborhood: "If you were to be very persevering and work very hard, you might live in that house one day." And now he does. He will live there until his death.

IVAN TURGENEV writes *Fathers and Sons*, 1862.

JAMES BARRIE's play about a boy who never grows up has its first performance in London at the Duke of York's Theatre, December 27, 1904.

BERT LAHR plays the Cowardly Lion in MGM's *The Wizard of Oz*, 1939.

IN November 1902 THEODORE ROOSEVELT goes on a bear hunt with the governor of Mississippi but refuses to shoot the bear. An admirer in Brooklyn sews two plush bears with button eyes and sends them to the White House. She subsequently makes a fortune in the toy bear business. The president has six children at home but does not give up hunting.

Benjamin Franklin has gout, 1750.

Norman Mailer is arrested while participating in an anti–Vietnam War march on the Pentagon, 1967. *Armies of the Night*, the book he writes about the protest movement, will win the Pulitzer Prize the following year.

John Updike gets a no-fault divorce from his wife of twenty-three years, 1976. His new novel is titled *Marry Me*.

Leo Tolstoy hears about a woman who's thrown herself in front of a train because of an unhappy love affair, 1872. He goes down to the train station to see her remains and afterward weaves the sad incident into a story. He names the main character Anna Karenina. The novel will begin: "All happy families are alike; each unhappy family is unhappy in its own way."

In December 1992 Charles and Diana split up.

Eleanor Hodgman Porter writes a book titled *Pollyanna* about a girl who always looks on the bright side of everything, 1913.

Edith Wharton refuses to write a happy ending for the stage version of *The House of Mirth*, and the play fails, 1906.

Diane Arbus photographs a pair of New Jersey identical twins, one frowning slightly, one almost smiling, 1967.

Dr. Josef Mengele obtains a divorce from his wife of sixteen years and purchases a half interest in a pharmaceutical company, 1955. He lives in Argentina, where few know him as the "Angel of Death."

The Cherry Orchard is premiered in Moscow on Anton Chekhov's forty-fourth birthday. It is his last play. He dies the following summer.

William Shawn succeeds founder Harold Ross as the editor of *The New Yorker* magazine, 1951.

Joseph Campbell's new book *The Hero with a Thousand Faces* explains, among other things, how it's the job of the young hero to murder and replace the old hero, 1949.

NICCOLÒ MACHIAVELLI loses his government post when the Medici unseat the Borgias and take power in Florence, 1512. The following year his name is put on a list. He is arrested, imprisoned, and tortured for twenty-two days. After his release he begins work on *The Prince*, in which he advocates utter ruthlessness as the most responsible way to govern a democracy.

RONALD REAGAN hosts live coast-to-coast TV coverage of the opening day at Disneyland, July 1955.

DOROTHY PARKER wins an Academy Award for the screenplay to the 1937 film *A Star Is Born*.

GEORGE WASHINGTON, wintering with his ragtag troops in Valley Forge, Pennsylvania, decides to cross the Delaware River on Christmas Eve 1776. His forces, many of them without shoes, surprise the Hessian troops at Trenton and defeat them. It is Washington's first victory.

AUNG SAN SUU KYI is placed under house arrest by the military government of Myanmar, 1989. She will remain under arrest for the next six years, while the democracy movement waits for its moment. She will win the Nobel Peace Prize in 1991.

In April 1962 JOHN F. KENNEDY entertains forty-nine American Nobel laureates at the White House and makes the memorable after-dinner remark: "I think this is the most extraordinary collection of human talent, of human knowledge, that has ever been gathered together at the White House, with the possible exception of when Thomas Jefferson dined alone."

While traveling in Italy, THOMAS JEFFERSON makes a drawing of a macaroni machine, 1787. Later in the year he receives a copy of the new U.S. Constitution in the mail. He suggests it be amended with a bill of rights.

On August 15, 1945, EMPEROR HIROHITO announces the surrender of Japanese forces in a radio broadcast to the nation. It is the first time the Japanese public has heard his voice, but since he is speaking in an archaic form of the language, no one can understand him. On New Year's Day 1946 he announces that he is not divine.

ARTIE SHAW retires his clarinet, 1954.

HUMPHREY BOGART is unhappily married when he meets and falls in love with nineteen-year-old Lauren Bacall on the set of *To Have and Have Not*, 1944. They will be married within the year and make four more pictures together.

PAUL NEWMAN plays the bandit Butch Cassidy opposite Robert Redford's Sundance Kid, 1969.

F. SCOTT FITZGERALD dies of a heart attack on December 21, 1940. In the last year of his life, the royalties for all his novels and stories amounted to $13.13, selling a total of seventy-two copies. It was Fitzgerald who said: "There are no second acts in American life."

Beat novelist WILLIAM S. BURROUGHS publishes *Naked Lunch*, 1958. He carries a journal around with him wherever he goes. In it, in three separate columns, he records what he is doing, what he is thinking, and what he is reading.

Grateful Dead guitarist JERRY GARCIA achieves another kind of immortality when Ben & Jerry's Ice Cream names a flavor after him, 1987.

TAMMY WYNETTE checks into the Betty Ford Clinic and joins the cast of a soap opera on CBS, 1986.

OLIVER GOLDSMITH writes *She Stoops to Conquer*, 1773.

JACKSON POLLOCK dies in a car crash in the Hamptons, 1956.

ROBERT LOUIS STEVENSON dies in Samoa, 1894.

CHAUCER begins writing *The Canterbury Tales*, 1387.

GEORGE III loses the American colonies, 1783. To paraphrase Oscar Wilde: Losing one colony is a misfortune, losing thirteen begins to look like carelessness.

Peasant poet JOHN CLARE is committed to an insane asylum in 1837. He will be confined, off and on, until his death in 1864.

ADOLF EICHMANN, having engineered the murder of six million Jews before and during World War II, has managed to elude the Allied authorities. In 1950, he escapes to South America and settles in Argentina.

HAL DAVID writes the immortal lyric "What's it all about, Alfie?" to a melody by Burt Bacharach, 1965.

MARIE CURIE wins her second Nobel Prize, this time for chemistry, 1911.

FRANK LLOYD WRIGHT builds a house on a hill in Wisconsin, which he names Taliesin, 1911.

Composer ROBERT SCHUMANN throws himself into the Rhine, 1854. He is rescued but will die in an asylum two years later.

After trying his hand at playwriting, journalism, selling door to door, and running a shop, L. FRANK BAUM sits down to write a children's book, 1900. He calls it *The Wonderful Wizard of Oz*.

RAYMOND CHANDLER leaves his job as an oil executive and writes his first detective story, 1933.

ƒorty-ƒive

Middle age is when you've met so many people that every new person you meet reminds you of someone else.

—OGDEN NASH, *Versus* (1949)

Comedian STEVE MARTIN buys Willem de Kooning's *Woman as Landscape* from Sotheby's for less than $6 million, 1990.

Landscape architect LANCELOT "CAPABILITY" BROWN begins work on the grounds of Blenheim Palace, Oxfordshire, 1760. It will be considered his masterpiece.

LANGSTON HUGHES writes the lyrics for the Kurt Weill musical *Street Scene*. The 1947 show is a hit, and Hughes buys a house in Harlem.

JOSEPHINE BAKER is refused service at New York's famous Stork Club, 1951. She and Grace Kelly storm out in protest. One New York columnist calls Baker a Communist.

Poems begin appearing, serially, under the name Webster Ford, 1914. Only later is it learned they were written, sometimes five or ten a day, by a Chicago lawyer, EDGAR LEE MASTERS, while defending a local waitresses' union against a strike injunction.

VOLTAIRE meets his patron, Frederick the Great of Prussia, for the first time in September 1740. Frederick is twenty-eight and hasn't yet shown a proclivity for invading his neighbors.

SAMUEL JOHNSON writes a sarcastic letter to Lord Chesterfield, who withheld his assistance until Johnson's *Dictionary* was finished, 1755. Johnson defines a patron as someone who watches while a person is drowning and then encumbers him with help once he has reached shore.

ALFRED TENNYSON writes "The Charge of the Light Brigade," celebrating the most famous cock-up in military history, 1854. He also grows a beard so he'll look more like the unshaven soldiers returning from the Crimea.

NAPOLEON is defeated at Waterloo, 1815. He is captured when his carriage gets bogged down in traffic. He will spend the rest of his life on St. Helena, a small island in the South Atlantic.

In 1981 JACK WELCH reaches the top at General Electric, the company where he has enjoyed job security for twenty-one years. During his twenty-year reign he will systematically fire more than 100,000 people, ten percent of the managers every year.

In August 1944 ERNEST HEMINGWAY participates in the liberation of the Ritz Bar in Paris, which has been occupied by the Germans since 1940.

On his forty-fifth birthday JOHN F. KENNEDY is serenaded by Marilyn Monroe at a large birthday party held at Madison Square Garden, 1962. It's rumored the president has been having an affair with the movie star for about a year.

JESSICA MITFORD investigates the funeral business in her book *The American Way of Death*, 1963.

In a letter to a friend MOTHER TERESA complains that Jesus isn't paying any attention to her, 1955.

PABLO PICASSO begins an affair with seventeen-year-old Marie-Therese Walter, whom he met in a department store, 1927.

JERRY SEINFELD ends his nine-year reign atop television comedy and spends the next year playing pool at Amsterdam Billiards, 1998. He is very rich.

HARLAND SANDERS is made an official member of the Honorable Order of Kentucky Colonels by Kentucky governor Ruby Laffoon,

1935. Sanders was in the army once, briefly, but was never promoted from the ranks.

GALILEO GALILEI perfects his telescope and trains it on the heavens in late 1609. He sees mountains on the moon, stars in the Milky Way, and moons around Jupiter. He gives the patents on the device to the Venetian Senate. The Senate thanks him by freezing his salary.

On June 12, 1964, NELSON MANDELA is sentenced to life imprisonment for plotting to overthrow the white South African government. His statement to the court receives international publicity.

Novelist THOMAS KENEALLY steps into a handbag store in Beverly Hills and hears a story about how a Nazi businessman named Oskar Schindler saved the proprietor and his wife from the death camps, 1980.

LAWRENCE STERNE begins writing *The Life and Opinions of Tristram Shandy, Gentleman*, 1759.

MARCO POLO, imprisoned by the Genoese, dictates his *Travels* to a fellow prisoner, 1299.

When SINCLAIR LEWIS receives a phone call from the Nobel Committee in Stockholm on November 5, 1930, he thinks it is someone playing a joke on him.

Because of spinal problems FRIDA KAHLO has been painting from her four-poster bed. In 1953 she and her bed are carried to Mexico's National Institute of Fine Arts for her first solo exhibition in her native country. She will live another four years.

NATHANIEL HAWTHORNE writes *The Scarlet Letter*, 1850. The story sends his wife to bed with a headache, which makes the author wonder if the ending he wrote is too unhappy, but the first printing sells out in ten days and the book goes on to be the first American best seller.

Senator JOE MCCARTHY is at the height of his influence when, on March 9, 1954, CBS's Edward R. Murrow broadcasts a *See It Now* program discussing the senator's red-baiting methods. Until now

McCarthy hasn't been widely seen on national television, and the medium doesn't flatter him. By summer he is openly rebuked in a Senate hearing. In December he is censured by the full Senate, and the witchhunt is over. He will die in 1957.

In 1948 GEORGE ORWELL writes his famous dystopian novel, *1984*. He gets the title by transposing the last two digits of the year on his calendar.

CHARLES DICKENS has a wall built down the middle of the bedroom he shares with Mrs. Dickens, 1857.

Former Python Michael Palin sets out from London's Reform Club to retrace the route of Jules Verne's Phileas Fogg, traveling around the world in eighty days, 1988. He does it in seventy-nine days and seven hours. The adventure is broadcast on the BBC.

ƒORTY-SIX

At forty-six one must be a miser; only have time for essentials.

—Virginia Woolf (1928)

The Duke of Windsor is in Paris when the Germans invade France, 1940. He and the duchess flee to Biarritz, with 222 suitcases, then to fascist Spain, and finally to Portugal. Years later it will emerge that the Nazis offered to put the Duke of Windsor back on the throne after they conquered Britain, and the duke was very interested in being king again. Instead he and the duchess are hustled aboard a British warship and spend the war in the Bahamas.

Shirley Temple is appointed U.S. Ambassador to Ghana, 1974.

Jorge Luis Borges is fired from his job as municipal librarian in Buenos Aires by the Peronists, 1946. He will spend the next eight years working as a poultry inspector.

Francisco Franco comes to power, 1939. He will rule Spain until his death in 1975.

Filmmaker Vittorio de Sica makes *The Bicycle Thief*, 1948.

Jascha Heifetz decides to take a long vacation, 1947. He has been performing almost nonstop for thirty-six years.

In 1752 (legend has it) Benjamin Franklin and his son William fly a homemade kite during a June thunderstorm to prove that lightning is electricity. Franklin also creates the first fire insurance company in America and invents the lightning rod.

T. E. Lawrence, better known as Lawrence of Arabia, crashes his motorcycle while avoiding two boys on bicycles in a country lane, 1935. He dies six days later.

Albert Camus dies in an automobile accident with a train ticket in his pocket—which is pretty existential if you think about it, 1960.

In 1952, Samuel Beckett finishes a play he began shortly after the war, about two guys named Vladimir and Estragon waiting for a third man who never arrives. The man who never arrives is named Godot. Beckett has little hope the play will ever be produced.

Ernest Hemingway divorces Martha Gellhorn for laughing at him, 1945.

Marcel Proust finishes writing *À l'ombre des jeunes filles en fleurs* and asks his housemaid, Céleste Albaret, to burn thirty-two black notebooks containing earlier drafts in the kitchen stove, 1917.

Julia Child's *French Recipes for American Cooks* is rejected by Houghton Mifflin, partly because it is seven hundred pages long, 1958. She rewrites it, and they reject it again, saying it would be too expensive to publish.

Richard Nixon has an impromptu debate with Soviet premier Nikita Khrushchev in the middle of the Dream Kitchen at the American Exhibition in Moscow, 1959. Khrushchev doesn't believe that the average American worker can actually afford to live in a house with such a marvelous kitchen. Nixon can't persuade him.

Ed Sullivan makes his television debut, 1948, prompting a New York critic to write, "One of the small but vexing questions confronting anyone in this area with a television set is why is Ed Sullivan on it every Sunday night?" The answer: He is an impresario, and impresarios don't need to be talented or good-looking.

Dr. Timothy Leary has lunch with pop culture guru Marshall McLuhan at the Plaza Hotel in New York, 1966. McLuhan advises Leary that the key to spreading his ideas is advertising, and advertising requires a catchy jingle. At a conference at Berkeley, Leary introduces his now-famous slogan: "Turn on. Tune in. Drop out."

Shortly after she publishes her third novel, *The Ponder Heart*, illness in the family forces EUDORA WELTY to set aside her writing in order to take care of her mother and two brothers, 1955. Publications cease for a decade and a half.

STEPHEN HAWKING publishes his book *A Brief History of Time: From the Big Bang to Black Holes*, which describes his Grand Unified Theory, what he likes to call his "Theory of Everything," 1988.

NORMAN MAILER runs for mayor of New York, 1969. He loses.

SAM SNEAD is the first player to shoot a 59 on the USGA tour, 1959.

LILLIAN HELLMAN is subpoenaed to appear before the House Un-American Activities Committee to testify on Communists in Hollywood, 1952. She tells the congressmen that she will not cut her beliefs to fit this year's fashions, hires a lawyer, is targeted by the IRS, and loses her farm in Pennsylvania.

In the movie *Rear Window*, 1955, JAMES STEWART plays a man laid up with a broken leg who passes the time by watching his neighbors through binoculars.

OSCAR WILDE dies in a cheap hotel in Paris, registered under the name Sebastian Melmoth, 1900. W. H. Auden writes, years later: "From the beginning Wilde performed his life and continued to do so even after fate had taken the plot out of his hands."

On October 24, 1937, COLE PORTER goes for a ride at the Piping Rock Club on Long Island. The horse shies and falls on top of him, crushing both of his legs. While waiting to be rescued, he tries to come up with witty lyrics to the song "At Long Last Love." He will live the remainder of his life in constant pain.

WILLIAM FAULKNER is hired by Howard Hawks to turn Ernest Hemingway's novel *To Have and Have Not* into a film script for Humphrey Bogart. It's the only film with two Nobel laureates in the credits.

ROBERT BENCHLEY makes his celebrated short film *How to Sleep*, 1935.

KATHARINE GRAHAM assumes control of the Washington Post Company after the suicide of her husband, 1963. She hasn't taken an active role at the newspaper in almost twenty years.

SAMUEL F. B. MORSE gives up painting when he fails to get the commission to paint the historic murals in the rotunda of the Capitol in Washington, 1837. He decides to devote all his attention to his "telegraph." He and an assistant successfully transmit messages over ten miles of wire strung around their laboratory.

THOMAS EDISON invents motion pictures, 1893.

HENRY VIII has his portrait painted by Hans Holbein the Younger, 1537. It is the first modern example of a royal portrait, at once flattering and realistic. The first example also of modern image management, as Henry orders copies made and distributed throughout the kingdom.

WILLEM DE KOONING starts to paint female figures into his garishly colored canvases, although you might not recognize them, 1950.

GEORGE S. KAUFMAN's many heroic entries in the explicit diaries of former girlfriend Mary Astor make the shy playwright a folk hero when the diaries are excerpted in the New York tabloids, 1936.

HORATIO NELSON writes in his diary: "At half past ten, drove from dear dear Merton, where I left all which I hold dear in this world." In a few hours he will embark on the flagship *Victory*. In three weeks he will celebrate his greatest victory, but only briefly, 1805.

*f*ORTY-SEVEN

Bias used to say that men ought to calculate life both as if they were fated to live a long and a short time.

—DIOGENES LAËRTIUS (circa A.D. 250)

HORATIO NELSON destroys the French fleet off Trafalgar, 1805, saving England from invasion by Napoleon. Twenty minutes into the battle he is hit by a sniper's bullet. He dies at four-thirty in the afternoon. "Thank God I have done my duty" are his last words.

PETER MAYLE buys a place in Provence, 1987.

AHMET ERTEGUN signs the Rolling Stones to a contract with Atlantic Records, 1971.

O. J. SIMPSON is a widower, 1994.

In 1929 VIRGINIA WOOLF publishes *A Room of One's Own*, a manifesto on women's autonomy, first delivered as a series of lectures at Cambridge.

MARLON BRANDO stuffs cotton balls in his cheeks to audition for the part of the old gangster Don Vito Corleone in Francis Ford Coppola's *The Godfather*, 1971. He gets the part and wins his second Oscar.

JACK KEROUAC dies of alcoholism, in Florida, 1969.

Adenoidal White House sage HENRY KISSINGER is dating Jill St. John, 1970. The red-haired former Bond girl is reputed to have an IQ of 162.

SHAKESPEARE retires and moves to Stratford-on-Avon, 1611.

GARY COOPER buys fifteen acres of land in a sleepy Colorado town and builds a house there, 1948. It has four bedrooms, five bathrooms, and an 18-by-38-foot living room. The town is called Aspen.

SIR ALEXANDER FLEMING leaves a culture plate on a windowsill in his laboratory and, almost by accident, discovers the antibiotic properties of penicillin, 1928.

While ill and confined to bed, LINUS PAULING figures out the alpha helix structure for proteins by folding pieces of paper, 1948.

Colombian author GABRIEL GARCÍA MÁRQUEZ gets a black eye from the Peruvian author Mario Vargas Llosa, Valentine's Day 1976. The two will not speak for another thirty years.

STENDHAL writes a first novel called *Le Rouge et le Noir*, 1830, basing it on a scandal he read about in the newspaper.

JAMES THURBER, now almost blind from the arrow wound suffered as a child, uses a Zeiss loop to do his drawings, 1942. Undaunted by this handicap, he begins an extramarital affair with a secretary at *The New Yorker*. To assist him with the complicated deception, he is given a flunky from the art department, an eighteen-year-old youth named Truman Capote.

MARCEL MARCEAU creates a mime-ballet based upon Voltaire's famous picaresque *Candide*, 1971.

TED WILLIAMS is inducted into the Baseball Hall of Fame, 1966. In his speech he makes a point of paying tribute to all of the Negro League stars "who are not here only because they weren't given the chance."

In December 1948 WHITTAKER CHAMBERS takes members of the House Un-American Activities Committee to his farm in Maryland and dramatically reveals a stash of microfilm he'd hidden inside a hollowed-out pumpkin the day before. Among the top-secret information are diagrams of fire extinguishers and life rafts, and details of the Nazi takeover of Austria ten years earlier. Prior to the pumpkin patch the microfilm had been hidden in a dumbwaiter in Baltimore.

NATHANIEL HAWTHORNE writes *A Blithedale Romance*, in which the narrator spies on the private behavior of other members of a commune from a secret tree house and from a hotel room across the street, 1852.

On November 22, 1963, in a special bulletin from CBS News, WALTER CRONKITE reports the grim news: "From Dallas, Texas, the AP flash, apparently official: President Kennedy died at 1 p.m. Central Standard Time—2:00 Eastern Standard Time, some 38 minutes ago."

PHAM XUAN AN is the last *Time* magazine reporter left in Saigon as the city falls to the Communists on April 29, 1975. He has less to worry about than his colleagues because he has been a spy for the North Vietnamese for the past thirty years.

Painter PAUL CÉZANNE finally inherits his father's money, 1886.

ANTHONY TROLLOPE already has twelve novels under his belt, 1862. Every morning he gets up before it's light and writes for three hours before going to work at the post office. He is very methodical, writing 250 words every fifteen minutes. If he finishes one novel before the three hours are up, he begins the next. He will write another thirty-five novels before he is through, plus his autobiography.

On Halloween 1954 W. H. AUDEN reviews a new book about a hobbit who inherits a magic ring and goes on an adventure. Auden likes the book very much and suggests it would be an excellent Christmas gift.

JUDY GARLAND dies two weeks after her forty-seventh birthday, 1969.

RAYMOND CHANDLER meets fellow novelist Dashiell Hammett for the first time at a party, on January 11, 1936. Hammett, forty-two, wrote his last detective novel four years earlier; Chandler won't write his first for another three years.

f O R T Y - E I G H T

Although I have come close on forty-nine,
I have no child, I have nothing but a book,
Nothing but that to prove your blood and mine.

—WILLIAM BUTLER YEATS, *Introductory Rhymes* (1914)

MICK JAGGER is a grandfather, 1992.

SHERLOCK HOLMES refuses a knighthood, 1902.

WINNIE THE POOH returns to England aboard the Concorde, 1969. It is a brief visit, the stuffed bear's first in more than twenty years.

In April 1971 PHILIP LARKIN writes "This Be the Verse," which will become an unofficial anthem for everyone who ever blamed their parents for everything.

MICHEL DE MONTAIGNE has spent the past year and a half traveling around Europe, but in 1581 he receives a letter from Henry III informing him that he has been elected mayor of Bordeaux. He will serve four years.

MOTHER TERESA instructs one of her regular correspondents to destroy all her letters, 1959. She worries that if her letters are made public, people will think more of her and less of Jesus.

WILLIAM SAFIRE wins the Pulitzer Prize for his commentary on corruption in the Carter administration, 1978. Safire was a speechwriter for President Nixon.

PAUL NEWMAN's name turns up on President Nixon's secret enemies list, 1972.

LAURENCE OLIVIER plays Shakespeare's Richard III in a movie, 1955.

MARGARET MITCHELL dies in Atlanta after being struck by a taxicab, 1949. She leaves the sequel to *Gone with the Wind* unwritten.

DOCTORS at Columbia Presbyterian Hospital in New York tell JOHN O'HARA he can either quit drinking or die from it, 1953. He goes on the wagon. "A hell of a way for booze to treat me after I've been so kind to it," he writes to a friend.

CARY GRANT quits smoking, 1952.

LEWIS CARROLL puts away his camera, 1880.

AFTER years toiling away in the great domed Reading Room of the British Museum, that vast institution funded by bourgeois capitalism, KARL MARX finally finishes volume one of *Das Kapital*, 1867.

W. S. GILBERT persuades Sir Arthur Sullivan not to retire by writing a libretto that the composer can't resist. He calls it *The Mikado*, and it premieres in 1885. Gilbert found his inspiration at a Japanese cultural exhibition at the Victoria and Albert Museum.

JOHN WAYNE stars in *The Conquerors*, 1955. It is filmed downwind from Yucca Flats, where the United States conducted eleven atomic bomb tests two years earlier. Almost half the cast and crew of the film will contract cancer in the following decades, and a fifth will die of it, including Wayne, in 1979.

ENGLISH archaeologist HOWARD CARTER stumbles across the opening to King Tut's tomb, November 4, 1922. While moving some rocks to set down a water jar, he discovers a staircase, a door, then a chamber containing the fabled treasure. He'd been searching for almost ten years. Lord Carnarvon, whose money paid for the expedition, will die within a year, some say because of an ancient curse, but Carter will die of natural causes in England at age sixty-four.

IN 1988 author BRUCE CHATWIN is wasting away from a mysterious disease. He describes it to some people as a fungus he ingested accidentally in central Asia. Sometimes he says it is a contagion from a bat that bit him while he was in China. He has AIDS and will die within a year. His memorial service is held in a Greek Orthodox church in London, on the same day the fatwa is declared on the life of his friend Salman Rushdie.

MIGUEL DE CERVANTES wins a poetry contest in Seville, 1595. His prize is three silver spoons.

ROBERT FROST's poem "Stopping by Woods on a Snowy Evening" is published in *The New Republic*, 1923. Frost wrote the first draft of the poem in one sitting, on a morning in June the year before.

Photographer DIANE ARBUS commits suicide in her apartment in a subsidized housing complex in New York City, 1971. The Museum of Modern Art will mount a major retrospective of her work in 1972. Arbus once said, "There is a quality of legend about freaks. Like a person in a fairy tale who stops you and demands that you answer a riddle."

WILLIAM JAMES finishes writing *Principles of Psychology*, on which he has been working for the past twelve years, 1890. In it he introduces the concept he calls "stream of consciousness."

Stream of consciousness novelist WILLIAM FAULKNER has fallen into obscurity, but he is about to be rediscovered by the editor Malcolm Cowley, 1945.

ZELDA FITZGERALD is trapped on the third floor when a fire breaks out at the Highland Hospital in Asheville, North Carolina. She and eight other women perish, 1948.

Vice President AARON BURR challenges Alexander Hamilton to a duel, which takes place on July 11, 1804, beside the Hudson River, in Weehawken, New Jersey. Hamilton fires in the air; Burr does not, wounding Hamilton, who dies the next day. Burr completes his term as vice president.

ƒORTY-NINE

KATHARINE GRAHAM is the guest of honor at Truman Capote's famous Black and White Ball, November 1966.

KENNETH GRAHAME, the secretary of the Bank of England, writes *The Wind in the Willows*, a picaresque novel about boating, 1908.

MARK TWAIN writes *Huckleberry Finn*, a picaresque novel about boating, 1884.

SHERLOCK HOLMES retires to a farm in Sussex to keep bees, 1903.

BEETHOVEN is completely deaf, 1819.

JANN WENNER comes out of the closet, 1995. He moves out of the New York townhouse he shares with his wife, Jane, and their three sons and moves in with a twentysomething clothing designer. The *Wall Street Journal* reports the split on the front page, but the Wenners remain married. Friends say Jann is a lot more fun to be with afterward.

GEORGE ELIOT begins *Middlemarch*, 1869. It will be her masterpiece.

JAMES JOYCE makes an honest woman of Nora Barnacle by marrying her in a London registry office on July 4, 1931. They have been together for twenty-seven years. Joyce is still opposed to marriage and marries Nora only "for testamentary reasons."

GERALD MURPHY and his wife, Sara, have returned home from their long idyll in France, 1937. Both of their sons have died, and Gerald has resumed the helm of the near-bankrupt Mark Cross luggage company. He describes the family business as "a monument to the useless." He no longer paints. In a 1935 letter to Fitzgerald, he writes: "Only the invented part of our life—the unreal part—has had any scheme, any beauty."

Paul Gauguin is living the idyllic life of a painter in Tahiti but tries to kill himself anyway, 1898.

Emily Post's publisher asks if she would like to write a book about etiquette, 1922. She says she'd be delighted. The book, titled *Etiquette: The Blue Book of Social Usage*, becomes a best seller.

Charles Schulz is divorced from his wife of twenty-one years, 1972.

Norman Rockwell's studio burns down, 1943.

Ivan Turgenev writes *Smoke*, 1867.

John Gielgud receives a knighthood from the newly crowned Queen Elizabeth II, 1953. Within months he is arrested outside a public lavatory in Chelsea on charges of "importuning for an immoral purpose." The press has a field day at his expense. He receives a standing ovation on his next stage appearance but is banned from entering the United States for four years.

Vladimir Nabokov takes a teaching post at Cornell University, where he has his students memorize Emma Bovary's hairstyle and the layout of the railway carriage from *Anna Karenina*, 1948.

Paul Verlaine can sometimes be found reciting his poetry in exchange for glasses of absinthe and grenadine in the bars and cafés of Paris's Latin Quarter, 1893.

Giacomo Casanova is allowed to return to Venice, from which he has been exiled for eighteen years, 1774. He will stay for nine years until another of his satires annoys the authorities.

Davy Crockett dies at the Alamo after he runs out of bullets, 1836.

WALLIS SIMPSON, the Duchess of Windsor, is riding out World War II in sunny Nassau, 1944, making lavish shopping trips to New York, visiting friends in Palm Beach, and writing complaining letters to sympathetic aristocrats, in which she compares their exile to Napoleon's on St. Helena.

RICHARD RODGERS collaborates with Oscar Hammerstein II (age fifty-six) on *The King and I,* 1951.

ISAK DINESEN publishes her first book, *Seven Gothic Tales,* 1934.

On August 20, 1858, a beardless former one-term congressman named ABRAHAM LINCOLN meets Illinois senator Stephen A. Douglas in the first of seven three-hour debates. Douglas has a strong voice while Lincoln's is high pitched and tends to squeak, but Lincoln is almost a foot taller. Lincoln speaks out against the profitable institution of slavery. He loses the first debate and the senatorial election, but he becomes a national figure.

f i f t y

There is a tide in the affairs of men,
Which, taken at the flood, leads on to fortune;
Omitted, all the voyage of their life
Is bound in shallows and in miseries.

—WILLIAM SHAKESPEARE, *Julius Caesar* (1599)

JULIUS CAESAR crosses the Rubicon, 49 B.C.

DIPLOMAT, presidential muse, and bon vivant HENRY KISSINGER tells the *New York Times* that "power is the ultimate aphrodisiac," 1973. It is a busy year for Kissinger. Besides dating actresses, he has negotiated an end to the Yom Kippur War between Israel and her neighbors, engineered a bloody overthrow of the elected government of Chile, and won the Nobel Peace Prize.

LEONARDO DA VINCI is employed as a military engineer for Cesare Borgia, 1502.

GUSTAV MAHLER has only a year left to live when he consults fellow Viennese Sigmund Freud about "a little problem," 1910. Freud determines that the composer's impotence is caused by a mother fixation, which dovetails neatly with Mrs. Mahler's father complex.

POL POT's army takes power in Cambodia, 1975. Within a year his government will begin its program of violent reforms, abolishing currency, religion, and private property. Millions will be forced from the cities to work in the fields. A Western journalist who has met Pol Pot describes him as "elegant, with a pleasing smile and delicate, alert eyes."

Jerome Kern writes the song "The Way You Look Tonight" for the movie *Swing Time*, 1935. In the picture Fred Astaire sings it to Ginger Rogers while she is shampooing her hair. The song wins an Academy Award.

In 1988 a collapsed spinal artery leaves photorealist painter Chuck Close paralyzed from the neck down. He is forced to learn entirely new ways of holding his brushes and applying paint to canvas. He will continue painting three enormous canvases a year from his wheelchair.

Grateful Dead guitarist Jerry Garcia introduces a line of neckties, 1992.

Rush Limbaugh announces to his radio audience that he can no longer hear anyone but himself, 2001. He begins to wear a hearing aid in his right ear.

Irving Berlin writes "God Bless America," 1938.

Evelyn Waugh goes insane while on a sea voyage to Ceylon, 1954. The experience will be put to use in a novel, *The Ordeal of Gilbert Pinfold*, 1957.

Henry Ford begins to build Model T automobiles on an assembly line, 1913. In 1914 he starts paying his workers an outrageous wage of five dollars per eight-hour day to increase productivity. The workers can suddenly afford to buy what they make.

Economist John Kenneth Galbraith publishes *The Affluent Society*, 1958.

Franklin D. Roosevelt wins the presidency and offers the nation "a New Deal," 1932.

In June 1954 J. Robert Oppenheimer, the father of the atomic bomb, loses his top security clearance at the Atomic Energy Commission over friendships he's had with people he knew to be Communists.

Igor Sikorsky, after thirty years of tinkering, flies his first helicopter on September 14, 1939. The steel-tube, open-cockpit VS-300 has a

65-horsepower Lycoming engine and a belt transmission turning a three-bladed main rotor. It can fly for only fifteen minutes at a time.

For much of 1693 ISAAC NEWTON is depressed and unable to sleep. He is convinced that best friends Samuel Pepys and John Locke are plotting against him.

EUGENE O'NEILL writes *The Iceman Cometh*, 1939.

MIGUEL DE CERVANTES is imprisoned in Seville, 1597.

SAMUEL F. B. MORSE runs for mayor of New York for the second time, as the candidate of the Nativist, or "Know-Nothing," Party, 1841. The platform is virulently anti-immigrant, anti-Catholic, anti-Semitic, and racist. He loses.

GEORGE IV has been named prince regent during his father's final bout of madness, 1812, but he is no George III. Leigh Hunt writes a poem calling the prince "a fat Adonis of fifty" and is sent to prison for two years. Charles Lamb writes worse, calling him "the Prince of Whales" but does so anonymously. The prince is reputed to spend £20 a week on cold cream and various perfumes.

WILHELM ROENTGEN places his wife's hand between a cathode ray tube and a photographic plate and gets a picture of her bones, 1895. He has discovered the X-ray.

The MARQUIS DE SADE publishes *Justine*, 1790. It is his first book. He has spent the previous eighteen years in prison.

Philosopher and nudie magazine publisher HUGH HEFNER is living with Sandra Theodore, a former Sunday school teacher, 1976.

SISTER WENDY BECKETT begins studying art, 1980.

Former sixties radical JERRY RUBIN is making a lot of money organizing networking seminars on Wall Street, 1988.

JULIA CHILD premieres her television program *The French Chef* from Boston, 1963; it's the first of 119 episodes that will appear over the next three years.

In the spring of 1922 MARCEL PROUST writes "*fin*" at the end of *À la Recherche du Temps Perdu*. In May he attends the premiere of Stravinsky's *Rénard* and has dinner afterward with the composer, the choreographer Diaghilev, Pablo Picasso, and James Joyce. Stravinsky tells him how much he hates Beethoven. Joyce falls asleep at the table.

CHARLES DARWIN publishes *The Origin of Species*, which posits the odd but beguiling notion that all living creatures have common ancestors, 1859.

EDWARD DE VERE, seventeenth Earl of Oxford, writes *Hamlet*, 1600. Or perhaps not.

Graphic artist EDWARD GOREY visits Loch Ness, 1975. "I did not see the monster, to my regret. The greatest disappointment of my life, probably."

CAPTAIN COOK discovers Hawaii, 1779, and is murdered there.

ƒɪ ƒ ᴛ ʏ - ᴏ ɴ ᴇ

He, in his developed manhood, stood,
A little sunburnt by the glare of life.

—Eʟɪᴢᴀʙᴇᴛʜ Bᴀʀʀᴇᴛᴛ Bʀᴏᴡɴɪɴɢ,
Aurora Leigh (1857)

Eʀɴᴇsᴛ Hᴇᴍɪɴɢᴡᴀʏ loses the Mumm champagne cork he's carried as a lucky piece since the war and replaces it with a Parisian chestnut, 1950. He and A. E. Hotchner and the Black Priest win big on a 19-1 long shot at the Auteuil racetrack.

Hᴇɴʀʏ Jᴀᴍᴇs, at the premiere of his play *Guy Domville*, responds to audience cries of "Author! Author!" but when he appears he is hissed off the stage, 1895. He goes back to writing novels.

French playwright Mᴏʟɪ̀ᴇʀᴇ dies, just after performing the lead in his play *The Imaginary Invalid*, 1673. He started out as a royal upholsterer. The word *farce* means "stuffing" in French.

Rᴀʏᴍᴏɴᴅ Cʜᴀɴᴅʟᴇʀ finishes *The Big Sleep*, 1939. It is his first novel.

Eʟᴍᴏʀᴇ Lᴇᴏɴᴀʀᴅ has his last drink, January 1, 1977.

Dʀ. Sᴇᴜss is given a list of 225 words to use in his new children's book, 1955. Two of the words on the list are *cat* and *hat*.

No longer partnered with Ginger Rogers, Fʀᴇᴅ Asᴛᴀɪʀᴇ dances with dumbbells, a hat rack, a framed photograph, a chandelier, and Jane Powell in *Royal Wedding*, 1951.

Pᴀᴜʟ Rᴏʙᴇsᴏɴ becomes the first person banned from American television when NBC cancels his appearance on *Today with Mrs. Roosevelt*, 1950.

RONALD REAGAN becomes a Republican, 1962.

Mathematician and philosopher RENÉ DESCARTES meets the philosopher and mathematician Blaise Pascal for the first time, 1647. Pascal shows Descartes his new computing machine.

Beat novelist WILLIAM S. BURROUGHS is living in London and dating a mathematician, 1965. Burroughs's grandfather and namesake invented the Burroughs adding machine.

GANDHI, to make a point, begins wearing only a loincloth, September 1921.

CHARLES SCHULZ is grand marshal of the Tournament of Roses Parade in Pasadena, 1974.

In February 1968 WALTER CRONKITE reports on the aftermath of the Tet Offensive in Vietnam. In a commentary following his report he says he is "more certain than ever that the bloody experience of Vietnam is to end in a stalemate." After watching the report, Lyndon B. Johnson decides that if he has lost Cronkite, he's lost Middle America. A month later Johnson announces that he will not seek reelection.

In October 1860 ABRAHAM LINCOLN receives a letter from eleven-year-old Grace Bedell of Westfield, New York, in which she advises him to grow a beard. He does so and a month later wins the presidency.

LEONARDO DA VINCI paints *La Gioconda*, which we know as the *Mona Lisa*, 1503.

In 1839 LOUIS DAGUERRE takes a photograph of a Paris boulevard. He has been taking similar pictures for the past couple of years, empty boulevards and streets and parks, but this one is different: in the lower left-hand corner you can see the figure of a man having his shoes shined. He is the first person ever to have his picture taken, because he stood still long enough for Daguerre to capture him.

ADOLF HITLER spends the morning of June 23, 1940, in Paris. He likes the Eiffel Tower, and has his picture taken there, but finds the Louvre disappointing. He has some quiet time at Napoleon's tomb.

He spends three hours in the city. He never comes back. A year later, almost to the day, he invades Russia.

TRUMAN CAPOTE publishes the first few chapters of his new book, *Answered Prayers*, in *Esquire* magazine, 1975. A scandal ensues. Gossip columnist Liz Smith writes: "He wrote what he knew, which is what people always tell writers to do, but he just didn't wait till they were dead to do it." Capote loses most of his friends and begins a downward spiral of drugs and alcohol use.

In November 1922 MARCEL PROUST dies of pneumonia. He had been at work rewriting one of his great death scenes. The surrealist Man Ray photographs his corpse.

EDMUND WILSON publishes *Memoirs of Hecate County* and divorces Mary McCarthy, 1946. He is disappointed when his European publishers decline to take his new book on grounds of its obscenity. Evelyn Waugh advises him that Cairo is a good place to get pornography published.

OVID is banished from Rome by Caesar Augustus for writing a sex manual, A.D. 8.

HONORÉ DE BALZAC marries his Polish countess, Evelina Hanska, after eighteen years of love letters, 1850. He dies a few months later. He has written ninety novels and tales and created more than two thousand characters, in just over twenty years.

ROBERT GRAVES begins circulating his new book to a few publishers, 1946. *The White Goddess*, which is about the wrathful deity who reigns over poetry, is rejected by the first editor, who drops dead shortly afterward. The second editor to reject the book hangs himself while dressed in women's underwear. The third editor likes the book and agrees to publish it. His name is T. S. Eliot; within the year Eliot wins the Nobel Prize for literature. All kneel to the White Goddess.

JOHN MILTON is imprisoned briefly after the restoration of the monarchy, 1659. He has been blind for several years.

The prophet MUHAMMAD has a vision in which he is taken to Jerusalem by night and meets with Jesus, Abraham, and Moses, 621. After leading them in prayer, he is taken up to Heaven to look around.

By 1890 JOHN D. ROCKEFELLER's Standard Oil Company is distributing its products to nearly every town in America and controls almost 90 percent of the market. In the next two years the Rockefeller combine will collapse and John D. Rockefeller will lose all of his hair, including his eyebrows.

VIRGINIA WOOLF publishes *Flush*, a biography of Elizabeth Barrett Browning's cocker spaniel, set in London and Florence, 1933.

T. S. ELIOT writes *Old Possum's Book of Practical Cats*, 1939. The author will die before it is made into a musical.

C. S. LEWIS publishes his Christian allegory for children, *The Lion, the Witch and the Wardrobe*, 1950.

After being tried for treason and acquitted, AARON BURR moves to Europe, 1807.

WAYNE MCLAREN, former Marlboro cowboy on TV, dies of lung cancer, 1992. He devoted the last two years of his life to a campaign opposing cigarette advertising.

f i *f* t y - t w o

True maturity is only reached when a man realizes he has become a father figure to his girlfriends' boyfriends—and he accepts it.

—Larry McMurtry, *Some Can Whistle* (1989)

Rolling Stones bass guitarist BILL WYMAN marries his nineteen-year-old girlfriend, Mandy Smith, 1989. The *New York Daily News* later reports that Wyman's twenty-eight-year-old son is dating Smith's forty-year-old mother, which means, should they marry, that Wyman's wife will be her own stepmother-in-law and Wyman will be his son's stepson-in-law.

VLADIMIR NABOKOV and his wife drive their Oldsmobile station wagon to Colorado, 1951. He's beginning work on a new novel about a girl named Lolita. During the winter months he begins to spy on girls riding on city buses, trying to learn how they talk. He is also reading teen magazines and the Girl Scout Manual.

Born-again Christian and presidential candidate JIMMY CARTER is interviewed by *Playboy* magazine, November 1976. He admits that sometimes he has lusted in his heart. He wins the presidency anyway.

Milkshake machine salesman RAY KROC learns that a hamburger restaurant in San Bernardino, owned by Richard and Maurice McDonald, is making forty milkshakes at a time, 1954. He goes there to learn their secret. Within a year he opens his own McDonald's restaurant in Des Plaines, Illinois. The hamburgers cost fifteen cents, milkshakes twenty cents, French fries a dime.

In February 1861 President-elect ABRAHAM LINCOLN attends the American premiere of Giuseppe Verdi's opera *Un Ballo in maschera*, which concludes with an American political assassination. His favorite opera is Gounod's *Faust*.

HARRY HOUDINI dies in Detroit on Halloween, 1926, of complications from a ruptured appendix. A few days earlier he'd invited a student to punch him in the stomach, hard, and he did. Houdini's funeral is held at the Elks' Clubhouse on West 43rd Street in New York City. Thousands attend.

In June 1999 STEPHEN KING is struck by a car while walking along Route 5 near Center Lovell, Maine. In the novel he's been working on, *From a Buick 8*, a character dies after being hit by a car. King survives. The vehicle that struck him was an '85 Dodge Caravan, not a Buick.

E. B. WHITE's classic children's book *Charlotte's Web* begins with the disconcerting sentence, "Where's Papa going with that ax?"

GENERAL DOUGLAS MACARTHUR ignores the advice of his aide, Dwight Eisenhower, and orders his troops to attack the ragtag "Bonus Army" of 1932. Thousands of veterans had come to Washington during the lowest point of the Great Depression seeking payment of their bonus from World War I. Some of them brought their wives and families with them. When MacArthur orders the torching of the encampment, many of the old soldiers lose all their belongings, everything they own in the world.

MICHELANGELO misses the Sack of Rome, because he's living in Florence, 1527.

HUNTER S. THOMPSON is arrested for possession of small quantities of marijuana and cocaine, some unidentified pills, thirty-nine hits of LSD, an antique Gatling gun, and four sticks of dynamite, 1990. He is charged with five felonies and three misdemeanors, with possible sentences of up to fifty years in prison. The cases are dismissed.

Asked how he feels after losing the 1952 presidential election to Dwight Eisenhower, ADLAI STEVENSON (quoting Lincoln) says that he's too old to cry, but it hurts too much to laugh.

RALPH WALDO EMERSON tells Walt Whitman that he enjoyed *Leaves of Grass* very much but suggests he edit out the naughty bits, 1855.

HENRY MILLER moves to Big Sur, 1944.

Poet EDNA ST. VINCENT MILLAY suffers a nervous breakdown. She will not write anything longer than a grocery list for two years, 1944.

Widowed and with her children grown, IRMA ROMBAUER finds herself at loose ends, facing a life by herself, so in 1930 she takes a sheaf of old mimeographed recipes and retreats to an inn in Charlevoix, Michigan, where no one knows her. She begins writing a cookbook. It will be aimed at women who've never really needed to cook before, and the Great Depression has created many of those. One of her instructions: "Stand facing the stove." The cookbook will be titled *The Joy of Cooking*.

When the people of Mecca do not like his message, the prophet MUHAMMAD flees to Medina, 622. The migration is called the Hegira and marks the beginning of the Muslim calendar.

SHAKESPEARE dies on his birthday, in Stratford, 1616. He leaves his second-best bed to his wife and threatens anyone who disturbs his mortal remains.

NOSTRADAMUS publishes his book of prophecies, 1555.

HO CHI MINH, who has been either in jail or on the run for the past decade, is jailed by the Chinese, 1942. He begins his prison diary, his hair turns gray, and he loses his teeth.

WILLIAM MAKEPEACE THACKERAY and Charles Dickens haven't been on speaking terms for five years, but shortly before Christmas 1863, in the doorway of London's Athenaeum Club, Thackeray decides to patch things up. The author of *Vanity Fair* dies a few days later on Christmas Eve.

FRANK WILLS, the security guard who discovered the White House burglars breaking into the Watergate Hotel in 1972, dies penniless in a hospital in Augusta, Georgia, 2000.

*ƒɪƒ*ᴛʏ-ᴛʜʀᴇᴇ

We cross our bridges when we come to them and burn them behind us, with nothing to show for our progress except a memory of the smell of smoke. . . .

—Tom Stoppard, *Rosencrantz and Guildenstern Are Dead* (1966)

On June 5, 1944, Dwight Eisenhower realizes that his success or failure in life, and the entire future of the free world, hinges upon the weather over the English Channel tomorrow morning. In his pocket he has a carefully worded address explaining his decision and is prepared to take full responsibility for what happens next.

Ernest Hemingway publishes his last novel, 1952. Titled *The Old Man and the* Sea, it begins, "He was an old man who fished alone in a skiff in the Gulf Stream and he had gone eighty-four days now without taking a fish." It was meant to be the epilogue of a much longer work; in the end the fish story is the only part the author is satisfied with. In the story the old fisherman catches the biggest fish of his life but cannot get it into the boat, and the sharks consume it before he can carry it to shore.

Charles Darwin grows a beard, 1862.

Evelyn Waugh buys himself a stately home, a suit of loud tweeds, and a coat of arms, 1956.

Walt Whitman writes his will, 1872.

Henry James hires a typist and rents a house on the south coast of England, 1896.

The prophet Muhammad has nine wives, 623.

BRIGHAM YOUNG has seventeen wives, 1855. He will have twenty-one wives altogether, and fifty-seven children.

FRANK SINATRA records "My Way," 1968.

OPRAH WINFREY is worth $2.5 billion and owns six homes, 2007.

FRANKLIN D. ROOSEVELT introduces the Social Security Act, 1935.

On November 3, 1954, while lecturing at Cornell University, LINUS PAULING learns that he has won the Nobel Prize for chemistry. He almost doesn't get to attend the award ceremony in Stockholm because the government has taken away his passport, citing his pacifist activities.

In June 1865 CHARLES DICKENS is returning from France with his mistress, Ellen Ternan, and her mother, when the train they are riding in leaves the rails and plunges off a bridge. Ten people die. The car Dickens is riding in is left hanging from the trestle. After escorting Miss Ternan off the train and safely away from reporters, the author climbs back inside the teetering railcar to retrieve the unfinished manuscript for *Our Mutual Friend*.

GENERAL ERWIN ROMMEL is recuperating from an automobile accident in France when he is implicated in a plot to assassinate Hitler, 1944. The führer sends a deputation to his bedside with the suggestion that Rommel commit suicide to avoid public embarrassment. He takes the poison he is offered and is buried with full military honors.

Famous reclusive novelist and short story writer J. D. SALINGER has a year-long love affair with eighteen-year-old writing prodigy Joyce Maynard, at the Cornish, New Hampshire, home that he shares with his children, some of whom are almost Maynard's age, 1972.

ALFRED KINSEY's *Sexual Behavior in the Human Male* tops the bestseller list, 1948.

TED TURNER marries Jane Fonda and is named *Time* magazine's 1991 Man of the Year, all within a couple of weeks, but the two events are unrelated.

John Constable, painter of hay wains and clouds, is elected to the Royal Academy, 1829.

Tory leader Margaret Thatcher becomes prime minister of Great Britain, 1979.

Samuel F. B. Morse strings a wire between Washington and Baltimore and taps out the words "What hath God wrought!" in 1844.

Walt Disney opens a theme park in California, 1955.

Pyotr Ilich Tchaikovsky premieres his Sixth Symphony in St. Petersburg on October 16, 1893. He is full of plans: to make trips to Odessa and Moscow and to write an opera based on a story by George Eliot, or perhaps on *The Merchant of Venice.* The symphony is a great success, but audiences are puzzled by how it ends. One critic senses a premonition of death in the Adagio. Nine days later the composer is dead of cholera.

In October 1912 Theodore Roosevelt is campaigning for president on the Bull Moose ticket when he is shot in the chest outside the Hotel Gilpatrick in Milwaukee, Wisconsin. He delivers a ninety-minute speech anyway but doesn't win the election.

Trick shooter Annie Oakley retires from show business, 1913.

Jerry Garcia dies of heart failure, 1995. Twenty-five thousand Deadheads attend a celebration of his life in San Francisco's Golden Gate Park. Garcia once said: "It's pretty clear now that what looked like it might have been some kind of counterculture is, in reality, just the plain old chaos of undifferentiated weirdness."

W. C. Fields plays Humpty Dumpty in the film *Alice in Wonderland,* 1933.

Sammy Davis Jr. does a commercial for Alka-Seltzer, 1979.

In the 1968 film *The Graduate*, the question is asked: "Where have you gone, Joe DiMaggio?" The retired ballplayer is living quietly in San Francisco and coaching part time for the Oakland A's.

f i f t y - f o u r

Early to rise and early to bed
Makes a male healthy wealthy and dead.

—JAMES THURBER, *Fables for Our Time* (1940)

CARY GRANT drops acid for the first time while filming *Houseboat* with Sophia Loren, 1958.

HENRY J. HEIMLICH invents the Heimlich Maneuver, 1974.

PAUL NEWMAN is one of the drivers of the second-place car at the Le Mans twenty-four-hour auto race, 1979.

THOMAS HARDY is learning to ride a bicycle, 1894. He is also working on *Jude the Obscure*. When that novel is published in 1895, its frank sexuality will cause an uproar. Booksellers will sell it wrapped in brown paper. Clergymen with a sense of humor will refer to it as *Jude the Obscene*.

CHRISTOPHER COLUMBUS dies, forgotten and in poverty, in Spain, 1506. He still believes he sailed to China in 1492. A few months after his death a map-maker in France names the New World after some-body else.

MOTHER TERESA is given a white Lincoln Continental by Pope Paul VI when he visits Bombay in 1964. She raffles the limousine off and uses the $100,000 to feed the poor.

BUSTER KEATON is paid $1,000 to play bridge with H. B. Warner, Anna Q. Nilsson, and Gloria Swanson's faded silent movie queen, Norma Desmond, in *Sunset Boulevard*, 1950.

While on safari in Africa in 1953, ERNEST HEMINGWAY survives two plane crashes. He suffers burns, a ruptured kidney, crushed vertebrae, various sprains, a paralyzed sphincter, and temporary blindness but enjoys reading his obituary in various newspapers.

OLIVER CROMWELL becomes lord protector of England, 1653. Within the year he sits to have his portrait painted, giving the painter Peter Lely the famous instructions: "I desire you would use all your skill to paint my picture truly like me, and not flatter me at all; but remark all the roughness, pimples, warts and everything, otherwise I will never pay a farthing for it." This is, in other words, the first "warts and all" portrait. Lely also painted the portrait of Charles I, whom Cromwell had recently ordered decapitated.

Alarmed by events in Germany, ALBERT EINSTEIN renounces his citizenship and leaves for the United States. In October 1933 he arrives at the Institute for Advanced Study at Princeton.

FREDERICK DOUGLASS is allowed to vote for the first time, 1872. His Rochester, New York, house is firebombed.

CHIEF SITTING BULL joins *Buffalo Bill's Wild West Show*, 1885. He is paid $50 a week to ride once around the arena but is earning a lot more for his autograph.

GANDHI has his appendix removed and is let out of jail, 1924.

JULIUS CAESAR returns to Rome victorious, has the fifth month of the year named July in his honor, and invents "leap year," 46 B.C.

FDR loses Maine and Vermont but wins the other forty-six states and reelection in 1936.

FRANK SINATRA discovers that he is on the Manson family's death list, along with Steve McQueen, Richard Burton, Elizabeth Taylor, and singer Tom Jones, 1969.

ROBERT E. LEE is offered command of the Union forces by Abraham Lincoln but declines, choosing instead to lead the armies of his native state of Virginia, 1861.

RALPH ELLISON's house burns down, along with the manuscript of the second novel he's been working on for the past fourteen years, 1967.

STROM THURMOND filibusters a civil rights bill on the Senate floor for a record 24 hours and 18 minutes, 1957.

On May 11, 1960, ADOLF EICHMANN is captured in Argentina by a small band of Israelis and is spirited out of the country to stand trial in Jerusalem for organizing the extermination of six million European Jews. His defense: "I was only following orders" and "Everybody killed the Jews."

ANDREW CARNEGIE publishes *The Gospel of Wealth*, in which he suggests that rich people have a moral obligation to look out for the less fortunate, 1889. Carnegie makes $25 million a year.

In April 1888 arms manufacturer ALFRED NOBEL reads his own obituary in a French newspaper. Upset to find himself described as "a merchant of death," he rewrites his will, leaving the bulk of his vast wealth to promoting peace.

The first Xerox 914 is shipped to the Standard Press Steel Company in Jenkintown, Pennsylvania, 1960. The machine weighs 650 pounds. The invention took CHESTER CARLSON twenty-four years to perfect.

SAMUEL JOHNSON and the painter Joshua Reynolds form a club, 1764. Some of the other members are David Garrick, Edmund Burke, Charles Fox, Richard Brinsley Sheridan, Adam Smith, Edward Gibbon, and James Boswell. In a burst of imagination they call it The Club. The main business to be conversation and drink.

CHRISTOPHER ROBIN MILNE publishes a memoir about the difficulties of his famous and poetic childhood, 1974.

WILLIAM STYRON's thirteen-year-old daughter decides to read his newest novel, 1979. The book is *Sophie's Choice*. She finds it pretty boring until she reaches the sex scene on page forty-five.

JOHN MILTON finishes writing *Paradise Lost*, 1665.

LAURENCE STERNE, author of *The Life and Opinions of Tristram Shandy, Gentleman*, dies in London, on March 18, 1768.

ALFRED HITCHCOCK appears in the film *Rear Window* as a man winding a clock in a neighboring apartment, 1954.

f i f t y - f i v e

That's no way for a man to do at his age:
He's fifty-five, you know, if he's a day.

—ROBERT FROST, "The Housekeeper" (1915)

CARY GRANT plays Roger Thornhill, an advertising executive, in *North by Northwest*, 1959. Jessie Royce Landis, the actress who plays his mother, is almost a year younger than he is.

On a train from New York to New Haven, W. H. AUDEN is mistaken for the eighty-four-year-old Carl Sandburg by a couple of Yale students, 1962. It spoils his day.

After more than five hundred performances of *Oklahoma!*, OSCAR HAMMERSTEIN II still cries every time he hears "The Surrey with the Fringe on Top," 1951.

The horse belonging to ELIZABETH, the queen mother, nearly wins the 1956 Grand National but collapses just before the finish. The jockey Dick Francis is unhurt.

Daredevil EVEL KNIEVEL donates his star-spangled jumpsuit and cape to the Smithsonian, along with one of the few Harley-Davidson XR-750 motorcycles left unwrecked at the end of his career, 1994.

RICHARD NIXON accepts the presidential nomination at the 1968 Republican Convention in Miami. The sight of him with Tricia and Julie causes Norman Mailer to reflect that "a man who could produce daughters like that could not be all bad."

JAMES ABBOTT MCNEILL WHISTLER titles his new book *The Gentle Art of Making Enemies*, 1890.

LYNDON JOHNSON is sworn in as president aboard *Air Force One*, 1963.

WILT CHAMBERLAIN publishes his memoirs, *A View from Above*, 1991. He devotes a chapter to his sex life, claiming to have had twenty thousand partners, 1.2 a day since he was fifteen.

ALEKSANDR SOLZHENITSYN's memoir of the Soviet penal system is published in Paris, 1973. The 260,000-word manuscript of *The Gulag Archipelago* was written in secret, with different parts of the manuscript kept at friends' homes around Moscow and its suburbs. Social calls were his opportunity to write.

WITH the removal of Juan Perón from power, JORGE LUIS BORGES is able to leave his position as poultry inspector in Buenos Aires and is appointed director of the National Library, 1955. But he is now almost completely blind. "I speak of God's splendid irony in granting me at once 800,000 books and darkness."

ROSE MARY WOODS, devoted secretary of President Richard Nixon, is carefully transcribing the secret White House tapes for the Senate Watergate Committee when she inadvertently, you might even say gymnastically, erases eighteen and a half minutes, 1973. In a year's time it will be Woods who tells the president's family about his decision to resign.

EMILY DICKINSON dies, 1886, having not left the house in almost twenty years.

AFTER the German Luftwaffe firebombs the Spanish city of Guernica in April 1937, PABLO PICASSO begins work on a 12-by-26-foot mural, depicting the horror of war in stark black and white. The painting, titled *Guernica*, is exhibited at the Paris World's Fair and serves as a warning of what is to come.

SCULPTOR, painter, and poet MICHELANGELO, one of the ornaments of the Italian Renaissance, is employed designing fortifications, 1530.

RACHEL CARSON writes *Silent Spring*, 1962, creating the modern environmental movement.

*f*i *f*t y - s i x

A life spent making mistakes is not only more honorable, but more useful than a life spent doing nothing.

—GEORGE BERNARD SHAW (1856–1950)

HENRY LUCE launches *Sports Illustrated*, 1954. The swimsuit issue won't arrive for another ten years.

ABRAHAM LINCOLN dies of an assassin's bullet, 1865. In his pockets are two pairs of spectacles, a linen handkerchief, a pocket knife, and a wallet containing a Confederate five-dollar bill and nine newspaper clippings.

JULIUS CAESAR is assassinated on the Ides of March, 44 B.C.

While visiting Key West, WALLACE STEVENS gets into a fistfight with Ernest Hemingway and breaks his hand on Hemingway's jaw, 1936.

FBI director J. EDGAR HOOVER is named Big Brother of the Year by Big Brothers of America, 1951.

CLINT EASTWOOD is elected mayor of Carmel, California, 1986. The job pays $200 a month.

In September 1957 LOUIS ARMSTRONG breaks his long silence on the race issue in an interview to a young reporter for the *Grand Forks Herald* in North Dakota. It comes as a shock to most Americans who are used to the trumpeter's ingratiating smile, but he is angry and has been angry for a long time. Two weeks ago black schoolchildren were barred from schools in Little Rock by National Guardsmen. And almost a century after Emancipation, Armstrong is the first black man to stay in Grand Forks' finest hotel.

Victor Fleming directs two pictures in 1939, a year that many consider to be the greatest in American filmmaking. The two pictures are *Gone with the Wind* and *The Wizard of Oz*. But today hardly anybody remembers Victor Fleming.

In March 1827 Ludwig van Beethoven writes a letter to a friend mentioning a new symphony "which lies already sketched in my desk." He dies a week later, leaving his Tenth Symphony unfinished and little more than a rumor for over a century until the sketch is found in the 1980s.

In February 1986 Imelda Marcos flees the Philippines with her husband, the deposed dictator Ferdinand Marcos, leaving behind 15 mink coats, 508 gowns, 888 handbags, and more than a thousand pairs of shoes.

Bankrupt after a disastrous opera season, George Frideric Handel is invited to spend the winter of 1741–42 in Ireland. In April, at a benefit performance for the aid of imprisoned debtors, he premieres a new oratorio he has titled *The Messiah*.

Henry Wadsworth Longfellow writes: "Listen my children and you shall hear / of the midnight ride of Paul Revere," 1863.

Dr. Seuss publishes *Green Eggs and Ham*, 1960. His publisher bet him $50 he couldn't write a book using only fifty different words; Seuss won. Only one of the words, *anywhere*, has more than one syllable. Only three children's books have sold more copies in hardcover.

Dr. Timothy Leary's daily regimen consists of "30 cigarettes, one marijuana biscuit, one bong hit, a half a cup of coffee, and a great deal of nitrous oxide," 1976.

Ian Fleming dies in 1964, having seen only one Bond film, *Dr. No*.

George Bernard Shaw writes *Pygmalion*, 1912–13. It is his twenty-eighth play; he will write another twenty-four. After he's dead, Lerner and Loewe will turn *Pygmalion* into a musical.

Gustav Eiffel builds the tower named for him in Paris, 1889. Many Parisians consider it an eyesore.

In September 1783 GIACOMO CASANOVA arrives in Paris. While visiting nearby Fontainebleau, he meets his son by a former housekeeper. He also meets Benjamin Franklin.

NOËL COWARD moves to Bermuda for tax purposes, 1956.

AARON BURR returns to America from Europe, 1812, hoping everybody has forgotten that he tried to make himself King of Louisiana a few years earlier. He sets himself up as a lawyer in New York, where he will live for another twenty-four years.

Algonquin Round Table wit ROBERT BENCHLEY dies from a cerebral hemorrhage, 1945. Asked about his health shortly before his death, he said, "Except for an occasional heart attack, I feel as young as I ever did."

f ɪ *ʃ* ᴛ ʏ - ꜱ ᴇ ᴠ ᴇ ɴ

The years between fifty and seventy are the hardest. You are always being asked to do things, and yet you are not decrepit enough to turn them down.

—T. S. Eʟɪoᴛ, *Time* magazine (1950)

Coco Cʜᴀɴᴇʟ has closed down her fashion house for the duration of the war and is living at the Ritz Hotel with a Nazi officer, 1941.

Aɴᴀïs Nɪɴ has two husbands, a New York banker and a forest ranger in California, 1960. She compares her life of deception to a trapeze.

Poet Jᴏʜɴ Bᴇʀʀʏᴍᴀɴ jumps to his death from a bridge into the Mississippi River in Minneapolis, 1972.

Jᴀᴍᴇꜱ Jᴏʏᴄᴇ celebrates his birthday by showing friends the first bound copies of *Finnegans Wake*, 1939.

Lᴀᴜʀᴇɴᴄᴇ Oʟɪᴠɪᴇʀ, at the peak of his fame, experiences a paralyzing episode of stage fright while performing at the National Theatre in London, 1964. This irrational terror will dog him for years.

Wearing a brown suit, Gᴇᴏʀɢᴇ Wᴀꜱʜɪɴɢᴛᴏɴ is sworn in as the first president of the United States of America, on Wall Street in New York City, 1789. Washington refuses to be called "your highness," preferring the less formal "Mr. President." He is a reluctant executive, afraid he might fail at the job, and is overheard saying, "I feel like a culprit who is going to the place of his execution."

Hᴜᴍᴘʜʀᴇʏ Bᴏɢᴀʀᴛ dies, 1957. Cause of death: Chesterfields. He made seventy-five feature films in his career, went to the electric chair twelve times, and was sentenced to more than eight hundred years in prison.

ARTHUR CONAN DOYLE declares that he believes in ghosts, 1916.

TWELVE years after returning to the Soviet Union from exile in Paris, SERGE PROKOFIEV is charged with the state crime of being too intellectual, 1948.

FRANK LLOYD WRIGHT moves to the Sun Belt, 1924.

HENRY JAMES finally writes a letter to Edith Wharton, who has been yearning to know him for years, 1900. James has avoided friendships with women admirers ever since one of them fell in love with him and subsequently killed herself.

AFTER a string of flops, COLE PORTER creates his masterpiece, *Kiss Me Kate*, 1948. He borrows the plot and characters from Shakespeare, but the songs are his own.

RICHARD NIXON receives the caped Elvis Presley in the White House, 1970. Presley surprises the president with a hug and asks to be made a federal agent-at-large for the Narcotics Bureau.

ISAAC NEWTON is named master of the mint, a convenient job for an alchemist, 1700.

ARISTOTLE ONASSIS purchases the Greek island of Skorpios, 1963.

FORMER German rocket scientist WERNHER VON BRAUN watches the Apollo 11 moon landing with other NASA scientists on the little TVs at Mission Control, October 4, 1969.

GENERAL GEORGE S. PATTON, having defeated Rommel's Afrika Corps at Kasserine Pass in North Africa and liberated Palermo and Messina in Sicily, nearly ends his career by slapping around two shell-shocked American GIs in a field hospital, 1943.

GERONIMO is captured south of Wilcox, Arizona, near the Mexican border, 1886. He has led the U.S. Cavalry on a chase lasting most of thirty years.

DUKE ELLINGTON plays the Newport Jazz Festival, 1956.

Sitting on a bed in his attic and typing with two fingers, Oxford professor J.R.R. TOLKIEN finishes *The Lord of the Rings*, 1949. The manuscript is more than half a million words long and took seventeen years to write.

f i f T Y - E I G H T

When I was very young and the urge to be someplace was on me, I was assured by mature people that maturity would cure this itch. When years described me as mature, the remedy prescribed was middle age. In middle age I was assured that greater age would calm my fever and now that I am fifty-eight perhaps senility will do the job. Nothing has worked.

—JOHN STEINBECK, *Travels with Charley: In Search of America* (1961)

WALLACE STEVENS publishes "The Man With the Blue Guitar," 1937.

ALFRED HITCHCOCK directs *Vertigo*, 1958. The movie is about an older man who persuades a younger woman to change the way she wears her hair.

ABRAHAM ZAPRUDER makes a keepsake film of the motorcade of John F. Kennedy as it passes the Texas Book Depository in Dallas, November 22, 1963.

PAUL COLE is on vacation in London when he sees four kooks with long hair crossing and recrossing at a street corner in St. John's Wood, 1969. A year later he sees himself in the background on the album cover of *Abbey Road*.

JOE DiMAGGIO agrees to become the television spokesman for Mr. Coffee, 1973. The former ballplayer drinks only decaffeinated.

In February 1987 ANDY WARHOL dies of heart failure after gallbladder surgery. He spent the last several years walking around New York's fancy neighborhoods buying tchotchkes with hundred-dollar bills he carried in a plastic bag.

One-eighth of all American househoulds with televisions are tuned to FRED ROGERS on *Mister Rogers' Neighborhood*, 1986.

MIGUEL DE CERVANTES publishes part one of *Don Quixote*, in Spain, 1605. He is a tax collector, ex-convict, and former soldier. The book is the first one to express itself as fiction, the first to wrestle with the difference between what is true and what is a figment of the author's imagination.

LANGSTON HUGHES has written twenty-six books in thirty-four years. Because people stop by and interrupt him during the day, he writes from midnight to six or seven in the morning, 1960.

JERRY LEWIS receives the Ordre Royale de la Legion d'Honneur in Paris, 1984.

DANIEL DEFOE publishes *Robinson Crusoe,* 1719. It's based on the actual shipwreck and survival of a man named Alexander Selkirk. Defoe made up the bit about Friday.

NICCOLÒ MACHIAVELLI dies, 1527. He wrote the book on political ruthlessness. *The Prince* will become required reading on many college campuses. He once said, "It is better to be feared than loved, if you cannot be both."

During student protests at Berkeley in 1969, California governor RONALD REAGAN says, "If there has to be a bloodbath, then let's get it over with."

IRVING BERLIN writes *Annie Get Your Gun*, 1946.

FYODOR DOSTOYEVSKY finishes *The Brothers Karamozov*, 1880.

HENRY ROTH's 1934 novel *Call It Sleep* comes out in paperback and sells enough copies on college campuses for Roth to sell his duck farm in Maine and move to a mobile home in Albuquerque, 1964.

THOMAS PYNCHON writes the liner notes to the album *Nobody's Cool*, by the band Lotion, 1996.

JAMES JOYCE dies in Zurich, of a perforated ulcer, 1941.

JOHN MILTON finds a publisher for *Paradise Lost*, 1667. The publisher pays him £10.

President GEORGE WASHINGTON has a set of dentures made out of hippopotamus teeth, 1790. They are made to fit around the one real tooth he has left, and the friction causes him constant pain, which requires regular doses of opium.

Most knowledgeable observers in the spring of 1949 think the Yankees' hiring manager CASEY STENGEL is a nutty idea or a publicity stunt. The team will win the pennant in the last game of the season and go on to beat the Dodgers in the World Series.

ƒıƒTY-NINE

I heard the old, old men say,
"All that's beautiful drifts away
Like the waters."

—WILLIAM BUTLER YEATS, "The Old Men
Admiring Themselves in the Water" (1903)

VIRGINIA WOOLF drowns herself in the River Ouse, having weighted her pockets with stones, March 28, 1941. She leaves a note for her husband: "I have a feeling I shall go mad. I cannot go on longer in these terrible times. I hear voices and cannot concentrate on my work. I have fought against it but cannot fight any longer. I owe all my happiness to you but cannot go on and spoil your life."

ELIZABETH TAYLOR marries for the eighth time, this time to an operator of heavy machinery, 1991.

WILLIAM SOMERSET MAUGHAM writes his last play, 1933. While otherwise forgettable, it contains a famous anecdote about a merchant who tries to evade Death by running away to the neighboring city of Samarra, only to discover that Samarra was where Death had planned to meet him the following day.

RICHARD NIXON goes to China and meets Mao Zedong, February 1972. In May he travels to Moscow. A month later some second-rate burglars he has hired break into the Democratic national headquarters at the Watergate Hotel.

VLADIMIR NABOKOV's *Lolita* is published in the United States, August 1958, three years after its publication in France. The novel is about a relationship between a besotted older man and a young girl. It quickly goes to the top of the best-seller list and allows Nabokov to quit teaching, which he loathes. The book's success pays for the Nabokovs' move to Switzerland, where the author will live out his life on the top floor of a luxury hotel.

ALFRED KINSEY publishes *Sexual Behavior in the Human Female*, 1953. His picture appears on the cover of *Time* magazine.

ALFRED HITCHCOCK directs *North by Northwest*, 1959. The famous last shot in the movie is of a train entering a tunnel.

On the night of October 16, 1834, painter J.M.W. TURNER hires a boat to watch the old Houses of Parliament go up in flames. He will paint two pictures of the event.

In March 1984 the *New York Times* reports that former president JIMMY CARTER "has been toiling in a callous-raising enterprise that may be unheard of for a former Commander in Chief." He is building houses for the homeless with Habitat for Humanity, an organization that has been virtually unknown until now.

TRUMAN CAPOTE dies, leaving no evidence that he's done any significant writing for several years, 1984. "Failure," he wrote "is the condiment that gives success its flavor."

Glitz, ELMORE LEONARD's twenty-third novel, is his first to make the best-seller list, 1985.

BUCKMINSTER FULLER is awarded U.S. Patent number 3197927 for the geodesic dome, 1954.

In June 1941 P. G. WODEHOUSE is invited to give a talk on German radio. He takes the opportunity to poke fun at the members of the master race who are holding him prisoner, but the English public isn't amused. He will be labeled a traitor, unfairly, and will never see England again.

During the worst year of the Great Depression, CHARLES WALGREEN increases his advertising budget to one million dollars, 1933.

RAY CHARLES does a television commercial for Pepsi, 1990.

The poet ROBERT LOWELL is confined in a hospital in London, where he entertains visitors with Benedictine that he hides in an aftershave bottle, 1976. His visit to two Harley Street acupuncturists reminds fellow poet Scamus Heaney of Gulliver in Lilliput, of Saint Sebastian stuck full of arrows, of a bull at the hands of the picador.

JONATHAN SWIFT's new book, *Travels into Several Remote Nations of the World, in Four Parts, by Lemuel Gulliver*, published in November 1726, has already gone into its fourth printing by mid-1727. It has also been translated into Dutch, German, and French. In Ireland, where Swift lives, there is a pirated edition. Swift visits London and stays with Alexander Pope.

GENERAL GEORGE S. PATTON breaks through German lines to relieve the 101st Airborne, who are besieged at Bastogne during the Battle of the Bulge, 1944. Less than a year later he dies in an automobile accident in occupied Germany. He always believed he was the reincarnation of historic generals, of Hannibal, whose elephants crossed the Alps and invaded Rome, and of a marshal in Napoleon's army.

On October 16, 1859, JOHN BROWN leads a raid on the Federal Arsenal at Harpers Ferry, West Virginia, hoping to trigger a slave revolt in the Shenandoah Valley. The raid captures the arsenal but fails to trigger the revolt. Brown is arrested by federal troops under the command of Colonel Robert E. Lee and is hung two months later. The Civil War will begin in nineteen months.

In October 1964 GIUSEPPE BONANNO, "Joe Bananas," is allegedly kidnapped by alleged mob rivals Peter and Nino Magaddino, while allegedly walking down Park Avenue in New York City. Bonanno is allegedly released after he agrees to retire. But according to Sam "The Plumber" Decavalcante, none of this ever happened.

HENRY FORD gives $70,000 to a new political party in Germany, 1922. The Nazi leader, Mr. Hitler, hangs Ford's picture in his office.

GERTRUDE STEIN writes *The Autobiography of Alice B. Toklas*, which of course is not about Alice B. Toklas at all, 1933.

SIXTY

The world is the house of the strong. I shall not know until the end what I have lost or won in this place, in this vast gambling den where I have spent more than sixty years, dice-box in hand, shaking the dice.

—DENIS DIDEROT, *Elements of Physiology*
(1774–80)

GIACOMO CASANOVA retires from swordsmanship and takes a job as a librarian at Castle Dux in Bohemia, 1785.

MICK JAGGER is knighted by Queen Elizabeth II, 2003.

SAMUEL PEPYS writes a letter to Isaac Newton asking for mathematical advice on how to bet safely on a dice game, 1693.

Three days after his sixtieth birthday, GROUCHO MARX premieres *You Bet Your Life* on television, 1950.

FRANK SINATRA is photographed with known mobsters, 1976.

HENRY FORD begins collecting antiques, 1923. Not only furniture but the very finest furniture, in bulk, and household items, and antique houses to put the antiques in. He actually buys historic houses and has them taken apart and reassembled in Dearborn, Michigan.

E. B. WHITE publishes *The Elements of Style*, 1959. It's a modest improvement upon a little book written by William Strunk Jr., who taught White years earlier at Cornell. The first Strunk and White edition will sell two million copies.

PAUL ROBESON performs to a packed house at Carnegie Hall, 1958. It is his first New York appearance in ten years.

Poet ROBERT LOWELL dies in a cab on his way into New York from JFK to visit his second wife, 1977. In the cab with him is a painting of his third wife by her first husband.

BOB DYLAN records a cover of the old Dean Martin hit "Return to Me," 2001.

CNN spends several days staking out the apartment of THOMAS PYNCHON, hoping to catch a glimpse of the reclusive novelist, 1997.

ALFRED HITCHCOCK directs the quintessential fright picture, *Psycho*, 1960. Americans begin locking the bathroom door before stepping into the shower.

Author JOHN O'HARA has lunch with Cardinal Spellman, 1965. O'Hara's Rolls-Royce fits as nearly through the cardinal's front gate as a camel through the eye of a needle.

VICTOR HUGO writes *Les Miserables*, 1862. Pope Pius IX puts it on a list of banned books, along with novels by Flaubert, Stendhal, and Balzac.

The prophet MUHAMMAD and his followers conquer Mecca, 630.

ISAAK WALTON goes fishing and writes a book about it, 1653.

SAMUEL TAYLOR COLERIDGE receives a visit from Ralph Waldo Emerson, 1833. Six names in one small room.

WINSTON CHURCHILL is a complete failure. He is mistrusted by both political parties. He is considered a blowhard, a warmonger, unreliable, disloyal, and prone to wild imaginings about the Bolsheviks and about the new Chancellor of Germany. Having lost all his savings in the Crash of '29, he supports his family with his pen, 1934.

HARRY TRUMAN has been vice president for eighty-two days when Franklin Roosevelt dies suddenly on April 12, 1945. Roosevelt is the only president many Americans can remember, and practically no one knows anything about this former haberdasher from Missouri.

Two years after declaring bankruptcy, MARK TWAIN is on a world lecture tour, hoping to repay his debts, 1896. For some time he has found Europe to be much more affordable than America. While in India, he meets Gandhi and sees the Taj Mahal.

ALFRED STIEGLITZ marries painter Georgia O'Keeffe, 1924. She is thirty-seven. He has taken hundreds of photographs of her, many of them nudes. Most people remember her as a crusty old painter, but in the photographs she is quite ethereal and lovely.

Two years after suffering a stroke, HUGH HEFNER marries his nurse, Kimberley Conrad, 1988. Remarkably, Conrad is chosen Playmate of the Year in 1989.

In 2004, a noted gerontologist estimates the life expectancy of Rolling Stones guitarist KEITH RICHARDS. Taking the average seventy-seven years of a white male, he subtracts eight years for smoking, nine for drug abuse, nine for sexual promiscuity, four for boozing, adds four for general hardiness and two for being right-handed, and comes up with fifty-two years, which means Richards should have been dead eight years ago. Using the same criteria, the doctor estimates Sting will live to age ninety-three.

JACK LALANNE swims from Alcatraz to Fisherman's Wharf in San Francisco, handcuffed and towing a half-ton boat, 1974.

GANDHI begins his two-hundred-mile walk to the sea to collect salt, March 1930.

Film director PRESTON STURGES begins writing his memoirs in February 1959 and finishes the last chapter on August 6, in his room at the Algonquin Hotel. He dies later the same afternoon.

SIXTY-ONE

The men who think of superannuation at sixty-one are those whose lives have been idle, not they who have really buckled themselves to work. It is my opinion that nothing seasons the mind for endurance like hard work. Port wine should perhaps be added.

—ANTHONY TROLLOPE, *Castle Richmond* (1860)

ORSON WELLES, who in 1941 cowrote, directed, and starred in the greatest movie ever made, performs card tricks on the Johnny Carson show, 1976.

In 1840, after a long career as a physician, PETER MARK ROGET decides to devote his retirement to compiling a compendium of words, organized by meaning instead of alphabetically. He sorts words into six categories: Abstract Relations, Space, Matter, Intellect, Volition, and Sentient and Moral Powers. He calls his book a thesaurus, which is the Greek word for "treasury." The project will take over ten years to complete.

JOHNNY CASH collaborates with the band U2 on the album *Zooropa*, 1993.

ALBERT EINSTEIN becomes a U.S. citizen, 1940. The FBI immediately begins investigating him as a subversive.

In 1729 JONATHAN SWIFT publishes *A Modest Proposal: For Preventing the Children of Poor People in Ireland from Being a Burden to Their Parents or Country, and for Making Them Beneficial to the Public*, in which he suggests that the poverty in Ireland could be alleviated by fattening

Irish children and feeding them to the rich absentee landlords living in England.

In the December 1920 issue of *Strand Magazine*, SIR ARTHUR CONAN DOYLE writes an article about two girls in Yorkshire who, he claims, have proven the existence of fairies by taking their photograph. His new friend Harry Houdini tells him he's nuts.

In early 1970, while on the plane to Washington to be interviewed for a seat on the Supreme Court, HARRY BLACKMUN does what he has always done when faced with a decision: he writes a list of the arguments against and in favor of what he is considering. He will decide to join the court, where he will have decisive influence in judging *Roe v. Wade*.

HENRY JAMES writes *The Golden Bowl*, 1904.

Painter GEORGIA O'KEEFFE moves to New Mexico for good, 1949.

GEORGE III survives a second assassination attempt while attending Mozart's *The Marriage of Figaro* at the Drury Lane Theatre in London, 1800. Hearing shots fired, the king stands up in the front of the royal box and looks through his opera glasses to see who is shooting at him.

WALKER EVANS, who so famously photographed Depression-stricken America in the 1930s, has spent the last twenty years taking pictures for *Fortune* magazine, 1965. He and his second wife live in Connecticut.

After several rounds of electroshock therapy for depression, ERNEST HEMINGWAY shoots himself with his shotgun in Ketchum, Idaho, on July 2, 1961.

SAUL BELLOW receives the Nobel Prize for literature. In his speech in Stockholm in December 1976, he says, "After years of the most arduous mental labor, I stand before you in the costume of a headwaiter."

Between 1960 and 1968, at the rate of one-sixteenth of a cent per copy, CHESTER CARLSON has made around $200 million in royalties on the Xerox copying process he invented, but he is still living in the modest three-bedroom house that he and his wife built just outside Rochester in 1946. He's given most of the money away.

DOLORES HART, who played Elvis Presley's love interest in *Kid Creole* (1958) and the "good girl" pursued by George Hamilton in *Where the Boys Are* (1960), is mother superior at the Benedictine Convent of Regina Laudis in Bethlehem, Connecticut, 2000. She chants the daily office in Latin eight times a day.

TITIAN paints the *Venus of Urbino*, 1538.

Homemaking maven and media mogul MARTHA STEWART is convicted of conspiracy, two counts of making false statements, and obstruction of justice related to the sale of stock in a company called ImClone, 2003. She's sentenced to five months' imprisonment.

W. C. FIELDS stars in the movie *Never Give a Sucker an Even Break*, 1941. He also wrote the screenplay.

MICHELANGELO begins painting *The Last Judgment*, 1536. It will take him five years.

THEODORE ROOSEVELT dies in his sleep at his home, Sagamore Hill, Long Island, 1919.

SIXTY-TWO

In youth it is the outward aspect of things that most engages us; while in age, thought or reflection is the predominating quality of the mind. Hence, youth is the time for poetry, and age is more inclined to philosophy. In practical affairs it is the same: a man shapes his resolutions in youth more by the impression that the outward world makes upon him; whereas, when he is old, it is thought that determines his actions.

—ARTHUR SCHOPENHAUER,
Parerga and Paralipomena (1851)

ARISTOTLE ONASSIS marries Jackie Kennedy, October 22, 1968. She is thirty-nine.

RICHARD FRANCIS BURTON completes his translation of *The Kama Sutra*, 1883.

MARK TWAIN meets Sigmund Freud, 1898.

CARL SANDBURG wins the 1939 Pulitzer Prize for his biography of Lincoln. The critic Edmund Wilson remarks that it is the cruelest thing done to Lincoln since he was assassinated.

PETER PAUL RUBENS paints *The Three Graces*, 1639. Within a year he will be dead.

SISTER WENDY BECKETT becomes a media darling with the broadcast of *Sister Wendy's Odyssey* on the BBC, 1992. She lives an otherwise quiet life in a trailer on the property of a Carmelite monastery in Norfolk, England.

Rolling Stones guitarist KEITH RICHARDS falls out of a palm tree while vacationing in Fiji, 2006.

CARY GRANT retires from movies, 1966. He once said, "I pretended to be somebody I wanted to be until finally I became that person. Or he became me." He will become a cosmetics executive.

WALKER EVANS publishes the photographs he took with a hidden camera, more than thirty years ago, of people riding the New York subway, 1966.

On Sunday evening, February 9, 1964, ED SULLIVAN says five words: "Ladies and gentlemen. The Beatles." Pandemonium ensues.

In March 1942 GENERAL DOUGLAS MACARTHUR abandons his command post in the Philippines, saying, "I shall return." He escapes with his wife, his son, his son's nanny, fourteen of his senior officers, and a half million dollars paid to him by the Philippine president Manuel Quezon.

LINUS PAULING becomes the only person to receive two unshared Nobel Prizes when he is awarded the Nobel Peace Prize for efforts and writings in opposition to nuclear armament, 1963. *Life* magazine calls the award "A Weird Insult From Norway."

PAUL SIMON jokes that letting Art Garfunkel sing lead in "Bridge over Troubled Water" was the biggest mistake of his career, but the two go on tour again in 2003. They seem to enjoy each other's company.

President GEORGE WASHINGTON dispatches an army to western Pennsylvania, where farmers have been refusing to pay a tax on whiskey, 1794.

EVELYN WAUGH dies at his country house, Combe Florey, in Somerset, 1966. His friend, the gossip and photographer Cecil Beaton, says he died of snobbery.

AGATHA CHRISTIE's new play, *The Mouse Trap*, begins its run in London's West End at the Ambassador's Theatre, 1952. It will outlive its author, playing to more than twenty thousand audiences through 2004.

At the end of World War I, in 1918, SIGMUND FREUD loses his entire fortune, which he'd invested in Austrian government bonds. The economy is depressed, and so is everybody who lives in Vienna, which would be great for Freud's practice except that nobody can afford to seek help. Freud is barely making a living.

MALCOLM COWLEY, the champion of so many lions of American literature in the twentieth century, is teaching creative writing at Stanford, 1960. In the class, among others, are Larry McMurtry and Ken Kesey. When the young writers strut their brave new material, Cowley smiles and turns off his hearing aid.

ORSON WELLES turns down the role of Darth Vader in the film *Star Wars*, 1977.

SIXTY-THREE

Age appears to be best in four things—old wood best to burn, old wine to drink, old friends to trust, and old authors to read.

—Francis Bacon, *Apophthegms* (1625), quoting
Alonso of Aragon

Novelist Arnold Bennett dies of typhoid, 1931. His companions at a Paris hotel didn't think the water was safe to drink; Bennett thought it was and said he would prove it. It wasn't.

Samuel Johnson vacations in Scotland with his biographer, James Boswell, 1773.

Thomas Paine meets Napoleon, 1800. Napoleon says that a gold statue of Paine should be erected in every city in the world. A statue of Thomas Paine will be erected in Parc Montsouris in Paris in 1949.

Walt Disney begins secretly acquiring land from orange growers in central Florida, 1965.

Lena Horne opens a one-woman show at New York's Nederlander Theatre, 1981. It will run for 333 performances, making it the longest-running solo show in Broadway history.

Vladimir Nabokov is on the cover of *Newsweek* magazine, 1962. Groucho Marx, asked for comment, says, "I plan to put off reading *Lolita* for six years—until she's eighteen."

Anaïs Nin publishes the first volume of her diaries, 1966.

Ulysses S. Grant, whose presidency ended in failure and scandal, recently bankrupted and now dying of cancer, sits down to write his memoirs, 1885. He finishes them a few days before dying in upstate New York. He had surrendered his pension when he entered the White House, and Congress had never paid for a president's retirement before, so Grant was entirely on his own. *The Personal Memoirs of U. S. Grant* will be published by Mark Twain and prove an enormous best seller. A famous general, a bad president, a remarkable author.

ROBERT E. LEE dies, 1870. His last words are "Strike the tent."

Sixty-*four*

Will you still need me, will you still feed me,
When I'm sixty-four?

— PAUL McCARTNEY, "When I'm Sixty-four" (1967)

PAUL McCARTNEY and his second wife, Heather Mills, split up, 2006.

KURT VONNEGUT publishes *Bluebeard*, 1987.

CHARLEMAGNE divides his kingdom among his three sons, 806.

KARL MARX dies in poverty in London, March 14, 1883. Eleven people attend the funeral.

Before the summer of 1948 is over, the pollsters have HARRY TRUMAN running so far behind that reelection to the White House seems impossible, and they stop taking polls. Truman embarks on a speaking tour aboard a private train, making whistle stops at hundreds of cities and towns. He goes to bed on election night believing he's lost but wakes up elected. A few days later he has his picture taken in St. Louis holding a newspaper with the headline DEWEY DEFEATS TRUMAN. Truman has a big smile on his face.

WILLIAM TECUMSEH SHERMAN retires from the army, 1884. There is talk of running him for president. Sherman says: "If nominated I will not run; if elected I will not serve."

In July 1962 BENNETT CERF travels to Oxford, Mississippi, for the funeral of William Faulkner, who was also sixty-four. Faulkner's relatives at the house treat the New York publisher with suspicion bordering on hostility, until one of them recognizes Cerf as a panelist on the

Sunday evening television program *What's My Line*. Suddenly everyone wants to be his friend.

NOVELIST and playwright SHERWOOD ANDERSON dies of peritonitis and a perforated bowel after swallowing a toothpick from an hors d'oeuvre at a cocktail party, 1941. Ironically, the cocktail party is in Colón, Panama.

ISAAC NEWTON is knighted by Queen Anne, 1705.

PHILO T. FARNSWORTH, the inventor of television, dies bankrupt, 1971. He never allowed his children to watch TV, believing the content was worthless.

RICHARD NIXON confides to David Frost and a television audience of millions that he was responsible for the Watergate break-in but that when a president orders something, it's not actually illegal, 1977.

MAO ZEDONG launches the Great Leap Forward, 1958. Before it's through, twenty million Chinese will die of starvation.

VOLTAIRE is comfortably settled in a garden villa overlooking Lake Geneva, 1759. Here he writes the satire *Candide*, which lampoons the popular notion that everything happens for the best in this best of all possible worlds.

HO CHI MINH's guerrilla army defeats the French at Dien Bien Phu, 1954. The French sign an armistice that divides the country at the seventeenth parallel. Now president, Ho refuses to move into the governor general's residence, instead choosing an electrician's cottage to live in. He likes to be called Uncle Ho and chain-smokes Salems.

IN 1959, while engaged in a life-or-death struggle with American leftists, FBI director J. EDGAR HOOVER is involved in a minor traffic accident, in which another vehicle strikes the left side of the car where he is sitting. Hoover issues orders that in the future he must never be seated in the left side of a car, nor should any car he is riding in make a left-hand turn.

HENRY FORD has produced fifteen million Model Ts by 1927.

Sixty-*five*

*I am no longer ******, clerk to the firm of &c. I am Retired Leisure. I am to be met with in trim gardens. I am already come to be known by my vacant face and careless gesture, perambulating at no fixed pace, nor with any settled purpose. I walk about; not to and from. . . . I grow into gentility perceptibly. When I take up a newspaper, it is to read the state of the opera,* Opus operatum est. *I have done all that I came into this world to do. I have worked task work, and have the rest of the day to myself.*

—CHARLES LAMB, "The Superannuated Man" (1825)

Former president LYNDON BAINES JOHNSON grows his hair long, till he looks a bit like the young people who protested against his war, 1971.

WINSTON CHURCHILL becomes prime minister for the first time, 1940. In his first speech in office he says, "All I have to offer is toil, blood, tears, and sweat."

JACK WELCH retires after twenty years as chairman and CEO of General Electric, 2001. Besides including a very comfortable income, his retirement package will pay for the telephone and computer service at his five homes; flowers, food, wine, and wait-staff when he's in New York; the dinners he eats out; memberships at three country clubs; Red Sox, Yankees, and Knicks tickets; a box at the Metropolitan Opera; very nice seats at Wimbledon, the French Open, and U.S. Open tennis tournaments; and dry cleaning, for the rest of his life.

President JOHN ADAMS moves into the new presidential residence, 1800. It won't be called the White House until they paint it white, which they'll need to do after the British burn it down in 1814. Adams doesn't live there long because he soon loses the 1800 election to his own vice president, and archrival, Thomas Jefferson.

JOHN O'HARA dies in his sleep on April 11, 1970. He'd just put in another good day of writing. *The New Yorker* published more of O'Hara's stories than anybody else's, 256 in all. One thing he did in his last year was learn to swim.

While experimenting with the refrigeration of meat, FRANCIS BACON catches cold and dies, 1626.

MIGUEL DE CERVANTES's European best seller *Don Quixote* reaches America in a 1612 translation by Thomas Shelton. Cervantes won't receive any royalties.

By the time of his death in 1939, CHARLES WALGREEN owns 493 drugstores in 215 cities in 37 states and has a net worth of $24,205,182.

After years of rejected submissions to the salons, PAUL CÉZANNE is given a retrospective in Paris, 1904.

DUKE ELLINGTON records songs from the Disney musical *Mary Poppins*, 1964. Even he cannot make them sound hip.

ANDREW CARNEGIE offers $5.2 million to the city of New York to build sixty-five branch libraries, 1901. Before he is through, he will pay for the building of more than 2,800 libraries in large and small towns all across the United States. The towns themselves will provide the books.

Vermonter IDA MAY FULLER applies for Social Security, 1939. She has been paying into the program for only three years. "It wasn't that I expected anything, mind you, but I knew I'd been paying for something called Social Security and I wanted to ask the people in Rutland about it." In January 1940 she receives Social Security check number 00-000-001 in the amount of $22.54.

In 1972 LAURENCE OLIVIER signs a contract to play an Italian-American gangster and goes to the trouble of perfecting the accent, but at the last minute he falls ill and the director has to replace him with Marlon Brando.

SIXTY-SIX

Thus the whirligig of time brings in his revenges.

—WILLIAM SHAKESPEARE, *Twelfth Night* (1599)

Former president, and Gentile, RICHARD NIXON is rejected by the coop board at New York's exclusive River House, 1979. Mr. Nixon's former adviser Henry Kissinger has an apartment there.

HUNTER S. THOMPSON invents shotgun golf at Owl Farm, Woody Creek, Colorado, 2004. The game is played in pairs, with one participant, a golfer, attempting to land an iron shot on the green, and the second player, armed with a shotgun, attempting to hit the ball in flight. A variation of trapshooting.

QUEEN ELIZABETH II has a very bad year; both of her sons' marriages are on the rocks, and one of her houses catches fire, 1992.

SIR JOHN GIELGUD's Mock Turtle dances on the beach with Malcolm Muggeridge's Gryphon in Jonathan Miller's film *Alice in Wonderland*, 1966.

SIR WALTER RALEIGH returns from his last voyage in search of El Dorado. The only gold he found happened to be in the hold of Spanish vessels. The king had forbidden him to attack the Spanish, so Raleigh loses his head, 1618.

After years spent in and out of mental institutions, the Princeton eccentric JOHN FORBES NASH is awarded the Nobel Prize for economics, 1994. Since the late 1960s he has been, as he describes it, "a person of delusionally influenced thinking but of relatively moderate behavior" and thus was able to stay out of hospitals. He also says, somewhat sadly: "Rationality of thought imposes a limit on a person's concept of his relation to the cosmos."

The *New York Times* announces that WINNIE THE POOH has become an American citizen, 1987. The stuffed animal has resided with several elderly friends at the New York Public Library for a number of years.

JOHNNY CARSON tapes his last *Tonight Show* on May 22, 1992. He can honestly claim that most of the children born in the United States in the previous three decades were conceived during his television show.

BRIGHAM YOUNG marries an attractive twenty-four-year-old, 1868. He has had twenty-one wives, but not all at one time.

FREDERICK DOUGLASS is criticized for marrying a woman a few shades lighter than himself, 1884. His wife of forty-four years died two years before.

PAUL REVERE builds the first mill for rolling copper in the United States, 1801. The name Revereware will be trademarked later.

JOHNNY MERCER dies, 1975. In his career he wrote or collaborated on more than a thousand songs and lyrics, including "Skylark," "Satin Doll," "Laura," "Autumn Leaves," and "I'm Old Fashioned."

Travel writer, lumberjack, parrot fancier, and former Python Michael Palin is elected president of the Royal Geographical Society, 2009.

SIXTY-SEVEN

Experience is a mere whiff or rumble, produced by enormously complex and ill-deciphered causes of experience; and in the other direction, experience is a mere peephole through which glimpses come down to us of eternal things.

—GEORGE SANTAYANA, letter to the
Marchesa Iris Origo (May 1933)

HENRI CARTIER-BRESSON has given up photography and gone back to drawing, 1975.

SAM SNEAD shoots his age in a PGA tour event, 1979.

MARY MCCARTHY is a guest on *The Dick Cavett Show* on PBS, 1979. The studio audience shifts nervously when she says that fellow writer Lillian Hellman is overrated. Asked to elaborate, she says, "Every word she writes is a lie, including 'and' and 'the.'" Hellman sues. The lawsuit ruins McCarthy's finances and her health. Randall Jarrell once wrote of McCarthy, "Torn animals were removed at sunset from that smile."

JOHN HUSTON plays a charming, dangerous, rich old man in Roman Polanski's *Chinatown*, 1974.

Disciples of the postimpressionist painter make pilgrimages to Aix-en-Provence to watch PAUL CÉZANNE at work on his monumental painting, *Bathers*. He will die on October 22, 1906.

GEORGE WASHINGTON dies of a sore throat at Mount Vernon, 1799.

Adventurer RICHARD FRANCIS BURTON completes his celebrated translation of *The Thousand Nights and a Night*, better known as *The Arabian Nights*, which is published in sixteen volumes in 1888. It has taken him the better part of three years, which comes to around a thousand and one nights if you do the math. So, around a story a day.

POET MARIANNE MOORE has been hired by the Ford Motor Company to help name their newest car-model, 1955. Among her suggestions are: Utopian Turtletop, Andante Con Tropo, the Anticipator, the Thunder Crester, the Silver Sword, the Regna Racer, the Magigravue, the Turcotingo, the Pastelogram, the Varsity Stroke, the Mongoose Civique, the Intelligent Whale, and the Resilient Bullet. Ford decides to name the new car the Edsel, after Henry Ford's son and heir.

LEONARDO DA VINCI dies in France, 1519. He wrote many of his ideas about engineering and art into a diary, which now resides in the library of billionaire Bill Gates. The most frequent entry in the diary is a simple question, written over and over again. "Tell me, tell me if anything got finished." The theory is that he wrote this as a way of testing a new quill.

RALPH WALDO EMERSON travels to California and meets John Muir, who is a big fan of his, 1871.

GEORGE IV dies at Windsor Castle, 1830. He was king for ten years, after being prince regent from 1811 to 1820. His executor, the Duke of Wellington, finds that his personal papers consist of mildly pornographic letters exchanged with his mistress, "dirty, snuffy pocket-handkerchiefs with old faded nosegays tied up in them," women's gloves, and other trinkets. The duke decides the best thing to do is to burn them. He gives the king's clothes to the servants, except the coronation robes, which are given to Madame Tussaud for her wax museum.

RALPH LAUREN owns nine red vintage Ferraris and six houses, 2007.

RECLUSIVE tycoon HOWARD HUGHES is living in Managua, Nicaragua, at the time of the December 1972 earthquake, in which five thousand people are killed. The inconvenienced multibillionaire is given refuge at the country palace of dictator Anastasio Somoza.

RICHARD NIXON finds an apartment in New York's Upper East Side, 1980.

Arch-conservative WILLIAM F. BUCKLEY JR. suggests that one of the few legitimate duties of government would be to pipe classical music into every home in America, 1993. That and public statuary.

In April 1926, two years after the composer's death, GIACOMO PUCCINI's *Turandot* is performed for the first time at La Scala Opera House in Milan, under the baton of Arturo Toscanini, from a score completed by Franco Alfano. During the opening performance Toscanini leaves the podium, in tears, at the point where Puccini had finished composing.

BUFFALO BILL CODY goes into the motion picture business, 1913.

SIXTY-EIGHT

Age is not a particularly interesting subject. Anyone can get old. All you have to do is live long enough.

—GROUCHO MARX, *Groucho and Me* (1959)

Playwright EUGENE O'NEILL premieres *A Long Day's Journey into Night*, 1956.

MIGUEL DE CERVANTES finishes part two of *Don Quixote*, in which quite a bit of the plot involves the hero talking about this fictional character Don Quixote who has become famous in the pages of a book written by an author named Miguel de Cervantes, 1615.

GROUCHO, Chico, and Harpo Marx perform together for the last time in *The Incredible Jewel Robbery* on CBS, 1959.

THOMAS EDISON starts taking a yearly vacation with friends Henry Ford and Harvey Firestone, 1915.

J.M.W. TURNER paints *Rain, Steam and Speed*, 1844.

CHARLES LINDBERGH breaks many years of silence to speak out on environmental issues, particularly the plight of whales and the threat posed to the atmosphere by supersonic aircraft, 1970.

RONALD REAGAN suggests that there is a suppressed study proving that most air pollution comes from plants and trees, 1979.

JOSEPHINE BAKER dies in Paris on April 12, 1975. She'd performed to a sold-out audience at Bobino the previous night. Twenty thousand Parisians turn out for her funeral.

In 1974, playwright LILLIAN HELLMAN appears in an advertising campaign for fur coats above the memorable copy-line "What becomes a legend most?" She is furious when she learns that she was chosen only after Ginger Rogers missed a photo shoot.

GEORGE BURNS retires from show business on the death of his wife and comedy partner, Gracie Allen, 1964.

ALEXANDRE DUMAS, author of *The Three Musketeers* and *The Count of Monte Cristo*, dies, 1870. He wrote 250 books in his lifetime, working with 73 assistants, earning as much as 200,000 francs a year, but always spending money more quickly than he earned it.

CLARENCE DARROW argues the case for the defense in the famous "Monkey Trial" in Dayton, Tennessee, 1925. The man on trial is John Scopes, who violated Tennessee law by teaching Darwin's theory of evolution in a public school. Darrow takes the case all the way to the Tennessee Supreme Court, where he wins, but only on a technicality, so creationism remains the law of the land. People in the southern United States are relieved to know they are not legally descended from monkeys.

In May 1934, in hopes of reviving his sexual vigor, poet WILLIAM BUTLER YEATS travels to London to receive an injection of monkey glands.

SIXTY-NINE

If I had any decency, I'd be dead. Most of my friends are.

—DOROTHY PARKER (1963)

LOUIS ARMSTRONG celebrates his birthday by playing at the Newport Jazz Festival, 1970.

SOCRATES is charged with not worshipping the gods and with corrupting Athenian youth. He is found guilty, 400 B.C. Sentenced to death, he drinks hemlock.

RALPH WALDO EMERSON's house burns down, 1872.

MARK TWAIN is invited to dinner at the White House by Theodore Roosevelt, 1905.

Prime Minister NEVILLE CHAMBERLAIN flies to Munich to appease Hitler, 1938. It is his first plane ride.

GALILEO is interrogated by the Inquisition and sentenced to prison for an indefinite period by Pope Urban VIII, 1633. In a formal ceremony at the church of Santa Maria Sopra Minerva, he abjures his errors, and the earth goes back to being the center of the universe. Galileo is sentenced to house arrest in his villa near Florence for the rest of his life.

Beat novelist WILLIAM S. BURROUGHS is writer in residence at the University of Kansas, where he spends his time gardening and experimenting with a new form of painting that involves shooting a handgun at cans of paint, 1983.

NORMAN ROCKWELL breaks his forty-seven-year run with *The Saturday Evening Post* and switches to *Look* magazine, 1963. Here he takes off his rose-colored glasses and paints subjects like poverty and civil rights. His audience isn't pleased.

FBI director J. EDGAR HOOVER instructs his agents to gather dirt on civil rights leader Martin Luther King Jr., 1964.

CHARLES PERRAULT publishes his *Tales of Mother Goose*, 1697.

Motorcycle daredevil EVEL KNIEVEL dies of natural causes, 2007.

Explorer, Orientalist, and translator of erotica RICHARD FRANCIS BURTON dies in Trieste on October 19, 1890. Hoping to save his reputation, his wife lights a bonfire in the backyard of their house in Mortlake outside London. Among the things she burns is his unpublished translation of the erotic classic *The Scented Garden*, which he'd been working on for fourteen years. She had been offered the astounding sum of £6,000 to publish it.

JAMES BARRIE donates the royalties from his play *Peter Pan* to the Great Ormond Street Children's Hospital, 1929.

After years of poverty, the poet, artist, and engraver WILLIAM BLAKE dies on August 12, 1827, and is buried in an unmarked grave with seven other people in Bunhill Fields; the burial was paid for with nineteen shillings borrowed for the occasion. Death, he once said, is "but a removing from one room to another."

In 1712 the Royal Society forms a special commission to decide whether ISAAC NEWTON or Gottfried Leibniz (age sixty-five) is the sole inventor of calculus. Newton is president of the Royal Society and chair of the special commission. The commission decides in favor of Newton.

When DOROTHY PARKER's husband dies in 1963, a West Hollywood neighbor asks if she can get her anything. "Get me a new husband," Parker says.

Seventy

If you find that you can't make seventy by any but an uncomfortable road, don't you go. When they take off the Pullman and retire you to the rancid smoker, put off your things, count your checks, and get out at the first way station where there's a cemetery.

—Mark Twain (1835–1910)

Long-range photos taken of Greta Garbo swimming seminude appear in *People* magazine, 1976. The retired actress is still quite svelte.

Noël Coward celebrates his birthday with a royal visit, an evening at the theater, a film retrospective, a television documentary, an authorized biography, and a special dinner at the Savoy, 1969. The knighthood arrives next, in the New Year's Honours List.

Reclusive bazillionaire Howard Hughes is living on the top floor of the hotel he owns in Las Vegas, 1975. He is pathologically afraid of germs and addicted to codeine and other painkillers; his hair is uncut and his fingernails are several inches long; and he wears tissue boxes for shoes. Within a few months he will be dead, leaving a confused estate that lawyers will grow wealthy fighting over.

President and former Supreme Allied Commander in Europe Dwight D. Eisenhower leaves office in 1961, but not before delivering a grave warning about the new "military industrial complex" that he believes holds far too much power in Washington.

Casey Stengel is fired by the Yankees after losing the 1960 World Series. In eleven years he led the team to nine World Series, and the

Yankees won seven of them. "I'll never make the mistake of being seventy again," he says.

CHARLES SCHULZ lets Charlie Brown hit a home run, 1993.

In a January 1814 letter to John Adams, THOMAS JEFFERSON says that the divine aspects attributed to Jesus are "the fabric of very inferior minds." With a penknife he begins editing all of the miracles and the hearsay out of the New Testament, leaving only Jesus' words and the more plausible episodes in his life. He calls this edition *The Jefferson Bible: The Life and Morals of Jesus of Nazareth Extracted Textually from the Gospels.*

WILLIAM SCHWENCK GILBERT, the surviving half of Gilbert and Sullivan, is the first dramatist to be given a knighthood, 1907.

The diarist and naval bureaucrat SAMUEL PEPYS dies, 1703. He once wrote in his diary, "For myself, chance without merit brought me in, and that diligence only keeps me so, and will, living as I do among so many lazy people, that the diligent man becomes necessary, that they cannot do anything without him." He had risen from nothing, you see, and knew it.

ANNIE SULLIVAN has spent fifty years spelling the world into the palm of Helen Keller's hand. Sullivan dies in October 1936; her pupil will live another thirty-two years without her.

GEORGE BERNARD SHAW is awarded the Nobel Prize for literature, 1926.

BUSTER KEATON receives a five-minute standing ovation at the 1965 Venice Film Festival. He has been making about $100,000 a year for the past few years, appearing in TV commercials.

JACK LALANNE swims the one and a half miles from Long Beach's Queen's Way Bridge to the *Queen Mary*, shackled and handcuffed and towing seventy boats carrying seventy people, 1984.

ROBERT FROST gets nineteen-year-old Truman Capote fired from his job at *The New Yorker* after Capote walks out of one of Frost's poetry readings, 1944.

HANS CHRISTIAN ANDERSEN dies, 1875. He had gone to live with some friends on the coast of Denmark. On the morning he died, he was served breakfast in bed but was found a little while later, still in bed. In his hand was a love letter that had been written to him forty-five years before. He never married.

Shortly after the successful end of the war in Europe, CHURCHILL is voted out of office by a grateful electorate, 1945.

SEVENTY-ONE

A man who is a politician at forty is a statesman at three score and ten. It is at this age, when he would be too old to be a clerk or a gardener or a police-court magistrate, that he is ripe to govern a country.

—WILLIAM SOMERSET MAUGHAM, *Cakes and Ale* (1930)

In May 1962 retired president DWIGHT D. EISENHOWER holds a press conference to criticize things that have happened since he left office. Current president John F. Kennedy says: "The thing I liked best was the picture of Eisenhower attacking medical care for the old under Social Security as 'socialized medicine'—and then getting into his government limousine and heading out to Walter Reed."

ZSA ZSA GABOR is arrested and tried for slapping a policeman in Beverly Hills, 1989. The judge sentences her to three days in jail and orders her to put her correct age on her driver's license.

On January 20, 1936, LORD BERTRAND EDWARD DAWSON M.D., physician to the British royal family, injects a lethal dose of morphine and cocaine into the jugular of the dying monarch, George V. If known, this act of kindness and high treason would have got him hanged. Instead he is made the first Viscount Dawson of Penn. He will continue as the personal physician to the next two kings.

The DUKE OF WINDSOR—former monarch, keen bridge player, and inventor of the Windsor knot—divides his time between his rent-subsidized, tax-free villa in Paris's Bois de Boulogne, guest bedrooms in Palm Beach, and cocktail parties on New York's Upper East Side, 1965. He is not welcome in the land of his birth, where his niece is queen.

SIR JOHN GIELGUD performs in Harold Pinter's *No Man's Land*, 1975.

SAUL STEINBERG's "View of the World from Ninth Avenue" appears on the cover of *The New Yorker* magazine, March 29, 1976.

SUSAN SONTAG dies in 2004, twenty-eight years after her doctor gave her only two years to live. In the intervening years she has written nineteen books and commented on many important causes of the day. Her personal library contains fifteen thousand books, arranged by historical period.

IN 1815 THOMAS JEFFERSON sells 6,487 of his books to the U.S. Congress for $23,950, the money approved by President James Madison. All the books belonging to Congress were burned by the British during the recent war.

MICHELANGELO is appointed chief architect of the new St. Peter's Basilica, 1546.

PIANIST ARTUR RUBENSTEIN visits his friend Pablo Picasso (age seventy-seven) and sits for twenty-one crayon portraits, 1958.

COCO CHANEL introduces her first fashion line since the war, 1953.

NOBEL laureate JOHN FORBES NASH and his wife, Alicia, are remarried, 2001. They divorced in 1963, at a time when the mathematician was in and out of mental institutions, but they have lived in the same house since 1970, a ménage Alicia describes as "like two distantly related individuals under one roof."

NELSON MANDELA is released from prison, 1990. He has spent a quarter century behind bars for his opposition to the South African apartheid system.

IN August 1962 the car carrying CHARLES DE GAULLE comes under a hail of bullets. The French president refuses to duck but emerges unhurt. He survives thirty-one assassination attempts between 1944 and 1966 and will die quietly in 1970.

IN April 1951 GENERAL DOUGLAS MACARTHUR is fired by President Harry Truman. On his return to America he is greeted by cheering crowds, then fades away like an old soldier.

SEVENTY-TWO

The past is what you remember, imagine you remember, convince yourself you remember, or pretend you remember.

—HAROLD PINTER, *Old Times* (1971)

SIGMUND FREUD flies in an airplane for the first time, 1928: "I found the sensation exciting and rather comfortable." The first note in his diary for 1929 is "Passed over for the Nobel Prize." Anti-Semitic disturbances are becoming a problem at Vienna University.

MICHELANGELO begins sculpting his own tomb, 1547.

GERTRUDE STEIN's last words, in 1946: "What is the question?"

ON his seventy-second birthday, ALBERT EINSTEIN has his picture taken while sticking his tongue out, 1951.

QUENTIN CRISP, self-described "stately homo of England," moves to New York and settles in the East Village, 1981.

COLETTE publishes her most famous novel, *Gigi*, 1945.

I. M. PEI plants a glass pyramid in the elegant forecourt of the Louvre, 1989.

KATHERINE ANNE PORTER receives a check for $27,000 for her long-awaited novel *Ship of Fools*, 1962. She immediately uses $2,000 of it as a down payment on a diamond and emerald ring costing $13,000.

THOMAS HARDY has been estranged from his wife, Emma, for some years; still, when she dies suddenly in 1912, the writer is filled with remorse. He begins to work out his feelings for her in poetry. Two years later he will marry his secretary, who is forty years his junior.

LUIS BUÑUEL directs *The Discreet Charm of the Bourgoisie*, 1972.

FRANK LLOYD WRIGHT completes Falling Water, 1939.

In 1966 MAO ZEDONG launches the Cultural Revolution. It is not a Chinese version of the Italian Renaissance.

BENJAMIN FRANKLIN meets Voltaire at the French Academy in Paris, 1778. The moment they embrace is seen by many as the high point of the Enlightenment.

AUGUSTE RENOIR's arthritis has made it impossible for him to paint, so he directs assistants who create his last sculptures, 1913. "The pain passes," he says. "But the beauty remains."

As of 2004 JOHN UPDIKE has produced thirty novels and story collections, six volumes of poetry, four enormous collections of criticism and miscellaneous journalism, as well as children's stories and memoirs, and four children. His only number-one best seller, *Couples*, came thirty-six years ago. He is still writing, waiting for a phone call from Sweden.

SEVENTY-THREE

But I have promises to keep,
And miles to go before I sleep.

—ROBERT FROST, "Stopping by Woods on a
Snowy Evening" (1923)

A year after he retires, FRED ROGERS's days are much the same, 2002. He swims, reads a lot, and listens to Beethoven. He's given his red sweater to the Smithsonian Institution.

SIR EDWARD ELGAR is receiving a driving lesson from his friend Percy Hull when the theme for a new march suddenly comes to him, 1929. He writes the music down on the margin of a map of Worcestershire. The theme, "Pomp and Circumstance no. 5," will be the last of the series often played at commencement ceremonies.

P. G. WODEHOUSE, the author of books about silly English earls and wise butlers, becomes an American citizen, 1955.

DOROTHY PARKER dies at the Hotel Volney in New York's Upper East Side, leaving all her worldly goods to the Reverend Martin Luther King Jr., 1967.

Architect LUDWIG MIES VAN DER ROHE coins a phrase when he says "Less is more," 1959.

ALBERT EINSTEIN is offered the presidency of Israel but turns it down, 1952.

ELIZABETH TAYLOR's dog dies, 2005.

SEVENTY-*four*

*Which of us is happy in this world? Which of us has his desire?
Or having it, is satisfied? Come, children, let us shut up the
box and the puppets, for our play is played out.*

—WILLIAM MAKEPEACE THACKERAY,
Vanity Fair (1848)

BING CROSBY dies just after finishing eighteen holes of golf at La Moraleja, outside Madrid, on October 14, 1977. He shot 85.

ISAK DINESEN meets Marilyn Monroe and Arthur Miller at a luncheon party at the New York apartment of Carson McCullers, February 5, 1959.

S. J. PERELMAN drives his 1949 MG from Paris to Peking, 1978. He reaches Peking with a case of pneumonia but minus his car and his two companions, recalling the transatlantic flight of the bearded aviators in the 1935 Marx Brothers film *A Night at the Opera.*

Poet WILLIAM WORDSWORTH writes a letter to the *Morning Post* protesting plans to run a railway from Kendal to Windermere in England's scenic Lake District, 1844. "Is then no nook of English ground secure?" he writes, rhyming every other line. The point the poet is making is that railroads may be well and good, but "not in my back yard." Railroads bring the poor into the countryside whose beauty they are not equipped to appreciate, he says. There will be no rail line into the Lake District.

ALFRED TENNYSON is offered a peerage by Queen Victoria, 1883. It is the first time an Englishman has been given a title simply for being literary, and it is why we know him as Alfred, Lord Tennyson to this day.

Tennyson was the last poet to sell as many books as the best-selling novelists of his time.

ALBERT EINSTEIN publishes an open letter endorsing civil rights and criticizing the committee chaired by Senator Joe McCarthy, 1953. McCarthy calls Einstein "an enemy of America."

SIGMUND FREUD's mother dies, 1930. She was ninety-five. Freud has a heart attack, which finally forces him to give up smoking.

GALILEO loses the vision in his left eye and is now totally blind, 1638. He petitions the Inquisition to be freed and is denied. He is granted permission to live in Florence and to go to church, but only on religious holidays and only so long as he doesn't talk to anyone. Later in the year he receives a visit from the poet Milton.

Poet EZRA POUND leaves St. Elizabeth's Hospital in Washington, D.C., after spending twelve years there, 1958. He was committed to the asylum for treason and is released on grounds of "incurable, permanent insanity." "How did it go in the madhouse?" he is asked. "Rather badly," he answers. "But what other place could one live in America?"

H. G. WELLS's name is put near the top of the list of persons to be immediately liquidated by the SS when the Nazis take over the government of Great Britain, 1940.

A month before his death in the summer of 1961, TY COBB enters Emory Hospital, in Atlanta, with a brown paper bag containing a million dollars in negotiable bonds and a loaded pistol that he places on the nightstand next to his bed.

CLINT EASTWOOD directs *Million Dollar Baby* and receives his second Oscar, 2005. He won his first directing Oscar in 1992.

COLONEL HARLAND SANDERS sells his stake in Kentucky Fried Chicken for $2 million, 1964. There are now more than six hundred restaurants bearing his name. He will spend the next decade visiting them all, dressed in his trademark white suit.

Japan's EMPEROR HIROHITO visits Disneyland, 1975.

SEVENTY-*five*

~~

I delight in men over seventy. They always offer one the devotion of a lifetime.

—OSCAR WILDE, *A Woman of No Importance* (1893)

On June 3, 1964, T. S. ELIOT sends a car to London's Savoy Hotel to bring Mr. and Mrs. Groucho Marx to dinner. Eliot tells Groucho that their friendship has greatly enhanced his credit with the grocer across the street.

DR. BENJAMIN SPOCK, on the advice of his second wife, makes a change from Brooks Brothers suits and begins wearing blue jeans, 1978. She also introduces him to yoga, massage, and a macrobiotic diet, among other things.

SIR EDMUND HILLARY is given the Order of the Garter by Queen Elizabeth II, 1995. He has not climbed Mount Everest again since being the first to do so in 1953. He has devoted himself to building schools in the Himalayas and to keeping bees.

GEORGE PLIMPTON appears as a corrupt spelling bee MC in episode number 303 of *The Simpsons*, 2003.

In three breaths PABLO PICASSO blows out seventy-five candles on a seventy-pound cake, 1956.

MICHELANGELO completes his frescoes in the Vatican's Pauline Chapel, 1550.

WILLIAM SOMERSET MAUGHAM sits for the portrait painter Graham Sutherland, 1949. The resulting picture, with the author cast against a garish yellow background, captures him just as Christopher Isherwood described him: "That old, old parrot, his flat black eyes, blinking and attentive, his courtly politeness and his hypnotic stammer."

EDMUND WILSON spends the summer in upstate New York, 1970. Wilson has never learned to drive. His dentist's wife teaches him how to French kiss.

CECIL B. DEMILLE directs *The Ten Commandments* for the second time, 1956.

GROUCHO MARX publishes *Memoirs of a Mangy Lover*, 1965. No one libeled in the book is alive to sue him.

EDITH WHARTON is living in France, 1937. Her last story, "All Souls," will be published after she dies later in the year.

S. J. PERELMAN says happiness is a brown paper bag of possessions and a room in a hotel. He's lived in the Gramercy Park Hotel for the past six years. On the wall is a picture by Saul Steinberg that the artist gave him in exchange for an autographed copy of *Ulysses*. He looks at the picture every day but hasn't read *Ulysses* in months. In September 1979 *The New Yorker* publishes Perelman's last story: "Portrait of the Artist as a Young Cat's-Paw." He dies a month later. His chief regrets were that he never played jazz piano and never learned to speak perfect French.

Poet MARIANNE MOORE, perhaps having suffered a mild stroke, says to a friend: "Nearly every word I write now lacks a final letter," 1963.

ALEKSANDR SOLZHENITSYN returns to Russia, 1994. He has lived in the United States for two decades but hates the culture and never mastered the language.

QUEEN ELIZABETH II sits for Lucian Freud, 2001. It is her 120th portrait. Besides sitting for her portrait, her other hobbies are riding, dog-rearing, Scottish dancing, and betting on horse races.

NELSON MANDELA is awarded the Nobel Peace Prize, 1993.

SEVENTY-SIX

It makes so little difference, at so much more
Than seventy, where one looks, one has been there before.

Wood-smoke rises through trees, is caught in an upper flow
Of air and whirled away. But it has been often so.

—WALLACE STEVENS,
"Long and Sluggish Lines" (1954)

Former president JOHN ADAMS makes up with former president Thomas Jefferson, 1812. The two haven't been on speaking terms for years, partly because of the terrible things Adams's people said about Jefferson and the terrible things Jefferson's people said about Adams when they were running against each other in 1796. The two men will exchange 158 letters over the next fourteen years and will die on the same day in 1826.

In 1928 ALICE HARGREAVES, née Liddell, auctions the original manuscript of *Alice's Adventures Underground*, which was a Christmas present to her from Lewis Carroll in 1864. An American collector purchases it for £15,400.

MARTHA GRAHAM retires from dancing but will continue to choreograph for another twenty years, 1970.

After years of boozing, WILLEM DE KOONING goes teetotal, 1980. Suddenly his paintings assume a serene, almost bland lassitude, which doesn't please everyone.

During lunch at the White House in 1987, President RONALD REAGAN asks the Soviet foreign minister if they would side with the United States in the event of an invasion from outer space.

CHARLES SCHULZ has seen *Citizen Kane* forty times, 1998.

ALBERT EINSTEIN dies, 1955. His body is cremated, but his brain is preserved for scientific study according to his wishes. His eyes are given to an ophthalmologist, who keeps them in a safe-deposit box.

VICTOR HUGO has a stroke, 1878. His mistress, Juliette Drouet, says it wouldn't have happened if the author weren't sleeping with his maid.

In 1935 the poet A. E. HOUSMAN soldiers on at Cambridge, continuing to lecture, admitting that the half-mile walk from home in Trinity to the hall in Magdalene is more work than the lecture. He sometimes thinks it was a mistake to live so long and runs up stairs hoping he might die at the top.

SEVENTY-SEVEN

At seventy-seven it is time to be in earnest.

—SAMUEL JOHNSON (1709–84)

MARC CHAGALL paints the ceiling of the Paris Opera, 1964.

ALICE B. TOKLAS publishes *The Alice B. Toklas Cookbook*, 1954. The most famous recipe is for "Hashisch Fudge."

KURT VONNEGUT is hospitalized for smoke inhalation after a fire breaks out in his New York townhouse. He'd been watching the 2000 Super Bowl.

The Egyptian novelist NAGUIB MAHFOUZ wins the Nobel Prize for literature, 1988. His novels have been banned throughout the Arab world, which is odd for the man who once worked as Egypt's director of censorship.

LOUIS XIV dies, amid much rejoicing, not just in France, 1715. His heir is a sickly five-year-old.

GANDHI celebrates the independence of India, July 1947. In January 1948 he will be assassinated on the way to evening prayer.

FRANZ JOSEF HAYDN, the retired Esterhazy court composer, dies in Vienna on May 31, 1809. In his lifetime he composed 108 symphonies, 24 operas, 14 masses, 57 canons, 83 string quartets, 47 divertimenti, 29 dances, 16 overtures, 126 string trios, 52 keyboard sonatas, and 32 pieces for mechanical clock.

WINSTON CHURCHILL's son Randolph has been an even bigger disappointment to Winston than Winston was to his own father. In 1952 Randolph writes in a letter: "ever since you first became Prime Minister you have repeatedly made it clear to me—& to others—that you no longer have that same desire for my company in private or in public which between 1923 & 1940 was the chief delight & pivot of my existence . . . I realize too that you regard me as a failure & that you cannot disguise this view." Randolph is a heavy drinker, mercurial, unpredictable, unpopular, and a bully, which at many points in his life would have been fair descriptions of Winston himself.

Retired *Playboy* magazine publisher HUGH HEFNER is living with seven blondes, aged between eighteen and twenty-eight, at the Playboy Mansion in Brentwood, California, 2002.

FREDERICK DOUGLASS dies at his home in Washington, D.C., shortly after attending a meeting of the National Council of Women, where he received a standing ovation, 1895.

SIR JOHN GIELGUD receives his first Oscar, playing the witty manservant to an alcoholic millionaire in *Arthur*, 1982.

GALILEO invents the clock pendulum, 1641.

Retired senator and former astronaut JOHN GLENN becomes the oldest man to orbit the earth, 1998.

BENJAMIN FRANKLIN witnesses the world's first successful balloon flight, in Paris in 1783. When someone asks, "What good is it?" Franklin replies, "What good is a newborn baby?"

JONATHAN SWIFT dies in October 1745, having outlived his friend Alexander Pope by a year. Swift suffered a stroke in 1742 and lost his ability to speak. Going mad was his worst fear. "I shall be like that tree," he said. "I shall die at the top." He is buried next to his beloved Esther Johnson, whom he'd known since she was a child of eight and had nicknamed Stella.

SEVENTY-EIGHT

You may have seen my mother waltzing on ice skates in Rockefeller Center. She's seventy-eight years old now but very wiry.

—JOHN CHEEVER, *The Angel of the Bridge* (1961)

MOSES is working as a shepherd for Jethro in Midian, 1448 B.C.

GRANDMA MOSES exhibits some of her paintings at Thomas's Drugstore in Hoosick Falls, N.Y., and is discovered by the art dealer Louis Caldor, 1938.

BENJAMIN FRANKLIN proposes the idea of daylight savings time, 1784.

WINSTON CHURCHILL wins the Nobel Prize for literature, 1953. He sees *Hamlet* performed for the first time but unnerves some of the actors by saying most of the lines a few seconds before they do.

GIUSEPPE BONANNO, "Joe Bananas," publishes his memoirs, 1983. Some of his most devoted readers are in the FBI. When they ask Bonanno to clarify certain events, he clams up and winds up in jail for fourteen months.

JOHN HUSTON directs *Prizzi's Honor*, 1985. His daughter Anjelica wins an Oscar for her performance.

SALVADOR DALI is made Marquès de Dalí de Púbol by King Juan Carlos of Spain, 1982.

PHILIP JOHNSON outrages the architecture world by putting a "Chippendale" scrolled top on the new AT&T headquarters in New York, 1984.

HENRY FORD, after years of spying on his employees and using strong-arm tactics and company police to prevent them from organizing, finally allows the UAW to unionize the workers at the Ford Motor Company, 1941. He will live six more years.

POET MARIANNE MOORE appears on the June cover of *Esquire* magazine, along with Joe Louis, Kate Smith, wristwatch huckster John Cameron Swayze, and others, 1966.

WILLIAM F. BUCKLEY retires from *The National Review* after fifty years at the helm, 2004. Old conservatives are seen wandering glassy-eyed and rudderless on the Upper East Side of Manhattan. Weeping is heard in Greenwich, Connecticut.

ELEANOR ROOSEVELT writes three books, one fewer than last year, 1962.

THE AYATOLLAH KHOMEINI returns to Teheran from Paris and overthrows the shah of Iran, 1979. His followers take forty-four Americans hostage at the American embassy.

GÜNTER GRASS is a world-famous novelist, poet, and playwright, a Nobel laureate, and a merciless critic of German hypocrisy. But in 2006 he reveals something he's kept hidden for over sixty years. As a teenager during the last months of World War II he served in the Waffen SS.

SEVENTY-NINE

[Bachelors'] approach to gastronomy is basically sexual, since few of them under seventy-nine will bother to produce a good meal unless it is for a pretty woman.

—M.F.K. FISHER, *An Alphabet for Gourmets* (1949)

In 1996, six months after leaving the French presidency and now dying of cancer, FRANÇOIS MITTERAND sits down to his last meal, the famous repast of ortolan, a yellow-throated songbird roughly the size of a man's thumb, weighing fifty-five grams. The bird is prepared in the traditional way, placed alive into armagnac until it is drowned, then plucked and eaten whole in one mouthful with a napkin worn over the head to prevent the aroma from escaping. He is joined by thirty close friends and family. Because the ortolan is endangered, the eating of it is illegal in France. Mitterand dies eight days later. His funeral is attended by both his families, the second one illegitimate.

GIUSEPPE VERDI writes his last opera, *Falstaff*, 1892.

GERONIMO, war chief of the Apaches, dies of pneumonia in 1909, after twenty-three years spent as a prisoner at Fort Pickens and Fort Sill. Having converted to Christianity three years earlier, he is buried in the Indian cemetery.

JEAN SIBELIUS burns his Eighth Symphony, 1945. He'd spent most of the 1930s composing it. A few colleagues report that much of it was written down; others say he had most of it in his head. He will speak of it occasionally and continue working on it into the 1950s, but it will never be performed. All that remain are a few sketches jotted in the margins of his Seventh Symphony.

Benjamin Franklin invents bifocals, 1785.

William Shawn is forced out as editor of *The New Yorker*, 1987. There is an atmosphere of resentful bewilderment on West 43rd Street, where 150 of his colleagues ask the chosen successor to refuse the appointment. Shawn had been editor for thirty-five years, supervising the work of John Cheever, John Hersey, John Updike, Pauline Kael, J. D. Salinger, and others.

In a 2003 interview Norman Mailer says American architecture has been in serious decline for the past fifty years. In fact he has a hard time praising any current art form, except MTV and advertising. He admires Madonna.

Lena Horne wins a Grammy, her fourth, 1996.

In 1963, a decade after leaving the White House, Harry Truman keeps to a strict routine. He's up at five-thirty each morning, taking a walk before breakfast, then walks to his office at the Truman Library. He returns home at three, often chatting on the porch with Mrs. Truman and her bridge club before going upstairs for a nap. After waking, he and Mrs. Truman call their daughter in New York. Dinner is at six. Evenings are spent on the screen porch talking with friends, or in the music room playing the piano, or reading in the study. Mr. Truman's favorite books are histories and biographies. Mrs. Truman prefers mysteries.

Eighty

Can't you see I'm dreaming?
In a dream you are never eighty.

—Anne Sexton, "Old" (1928–74)

Poet Marianne Moore throws out the first ball at the Yankees opener, 1968.

Beat novelist William S. Burroughs does a television commercial for Nike, 1994.

Queen Elizabeth II has outlasted four Archbishops of Canterbury, 2006.

In January 2000 a portrait of author Doris Lessing is hung in the National Portrait Gallery in London. The government offers to make her a Dame of the British Empire, but she refuses on the grounds there isn't a British Empire anymore. She says being "a dame" is "a bit pantomimey" anyway.

Victor Hugo's birthday is celebrated as a national holiday in France, 1882.

Count Leo Tolstoy rewrites his will, leaving the copyrights to all of his books to the public, 1908. His family isn't happy when they find out about this. He also says he wants to be buried in the Zakaz Forest.

Alfred, Lord Tennyson writes "Crossing the Bar," 1889.

Sigmund Freud receives birthday cards from James Joyce, Virginia Woolf, Pablo Picasso, Albert Einstein, Albert Schweitzer, H. G. Wells, and others, 1936.

HELEN KELLER meets John F. Kennedy at the White House, 1961. Asked how many presidents she's met, she answers that she can't recall, but she's met every one since Grover Cleveland.

ROMAN politician and general CATO THE ELDER begins studying Greek, 154 B.C.

Inventor SAMUEL F. B. MORSE sees a statue of himself erected in Central Park, 1871.

ALFRED HITCHCOCK dies without ever winning the Best Director Oscar, 1980. He told an interviewer the four things that frightened him most were children, policemen, high places, and that his next picture wouldn't be as good as his last one.

GRANDMA MOSES has a one-woman show in New York and is featured in a special presentation at Gimbels department store, 1940.

Crime novelist DICK FRANCIS loses his wife of fifty-three years, 2000. She was seventy-six. There had long been rumors that Mary Francis wrote the novels and that the former jockey provided the race-course atmosphere and the name. He always called her the brains of the operation. If so, they wrote thirty-nine novels together, all of them best sellers. The books stop coming, for a while.

Eighty-one

He had as white a head and fresh a cheek
As ever were produced by youth and age
Engendering in the blood of hale fourscore.

—William Wordsworth, "The Brothers" (1800)

In an interview in *Newsweek*, Robert Frost compares writing free verse to playing tennis with the net down, 1956.

French writer André Gide dies in Paris, 1951. A few days later a telegram appears on a bulletin board in the Sorbonne bearing his signature. It reads: "Hell doesn't exist. Better notify Claudel." His colleague, poet Paul Claudel, had once tried to convert Gide to Catholicism.

George Burns plays the title role in the film *Oh God!*, 1977.

Groucho Marx performs in a one-man show at Carnegie Hall, 1972. He is also made a *Commandeur des Arts et Lettres* by the French government.

Victor Hugo mourns the death of his mistress, 1883.

Paul Revere has become quite rich manufacturing church bells, 1816.

John Kenneth Galbraith publishes *A Short History of Financial Euphoria*, 1990.

John Huston dies on location, 1987. His last film, *The Dead*, was adapted from a story by James Joyce.

When his daughter writes a memoir, J. D. Salinger says to a Cornish, New Hampshire, neighbor: "Never have children." *Catcher in the Rye* still sells about 250,000 copies in 2000, a half-century after publication.

JAMES BEARD, the doyen of American cookery, dies, 1985. He once said, "I believe that if ever I had to practice cannibalism, I might manage if there were enough tarragon around."

EIGHTY-TWO

*My will contains directions for my funeral, which will be fol-
lowed not by mourning coaches, but by oxen, sheep, flocks of
poultry, and a small traveling aquarium of live fish, all wearing white scarf's in honor of the man who perished rather
than eat his fellow creatures.*

—GEORGE BERNARD SHAW (1856–1950)

GRETA GARBO is often seen walking in her quiet New York neighborhood, 1988. She's shared the seven-room apartment at 450 East 52nd
Street with her Renoir and her Bonnard since 1953.

TOLSTOY dies, 1910.

THEODOR SEUSS GEISEL is named a literary lion by the New York
Public Library, 1986. At the reception, Jackie Onassis asks him where
he gets his ideas.

SALVADOR DALI receives a pacemaker, 1986.

THOMAS EDISON celebrates his eighty-second birthday with President
Hoover, Henry Ford, and Harvey Firestone at Edison's winter place in
Florida, 1929. He is living on a strict diet of one pint of milk every
three hours, nothing else.

JOHANN WOLFGANG VON GOETHE dies, 1832.

MAO ZEDONG dies, 1976. His little red book of sayings was a
perennial best seller. Among his more memorable homilies: "People of
the world, unite and defeat the U.S. aggressors and all their running
dogs!"

In 1938, after the Gestapo raid his apartment in Vienna, SIGMUND FREUD flees to London via Paris, where Salvador Dali takes the opportunity to sketch his portrait. Twenty Maresfield Gardens, Hampstead, is Freud's "last address on this planet."

Eighty-three

And Moses was fourscore years old, and Aaron fourscore and three years old, when they spake unto Pharaoh.

—Genesis 7:7

Thomas Jefferson dies at Monticello on July 4, 1826, fifty years after his Declaration of Independence was adopted. John Adams, his old political rival and friend, dies a few hours later on the same day in Quincy, Massachusetts, at age ninety.

Journalist Martha Gellhorn has to give up writing because she can no longer see the keys of her typewriter and it's too late to learn to dictate. She still smokes and drinks and eats what she likes.

Film director Billy Wilder sells some of his famous modern art collection for $32.6 million, 1989. He still owns more than sixty cashmere sweaters.

In 2007 Norman Mailer lives in the fourth-floor walk-up in Brooklyn Heights where he's lived since 1962. Because of the arthritis in his knees, he climbs the stairs using a cane and a silver-knobbed walking stick.

Record mogul Ahmet Ertegun dies after falling off the stage at a Rolling Stones concert, 2006.

In 1778 Voltaire returns to Paris after twenty-eight years of exile. He meets Benjamin Franklin and attends a staging of his last play, *Irene*, where he is crowned with laurels and applauded by the audience. He dies soon after.

EMPEROR HIROHITO very nearly apologizes to President Chon Du-hwan of Korea for what Japan did during World War II, 1984. He says he hopes it never happens again.

WINSTON CHURCHILL finishes writing *A History of the English Speaking Peoples*, 1958. It is almost fifteen hundred pages long, around a million words, and fills four volumes, but much of it was composed by a team of employees. Because of various interruptions, the writing has taken a quarter-century. The contract he signed in 1932 was for the sum of £20,000, which comes out to around five pence a word.

EIGHTY-*four*

To me, old age is always fifteen years older than I am.

—BERNARD BARUCH (1955)

FREDERIC, the indentured slave of *The Pirates of Penzance*, having been born on the twenty-ninth of February, finally celebrates his twenty-first birthday, 1940.

JOE JOHNSTON, a former Confederate general, refuses to wear a hat while serving as pallbearer for his old foe, William Tecumseh Sherman, 1891. The weather is cold and rainy, and Johnston dies of pneumonia ten days later.

SAUL BELLOW has a new daughter, his first, 1999.

PABLO CASALS plays the cello at the Kennedy White House, November 13, 1961.

GEORGIA O'KEEFFE stops painting in oils because of deteriorating vision, but she continues drawing, 1972.

BENJAMIN FRANKLIN dies, 1790. Twenty thousand people attend his funeral in Philadelphia.

THOMAS EDISON opens the electrically operated Lackawanna Railroad, 1931. He drives the inaugural train, personally, all the way from Hoboken to Dover, New Jersey. He dies on October 18. Henry Ford captures Edison's last breath in a test tube as a keepsake.

GRETA GARBO finishes writing her autobiography and dies shortly afterward, 1990.

COCO CHANEL criticizes the clothes sense of Jackie Kennedy, 1967. "She's got horrible taste and is responsible for spreading it all over America." Jackie wore a raspberry Chanel suit the day her husband was assassinated.

PABLO PICASSO loses his third lawsuit against Françoise Gilot over her book *Life with Picasso*, 1965. He telephones his congratulations, but it's the last time the two speak to each other.

WINSTON CHURCHILL wins his last election to the House of Commons, 1959.

Eighty-*five*

Like this insubstantial pageant faded,
Leave not a rack behind. We are such stuff
As dreams are made on, and our little life
Is rounded with a sleep.

—William Shakespeare, *The Tempest* (1611)

Prince Philip has been walking two paces behind Queen Elizabeth II for the past sixty years, 2007. Rumor has it that he has slept with a princess, a duchess, two or three countesses, and assorted other women-not-his-wife, but they are only rumors.

God appears to Abraham in a dream, 1906 b.c.

Ezra Pound lives with his mistress of many years, violinist Olga Rudge, dividing the year between Rapallo and Venice, 1971. They share a love of Vivaldi and a dislike of biographers.

Titian paints *The Rape of Europa*, 1562.

Golfer Sam Snead shoots a 78 on his eighty-fifth birthday, 1997.

Linus Pauling publishes *How to Live Longer and Feel Better*, 1986. The book lands on the *New York Times* best-seller list.

Comic novelist P. G. Wodehouse is a creature of habit. Every morning he walks the dogs, spends a few hours at the typewriter, then has cocktails and lunch, followed by a half hour watching his favorite soap opera, *The Edge of Night*. Afternoons are spent napping and thinking up plots. In the evening he likes to read Perry Mason novels. He lives in suburban Long Island, 1966.

AGATHA CHRISTIE dies, unsuspiciously, 1976. She has written seventy-nine crime novels, several collections of stories, and fifteen plays, which have been translated into 103 foreign languages.

J. D. SALINGER hasn't published anything in forty years, but there are rumors of a room-sized safe full of unpublished stories in his New Hampshire house, 2004.

AARON COPLAND has a house in the Hudson River Valley an hour north of New York, 1986. He is working on his memoirs.

DR. BENJAMIN SPOCK is arrested, along with 376 others protesting the plight of the homeless, on Capitol Hill, 1988.

HISTORIAN THOMAS CARLYLE dies, 1881. He once said, "A well-written life is almost as rare as a well-spent one."

EIGHTY-SIX

And Abram was fourscore and six years old, when Hagar bare Ishmael to Abram.

—Genesis 16:16

ROBERT FROST reads his poem "The Gift Outright" at John F. Kennedy's inauguration, 1961. He'd planned to read a poem he'd written for the occasion, but the ink on the piece of paper is too faint and the winter sunshine is too bright, so he recites the other poem from memory instead.

Novelist GRAHAM GREENE dies in Vevey, Switzerland, 1991. Greene once wrote, in the voice of one of his fictional heroines, "I believe there's a God—I believe the whole bag of tricks; there's nothing I don't believe; they could subdivide the Trinity into a dozen parts and I'd believe."

MURIEL SPARK still writes her stories in composition books, in longhand, with pens no one else has touched, and she seldom revises, 2004. She makes her own bed and every morning takes tea in to Penelope Jardine, who does her typing and makes the domestic arrangements. The two have lived together in Tuscany for many years.

In 1561 MICHELANGELO receives commissions to design the Porto Pia and Santa Maria degli Angeli in Rome. He still hasn't finished the Sforza Chapel in Santa Maria Maggiore from last year. He dies two weeks shy of his eighty-seventh birthday. He has outlived twelve popes and worked for nine of them.

Director INGMAR BERGMAN celebrates his eighty-sixth birthday by announcing his retirement from the stage, July 14, 2004. His last production is Henrik Ibsen's *Ghosts*.

PIERRE MONTEUX signs a twenty-five-year contract, with a twenty-five-year renewal option, to conduct the London Symphony Orchestra, 1961. Monteux conducted the premiere performance of Stravinsky's *Rite of Spring* in 1913, which resulted in a famous riot.

JASCHA HEIFETZ dies, 1987. He played the violin almost every day since picking up the instrument at age three. He said, "Child prodigism—if I may coin a word—is a disease which is generally fatal. I was among the few to have the good fortune to survive."

E. B. WHITE, essayist and author of *Stuart Little* and *Charlotte's Web*, dies, 1985. The author always hated formal occasions; if it were possible to skip his own funeral, he would.

EIGHTY-SEVEN

*So long as a man rides his hobbyhorse peaceably and quietly
along the King's highway, and neither compels you or me to get
up behind him—pray, Sir, what have either you or I to do
with it?*

—LAURENCE STERNE, *The Life and Opinions of
Tristram Shandy, Gentleman* (1759–67)

SIR JOHN GIELGUD plays his first nude scene in the film *Prospero's
Books*, 1991.

PABLO PICASSO creates more than eight hundred new works in 1968
and 1969.

SAM SNEAD plays in his last Masters Tournament, 2000. He has played
sixty-three Masters in a row since 1937.

ALICE B. TOKLAS is evicted from the apartment she shared with
Gertrude Stein at 5 Rue Christine, 1964. Stein's nephew has already
appropriated the paintings by Picasso, Gris, and others that Stein had
willed to Toklas for her lifetime. The executor of Stein's will is a lawyer
named Edgar Allan Poe, the great-nephew of the poet.

EUDORA WELTY receives the French Legion of Honor, 1996.

IN 1993 BILLY WILDER is working with Steven Spielberg on a film
project about the Holocaust, which Wilder escaped by coming to
America in 1934.

EIGHTY-EIGHT

The great secret that all old people share is that you really haven't changed in seventy or eighty years. Your body changes, but you don't change at all. And that, of course, causes great confusion.

—DORIS LESSING (1992)

HARRY TRUMAN has been married to Bess Truman for fifty-three years and known her since they were kids, 1972.

TITIAN paints *The Education of Cupid*, 1565.

GEORGE BERNARD SHAW gives Shaw's Corner, his house of almost forty years, to the National Trust, 1944.

In 1970 PABLO PICASSO invites his three nephews and his niece to his home at Mas Notre-Dame-de-Vie in the south of France and informs them that all the paintings their mother had saved for them, around a thousand in all, will be given instead to the new Museo Picasso in Barcelona. They are not happy about it, so he gives them a painting each.

ALEKSANDR SOLZHENITSYN is visited at home by the latest absolute ruler of mother Russia, 2007. Vladimir Putin wants to pin a medal on him.

ROBERT FROST prefers to cut his own hair so he doesn't have to listen to the barber's conversation, 1962.

SYBILLE BEDFORD begins writing her memoirs, 1999. She says of her younger life, and its distractions: "Often choice had led me to spend the squandered years in beautiful or interesting places: to learn, to see, to travel, to walk in nocturnal streets, swim in warm seas, make friends and keep them, eat on trellised terraces, drink wine under summer leaves, to hear the song of tree-frog and cicada, to fall in love . . . (Often, too often.)"

WALTER CRONKITE still has an office and a staff of four at CBS headquarters in New York, 2005. He has a consulting contract with the network but is rarely consulted. He thinks about starting a blog.

Eighty-nine

I had all my life a curious sense of immunity that nothing would happen to me. And nothing ever did.

Louis Auchincloss (2008)

The Duchess of Windsor dies, 1986. The former Mrs. Wallis Simpson was best known as "the woman I love" for whom Edward VIII abdicated the English throne in 1936. Noticing that all the flowers are from couturiers, jewelers, and hairdressers, the Duchess of Marlborough explains, "Her life's work was shopping."

Polish-born pianist Mieczyslaw Horszowski marries Italian pianist Beatrice Costa, 1981. It is his first marriage. His repertoire is chiefly Bach, Beethoven, and Chopin.

The shy and retiring Jean Sibelius invites Eugene Ormandy to tea at his home outside Helsinki, 1955. Ormandy surprises him by bringing along the 110-member Philadelphia Orchestra to say hello.

The Reverend Billy Graham has prayed with ten presidents of the United States, 2008.

Nine years after his death, the skull and bones of Geronimo are stolen from the Indian cemetery at Fort Sill, Oklahoma, and placed in the crypt at Skull and Bones, a famous secret society at Yale, 1918.

NINETY

I advise you to go on living solely to enrage those who are paying your annuities.

—Voltaire (1694–1778)

George Bernard Shaw celebrates his birthday by going on television, 1946. Dublin gives him the key to the city.

Sarah gives birth to Isaac, 2040 b.c.

Bertrand Russell is interviewed by *Playboy* magazine, March 1963.

Julia Child gives her Cambridge, Massachusetts, kitchen to the Smithsonian, 2002.

John D. Rockefeller Sr. loses half of his fortune in the stock market crash of 1929. But there's still enough Rockefeller money around to found the Museum of Modern Art, build Rockefeller Center, restore Colonial Williamsburg, and buy enough of Jackson Hole, Wyoming, for a national park.

Millard Kaufman's first novel, *A Bowl of Cherries*, is published by McSweeney's, 2007.

Frank Lloyd Wright is asked to design an opera house, two museums, and a post office in Baghdad, 1957.

The memoirist and gadfly Quentin Crisp dies, leaving behind many charmed acquaintances, a handful of charming books, and a messy apartment, 1999.

Ninety-one

～

Pozzo: I don't seem to be able . . . [long hesitation] to depart.
Estragon: Such is life.

—Samuel Beckett, *Waiting for Godot* (1953)

On his deathbed William Somerset Maugham asks a friend to reassure him that there is no afterlife, 1965.

Katharine Hepburn still digs her own back garden at 44 East 49th Street, Turtle Bay Gardens, New York City, 1998. She's lived in the four-bedroom house for more than sixty years.

Frank Lloyd Wright is still at work on his designs for the Guggenheim Museum in New York when he dies in April 1959.

NINETY-TWO

I often wonder: suppose we could begin life over again, knowing what we were doing? Suppose we could use one life, already ended, as a sort of rough draft for another? I think that every one of us would try, more than anything else, not to repeat himself, at the very least he would rearrange his manner of life, he would make sure of rooms like these, with flowers and light.

—ANTON CHEKHOV, *The Three Sisters* (1901)

PAUL COLE, who appears on the album cover photograph that was snapped in St. John's Wood, has still never listened to *Abbey Road*, preferring classical music, 2004.

Painter WILLEM DE KOONING dies in East Hampton, Long Island, 1997.

EUDORA WELTY dies, 2001. She lived in Jackson, Mississippi, most of her life, much of it in the house her father built in 1925. She never married.

NINETY-THREE

The wrinkled smile of completeness that follows a life lived undaunted and unsoured with accepted lies they would ripen like apples, and be scented like pippins in their old age.

—D. H. LAWRENCE, "Beautiful Old Age" (1929)

In 1972 P. G. WODEHOUSE receives a long-deferred knighthood from the country that exiled him thirty years ago. He dies in suburban Long Island six weeks later. He wrote 96 books in his long career, as well as 250 songs for 30 musical comedies, 15 plays, and 44 film scripts. Despite being an author of light comedy, he was admired as a supreme stylist by the likes of George Orwell, Evelyn Waugh, Rudyard Kipling, and Max Beerbohm.

Scientist, pacifist, and double Nobel laureate LINUS PAULING dies on August 19, 1994. He once said, "Satisfaction of one's curiosity is one of the greatest sources of happiness in life."

On October 27, 1987, MAO ZEDONG is played by a tenor wearing a Mao suit in the premiere of John Adams's *Nixon in China* at the Houston Grand Opera. Mao has been dead for eleven years. Nixon is seventy-four and still living but does not attend; nor does Madame Mao, who is in a Chinese prison for her part in the Cultural Revolution. The Nixon part is played by a baritone.

After having four car accidents in a month, GEORGE BURNS hires a chauffeur, 1989. In an interview on the TV program *60 Minutes*, he says that he has visited wife Gracie Allen's grave at least once a week for over twenty-five years and has spoken with her each time. Their TV show, which ended in 1958, ran a year longer than *I Love Lucy*.

N i n e t y - *f o u r*

~❧~

The glorious chariots of the kings wear out;
the body also comes to old age;
but the virtue of good people never ages;
thus the good teach each other.

—The Buddha

George Bernard Shaw falls out of a fruit tree he has been pruning and breaks his leg, 1950. While he is in the hospital, doctors discover the long-standing kidney disease that will finally do him in in early November.

In a 2003 interview, economist John Kenneth Galbraith says: "I do a lot of my reading not for the sake of information but because it is a bridge over idleness. Idleness is the one thing I can't live with."

John Gielgud plays Pope Pius V in *Elizabeth*, 1998.

Bandleader Artie Shaw dies on December 30, 2004. His obituary in the *New York Times* bears the byline of a reporter who died in 2002.

Ninety-five

Who lives longer: the man who takes heroin for two years and dies, or the man who lives on roast beef, water and potatoes till ninety-five? One passes his twenty-four months in eternity. All the years of the beef-eater are lived only in time.

—Aldous Huxley, *Antic Hay* (1923)

Eubie Blake plays the piano on the lawn of the White House, 1978.

Elizabeth, the queen mother, has cataract surgery and two hip replacements and is given a golf cart by her daughter the queen, 1995.

Senator Strom Thurmond, who secretly fathered an out-of-wedlock child with a black fifteen-year-old housekeeper sixty-five years earlier, swears in the chief justice presiding over the impeachment trial of President Bill Clinton, who is charged with having consensual sex with a twenty-two-year-old intern in the Oval Office and trying to cover it up.

Studs Terkel polishes off another volume of memoirs, 2007. He has written about the Roaring Twenties, the Depression, World War II, and the Blacklist (which he was on), all of it on a typewriter.

Grandma Moses is interviewed on television by Edward R. Murrow, 1955.

Leopold Stokowski records Brahms's Second Symphony and Mendelssohn's Fourth (the *Italian*), 1977. He dies a few weeks later.

Titian writes a letter to Phillip II of Spain, to pester him about a portrait that hasn't been paid for, 1571.

Film director Michelangelo Antonioni's Rome apartment is burgled during Christmas 1996. Among the items stolen is his Oscar statuette, awarded for lifetime achievement.

Henri Cartier-Bresson dies on August 3, 2004, a couple of weeks before his ninety-sixth birthday. He once said, "Photographers deal in things which are continually vanishing and when they have vanished there is no contrivance on earth which can make them come back again."

Dorothy Parker's ashes have spent the past fifteen years in a filing cabinet in her lawyer's office at 99 Wall Street, but in 1988 the NAACP arranges to have the remains sent to Baltimore, where a memorial garden has been built. The plaque includes the epitaph she wrote for herself twenty-two years earlier, "Excuse My Dust."

NINETY-SIX

By Spoon River gathering many a shell,
And many a flower and medicinal weed—
Shouting to the wooded hills, singing to the green valleys.
At ninety-six I had lived enough, that is all,
And passed to a sweet repose.

—EDGAR LEE MASTERS, "Lucinda Matlock,"
Spoon River Anthology (1916)

KATHARINE HEPBURN dies in the house where she grew up in Old Saybrook, Connecticut, 2003.

In 2002 PHILIP JOHNSON can be found quite often at table number 32 at the Four Seasons, the ground-floor restaurant located in the Seagram Building he designed with Mies van der Rohe in 1954.

MARTHA GRAHAM is choreographing a new dance called *The Eye of the Goddess* for the Barcelona Olympics, when she dies in 1991.

Thirteen years after his death in 1778, VOLTAIRE's body is removed from the private grave near Troyes to the Pantheon in Paris, where he is interred with the honors he was deprived of before, 1791.

GEORGES BIZET's Symphony in C is premiered on February 26, 1935, almost sixty years after the composer's death. Conductor Felix Weingartner had discovered a copy of the score at the Paris Conservatory.

N I N E T Y - S E V E N

No wonder you rise in the middle of the night
to look up the date of a famous battle in a book on war.
No wonder the moon in the window seems to have drifted
out of a love poem that you used to know by heart.

—BILLY COLLINS, "Forgetfulness" (2000)

Philosopher BERTRAND RUSSELL dies, February 2, 1970.

In October 2006, film director MANOEL DE OLIVEIRA premieres *Belle Toujours* at the New York Film Festival. What he puckishly describes as his "last film" is an homage to the Luis Buñuel film *Belle de Jour.* De Oliveira has been working on it for decades.

GIUSEPPE BONANNO, "Joe Bananas," of 1847 East Elm Street, Tucson, Arizona, dies of natural causes, 2002. He headed one of the notorious "Five Families" of New York City. After his demise Joseph "Big Joey" Massino and Richard "Shellackhead" Cantarella start singing to the feds.

Composer ELLIOTT CARTER walks onstage at Avery Fisher Hall to share the applause for his 1996 composition *Allegro Scorrevole*, performed on this evening in 2006 by the New York Philharmonic. The conductor is thirty-two.

NINETY-EIGHT

"You are old, father William," the young man said,
"And your hair has become very white;
And yet you incessantly stand on your head
Do you think, at your age, it is right?

"In my youth," father William replied to his son,
"I feared it might injure the brain;
But, now that I'm perfectly sure I have none,
Why, I do it again and again."

—LEWIS CARROLL, *Alice's Adventures*
in Wonderland (1865)

AL HIRSCHFELD will soon have a Broadway theater named after him, 2002. The theater located at West 45th Street was built two years before Hirschfeld began caricaturing the New York theater scene in 1926. Since 1945 every Hirschfeld drawing has had a number on it indicating how many times his daughter Nina's name has been written into the linework.

IRVING BERLIN gets a phone call from director Steven Spielberg, who wants to use one of his songs in a movie, 1986. Berlin refuses, saying he's planning to use it in a new project of his own.

RIN TIN TIN dies at his home in Los Angeles, 1932. In human years he would have been fourteen. Popular legend has him dying in the arms of screen siren Jean Harlow. He never married. Tin had retired from pictures the year before. He starred in forty feature films, twenty-six of them for Warner Brothers, and is credited with saving the studio from bankruptcy.

Ninety-nine

Eat less when you dine; live to age ninety-nine.

—Chinese proverb

Bob Hope owns an 85,000-page joke file, digitally scanned and broken down into categories, which he stores in file cabinets in a theft- and fire-proof walk-in vault in the office next to his North Hollywood home, 2002. The jokes were written by more than a hundred professional joke writers, but some of them were stolen from other comedians, most of them now dead.

Mieczyslaw Horszowski performs his last piano recital, 1992. Because of impaired eyesight, Maestro Horszowski is no longer performing concertos or chamber works but has continued performing a solo repertoire, playing from memory. He was taught the piano by his mother, in Poland. His mother was taught by a former student of Chopin.

Al Hirschfeld dies, 2003. The last uncompleted drawing on the board in his studio is of the Marx Brothers, who were personal friends of his.

ONE HUNDRED

I am this month one whole year older than I was this time twelve-month; and having got . . . almost into the middle of my fourth volume—and no farther than to my first day's life—'tis demonstrative that I have three hundred and sixty-four days more life to write just now, than when I first set out . . . write as I will . . . I shall never overtake myself . . . At the worst I shall have one day the start of my pen—and one day is enough for two volumes—and two volumes will be enough for one year.

—Laurence Sterne, *The Life and Opinions of Tristram Shandy, Gentleman* (1759–67)

Elizabeth, the queen mother, still walks her dogs for twenty minutes three times a day, 2000.

Comedian Bob Hope dies on July 27, 2003.

Moses is still wandering with the Jewish people in the wilderness, 1425 B.C. He will never arrive in the Promised Land, but he will see it from a distance.

Ida May Fuller, a classmate of Calvin Coolidge and the first person to receive Social Security in 1940, is still living in Ludlow, Vermont, 1974. She will die in 1975. In thirty-five years of retirement, her Social Security benefits will total $22,888.92. A nice return. Miss Fuller paid in $24.75 during the last three years of her working life. She was a lifelong Republican and never thought much of the New Deal.

Irving Berlin lives very quietly in his New York City apartment, avoiding the public eye, 1988. He still cannot read or write music and can only play in one key, F-sharp. He prefers playing only the black keys.

GEORGE BURNS dies on March 9, 1996. He once observed that it was "too bad that all the people who know how to run the country are busy driving taxi-cabs and cutting hair."

In January 1967, thirty-five years after the author's death, JOHN GALSWORTHY's *The Forsyte Saga* begins its broadcast run on BBC-TV. Despite being in black and white, it is the most expensive television production yet made, inaugurating a whole new television format called the miniseries. In America it is the initial selection of the program *Masterpiece Theatre* on PBS.

DR. ALBERT HOFMANN celebrates his one hundredth birthday, 2006. Seven decades after he invented LSD, he claims to have a remarkable memory but makes no reference to flashbacks.

ACKNOWLEDGMENTS

I want to thank the biographers who spend years on one subject and the anthologists of anecdotes. I would also like to acknowledge the usefulness of print periodicals: especially *The New Yorker, Smithsonian, Rolling Stone, Vanity Fair, The Atlantic, Harper's,* the *New York Times*, and other publications that arrive like clockwork full of unexpected riches. Also, my acknowledgments to Garrison Keillor's *Writer's Almanac* and the people at the *Oxford Dictionary of National Biography,* who send me tidbits and short biographies every day via e-mail.

Finally, many thanks to my editors, Julia Pastore and Shaye Areheart, and to my agent, Marly Rusoff.

INDEX

ABOUT THE AUTHOR

ERIC HANSON has been an illustrator and writer for more than twenty years.

His art has appeared in *The New Yorker, Vanity Fair, Rolling Stone, Spy, The Atlantic, Harper's,* the *New York Times, Gourmet,* and other publications.

His fiction and satire have been published in *McSweeney's.* His articles have appeared in *Smithsonian, National Geographic Traveler, Hemispheres,* and *Minnesota Monthly.* He lives in Minneapolis with his wife and two children.

www.abookofages.com

www.cr-h.com